MW01175020

Integrated Spelling

Teacher's Edition

GRADE 1

Harcourt Brace & Company

Orlando Atlanta Austin Boston San Francisco Chicago Dallas New York Toronto London

Printed in the United States of America

ISBN 0-15-310826-6
1 2 3 4 5 6 7 8 9 10 054 2001 2000 99 98

Contents

Integrated Spelling

INTEGRATED SPELLING *is spelling and vocabulary instruction that is developmental in sequence, complete in scope, and fully integrated with the literature-based instruction in Signatures. Based on extensive research, the program offers teachers practical strategies for maximizing children's learning of spelling and provides numerous opportunities for children to learn and apply a variety of spelling strategies to all their writing.*

Integrated Spelling *is based upon these beliefs:*

- Spelling instruction is most effective when it takes place within the broader context of reading and writing.

- There is a meaning basis for spelling: knowledge of spelling and word meaning should be developed through reading and responding to literature.

- Use of an organized, developmental spelling curriculum and purposeful activities promotes spelling growth.

- A diagnostic tool that gives teachers insight into each child's stage of development is an integral part of an effective spelling program.

- A spelling program should help children develop a spelling consciousness—an ability to examine their own writing and identify misspelled words.

- Allowing young children to invent spellings or to use temporary spellings in their writing, while gradually helping them arrive at more standard spellings, is reflective of the natural developmental process for learning spelling.

- Knowledge of the history and heritage of the English language, along with language play, is an essential component of a spelling program.

▶ INTEGRATION WITH Signatures

For each selection in *Signatures,* a corresponding spelling lesson links reading, writing, vocabulary, and spelling, providing a meaningful approach to spelling instruction. Lesson 1 covers initial consonants, thereafter each core lesson in Lessons 2–18 of *Integrated Spelling* includes

- a focus on developing phonemic awareness of a phonogram and concept of word.

- language activities in which children "play" with the phonogram.

- writing activities in which children spell words using the phonogram.

Each core lesson in Lessons 19–36 includes

- a spelling generalization.

- a list of Spelling Words prompted by the literature and gathered from research.

- a *Strategy Workshop* with spelling strategies that children practice and apply.

- a *Vocabulary WordShop* that includes concept words from the literature, and vocabulary activities to develop children's knowledge of concepts and words.

- activities related to story themes and concepts from *Signatures,* and writing applications that encourage personal responses.

Developmental Levels of Spellers, Grades 1–6

▶ EMERGENT SPELLERS

- Children first begin to use alphabet symbols to represent words or messages, but they do not always know what sounds match the letters.

- Spelling attempts are often not readable by anyone other than the child who produces them, because the letters do not consistently represent sounds.

- Children may or may not understand the concept of word. They string letters together at random, sometimes in left-to-right fashion.

- Children frequently mix uppercase and lowercase letter forms, although they generally show a preference for uppercase, such as in *IEOOS*.

▶ SEMI-PHONETIC SPELLERS

- Children use invented spellings.

- They conceptualize that letters represent the sounds in words, but they may omit major sounds (often vowel sounds) in words—such as writing *bt* for *boat*.

- They understand the concept of word and of left-to-right progression.

▶ PHONETIC SPELLERS

- Children refine their invented spellings.

- They use a phonetic or letter-name system of spelling in which they make a one-to-one match between the sequential sounds they hear in words (/m/ /ā/ /k/) and the alphabet letter names that represent these sounds (*MAK*).

- Children spell words the way the words sound. Although the spelling may be unconventional, the words are usually readable.

- Children may or may not be aware of word segmentation—the breaking of words into smaller parts.

- The matching of letters to sounds is systematic and perceptually accurate, such as in *shuts* for *shoots* and *ses* for *says*.

> Opportunities for teacher choice allow instruction to be tailored to fit the various developmental levels of children in the class.

▶ TRANSITIONAL SPELLERS

- Children move from concrete to more abstract representation, which requires greater reliance on visual memory—spelling words the way they look rather than the way they sound.

- By reading, writing, and thinking about spelling, children develop a sense of when a particular spelling looks correct.

- Children may still invent spellings, but they have learned many of the conventions of English spelling. They put vowels in every syllable, use *e*-marker and vowel digraph patterns, spell inflectional endings correctly, and use English letter sequences that occur frequently.

- Transitional spellers may include all the appropriate letters in a word, but they may reverse some letters—such as in *TAOD* for *toad* or *FETE* for *feet*.

Children progress through these stages in each lesson: discovery of spelling patterns through sorting, consideration of relevant rules and strategies, application of these rules and strategies, and confirmation of understanding.

▶ SYNTACTIC-SEMANTIC SPELLERS

- Children are competent and correct spellers. They understand the English spelling system and its basic rules.

- Children understand the accurate spelling of prefixes, suffixes, contractions, compound words, and many irregular spellings; they usually use silent letters and double consonants correctly; they are able to distinguish homophones.

- Through understanding the principles of syllable juncture and applying what they know about one-syllable words, children are able to spell multisyllabic words accurately.

- When spelling a new word, children think of alternative spellings and visualize the word.

- Children begin to recognize word origins and use this information to make meaningful associations as they accumulate a large corpus of known spellings.

▶ STRATEGIC SPELLERS

- Children have already mastered basic spelling patterns and are able to apply them automatically.

- Children have developed a "spelling consciousness" that allows them to adapt and integrate spelling strategies as a natural part of the writing process.

- Their understanding of meaning relationships enables children to be confident language users and serves as a powerful spelling resource.

Developmental Levels of Spellers, Grade 1

CHILDREN BENEFIT most from instruction that is appropriate to their developmental levels. The developmental levels of most first graders, as shown below, may be determined by using the Spelling Placement Inventory on pages T16–T17 of this Teacher's Edition. See pages T8–T9 for information on developmental levels of spellers, Grades 1–6.

DEVELOPMENTAL LEVEL	CHARACTERISTICS
Emergent Spellers	• begin to use alphabet symbols to represent words but do not always know which sounds match the letters. • produce spelling that is often not readable by anyone other than the child. • may or may not have the concept of word. Letters are strung together at random, sometimes in left-to-right fashion. • frequently mix uppercase and lowercase letter forms but show a preference for uppercase.
Semi-Phonetic Spellers	• use knowledge of sounds represented by letters to invent spellings. • may omit major sounds, particularly vowel sounds, in some words, such as in *camr* for *camera*. • write some words that are decipherable. • understand the concept of word and left-to-right progression.
Phonetic Spellers	• refine their invented spellings. • use a phonetic or letter-name system of spelling in which they make a one-to-one match between each of the sequential sounds they hear in words. • spell words the way the words sound. Although the spelling may be unconventional, the words are usually readable. • may or may not be aware of word segmentation—breaking words into smaller parts. • match letters to sounds in a systematic and a perceptually accurate way.
Transitional Spellers	• move from concrete to more abstract representation, which requires greater reliance on visual memory—spelling words the way they look rather than the way they sound. • develop a sense of when a particular spelling looks correct. • may still invent spellings but have learned many of the conventions of English spelling. • may include all the letters in a word but may reverse some letters, such as in *taod* for *toad* or *fete* for *feet*.

Assignment Guide

USE THIS ASSIGNMENT GUIDE *to adjust assignments to the developmental levels of children.*

3-DAY PLAN	MATERIALS	DEVELOPMENTAL LEVELS	5-DAY PLAN
Day 1 Phonogram Picture Search Activity*	*First Page of Pupil's Edition Lesson* *Home Activities Master*	*Emergent Spellers (Below Level)* *Semi-Phonetic Spellers (On Level) and Phonetic Spellers (Above Level): Introduce Phonogram***	**Day 1** Phonogram Picture Search Activity*
Strategy Workshop	*Second Page of Pupil's Edition Lesson*		**Day 2** Strategy Workshop
Day 2 Vocabulary WordShop	*Third and Fourth Pages of Pupil's Edition Lesson*	*Phonetic Spellers (Above Level): Assign Vocabulary WordShop Words*	**Days 3 & 4** Vocabulary WordShop
Day 3 Wrap-Up		*Emergent Spellers (Below Level) and Semi-Phonetic Spellers (On Level) and Phonetic Spellers (Above Level): Reinforce Phonogram***	**Day 5** Wrap-Up

LESSONS 1–18

3-DAY PLAN	MATERIALS	DEVELOPMENTAL LEVELS	5-DAY PLAN
Day 1 Pretest and/or Sorting Activity	*First Page of Pupil's Edition Lesson* *Home Activities Master*	*Emergent and Semi-Phonetic Spellers (Below Level): Introduce Spelling Words* *Phonetic Spellers (On Level) and Transitional Spellers (Above Level): Pretest Spelling Words*	**Day 1** Pretest and/or Sorting Activity
Strategy Workshop	*Second Page of Pupil's Edition Lesson*		**Day 2** Strategy Workshop
Day 2 Vocabulary WordShop	*Third and Fourth Pages of Pupil's Edition Lesson*	*Transitional Spellers (Above Level): Assign Vocabulary WordShop Words*	**Days 3 & 4** Vocabulary WordShop
Day 3 Posttest		*Emergent and Semi-Phonetic Spellers (Below Level) and Phonetic Spellers (On Level): Test Spelling Words* *Transitional Spellers (Above Level): Test Spelling Words and Vocabulary WordShop Words*	**Day 5** Posttest

LESSONS 19–36

* Lesson 1, Initial Consonants Picture Search Activity
** Lesson 1, Review/Reinforce Initial Consonants

Planning Instruction

IN INTEGRATED SPELLING *the instructional plan of the developmental lessons is both consistent and flexible. Each core lesson in Lessons 2–18 focuses on a target phonogram and the concept of word. Each core lesson in Lessons 19–36 focuses on a spelling generalization and a corresponding list of Spelling Words.*

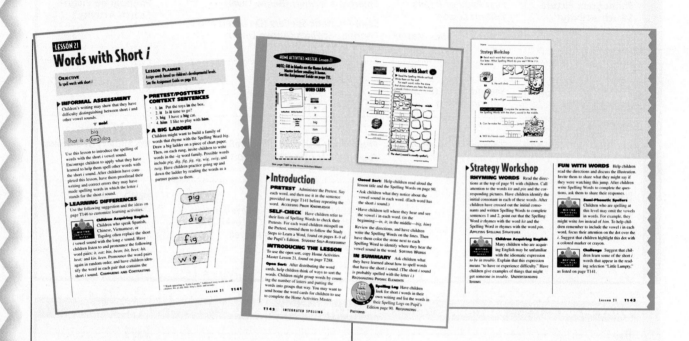

▶ PART 1: Introduction

The first page of each Teacher's Edition lesson provides tools for making instruction appropriate for children and includes the objectives and lesson-planning information, an informal assessment procedure, and suggestions for children who are acquiring English. A suggestion is also provided for an ongoing group activity, such as a bulletin board activity, to introduce the phonogram or spelling generalization. In Lessons 19–36, Pretest/Posttest Context Sentences also appear on this page.

The second page of each Teacher's Edition lesson, labeled *Introduction*, relates to the first page of the corresponding Pupil's Edition lesson. In Lessons 2–18, this Teacher's Edition page provides background-building suggestions and sentences to assess

children's prior knowledge of the phonogram (Preview), specific steps for introducing the phonogram, and ideas for engaging children in applying the focus phonogram. In Lessons 19–36, this Teacher's Edition page offers the following: a Pretest and a Self-Check procedure; a choice of an open-sort or a closed-sort activity, either of which may be used to help children discover patterns and common elements in the Spelling Words; a summarizing activity (In Summary); and an extension activity (Your Own Words).

A Home Activities Master, provided for each lesson, may be used in class or distributed to be completed as homework.

▶ PART 2: Strategy Workshop

This Teacher's Edition page relates to the second page of the corresponding Pupil's

Edition lesson. A description of the strategy children use in the workshop activities is provided. Suggestions for ways to help children complete the activities are also given. In Lessons 2–18, practice is provided in reading, writing, and saying words with the target phonogram. In Lessons 19–36, useful strategies and structural information about the Spelling Words are presented. Children put this new knowledge to use in the workshop activities, which they may work on cooperatively or independently.

▶ PART 3: Vocabulary WordShop

These two Teacher's Edition pages relate to the third and fourth pages of the corresponding Pupil's Edition lesson. The Pupil's Edition pages guide children to think critically about the spellings and meanings of high-utility words and topically related words from the literature. The Teacher's Edition pages provide suggestions for hands-on activities and/or optional writing activities.

▶ PART 4: Lesson Wrap-Up

For all lessons, a Reteach procedure structured to help children with learning differences is provided on the final Teacher's Edition page. Suggestions for one or more activities that integrate the curriculum areas are also provided. These lively activities involve one or more learning modalities and encourage creativity. In Lessons 19–36, children have the opportunity to demonstrate spelling proficiency by taking the Posttest.

▶ REVIEW LESSONS

Review lessons give children another opportunity to work with the Spelling Words, to review strategies and rules, and to apply their accumulated knowledge in writing activities. The lessons also provide practice in using a standardized test format.

Spelling Placement Inventory

DETERMINING A CHILD'S DEVELOPMENTAL LEVEL *can best be done through a combination of observation, evaluation of written work, and administration and interpretation of a placement instrument.*

THE SPELLING PLACEMENT INVENTORY establishes a benchmark of spelling awareness for each child and serves as an indicator of his or her developmental level at a specific time. You can determine progress throughout the year by comparing performance on lesson assignments to performance on the inventory, or you may want to have children take the inventory periodically and at the end of the year.

▶ DIRECTIONS FOR ADMINISTERING THE SPELLING PLACEMENT INVENTORY

Administer the Spelling Placement Inventory on pages T16–T17 at midyear of first grade. Follow these directions:

1. **Dictate the ten words to children by pronouncing each word, using it in a sentence, and then pronouncing the word again.**

2. **Collect children's papers, and score each Spelling Placement Inventory by writing the correct spelling beside each incorrect spelling. For example:**

Child		
1.	fn	fan
2.	pt	pet
3.	dg	dog

By correcting the Spelling Inventories in this manner, you will gain valuable knowledge of each child's developmental understanding of one-syllable spelling words.

3. Although a numerical score can be assigned to each child's Spelling Placement Inventory (0 to 100 percent range, with 10 points taken off for each incorrect spelling), it is also important at the first-grade level to note the child's stage of spelling development.

For example, do the child's spelling attempts show a pattern of representing the beginning and ending consonants but leaving out the vowel (Semi-Phonetic stage), or does the child include vowels in his or her spellings but represent them unconventionally? For example, a child who spells *dig* as *deg* has substituted the phonetically similar letter-name *e* for the short *i* sound. This is characteristic of the Phonetic stage of spelling.

4. By administering the same ten-word Spelling Placement Inventory at the end of first grade and scoring it in the manner described, you will be able to document, for each child, Pretest-Posttest gains in the number of correct spellings, as well as qualitative gains in spelling knowledge (e.g., movement from the Semi-Phonetic stage to the Phonetic stage).

Suggestions for meeting individual needs help ensure that every child benefits from every lesson.

Spelling Placement Inventory, Grade 1

Follow the directions on pages T14–T15 for administering this Spelling Placement Inventory.

WORDS	STAGES		
	On level PHONETIC SPELLERS	Below level SEMI-PHONETIC SPELLERS	Above level TRANSITIONAL SPELLERS
1. fan	fan	f, fn	
2. pet	pat	p, pt	
3. dig	deg	d, dg	
4. hot	hit	h, ht	
5. sun	son	s, sn	

NOTE: In words 2–5, the Phonetic stage spellings illustrate the appropriate phonetic substitutions for short vowel sounds (*a* for /e/; *e* for /i/; *i* for /o/; *o* for /u/).

| | STAGES | | |
WORDS	On level PHONETIC SPELLERS	Below level SEMI-PHONETIC SPELLERS	Above level TRANSITIONAL SPELLERS
6. name	nam	n, nm	naem
7. like	lik	l, lk	lice
8. home	hom	h, hm	hoam
9. is			
10. the			

NOTE: In words 6–8, the Transitional stage spellings illustrate attempts to make the long vowel sound with a second vowel letter. Words 9 and 10 are high-frequency words.

Spelling Log

THE SPELLING LOG *provides an excellent opportunity for children to write words from the spelling lessons, to keep an ongoing record of words they have misspelled on Pretests or in other writing, and to note troublesome words as an aid to writing and proofreading.*

THE SPELLING LOG also encourages children to record words that are of special interest to them, such as words having to do with a favorite activity, place, or topic. The Pupil's Edition of *Integrated Spelling* includes a Spelling Log in which children may record words.

▶ INTRODUCING THE SPELLING LOG

Ask children to name some different ways they learn new words. (by reading books, signs, and menus; by listening to the radio; by watching TV; by talking with friends and family) To introduce the idea of a Spelling Log, ask children to name some things they can do to remember new words they learn. Explain that there is a special section in their spelling book that they can use for recording new words. Read page 5 of the Pupil's Edition with children.

Introduce the Spelling Log by having children look at pages 6–7 in their books. Explain that there are three parts to the Spelling Log: Spelling Words to Study, Vocabulary WordShop Words, and My Own Word Collection. Then read pages 6–7 with the children to help them find out about these parts. Ask the following questions:

• Where will you find the words to write in the first part of the Spelling Log? Name some words that might belong on the page labeled *Science Words*.

• What words will you write in the third part of your Spelling Log? *Play Words* is one group of words you might want to list. What are some word groups you might create?

Invite children to examine the Spelling Log which begins on page 183 in their books. Have volunteers identify the two parts of the Spelling Log and tell on which page each begins and ends.

▶ CREATING SPELLING LOGS

You might also have children create additional or separate individual Spelling Logs. Suggest that they use sheets of lined paper that they can keep in a notebook. To be useful, each Spelling Log should be organized so that children can easily find words they have written and can systematically add new words. Children might organize their logs alphabetically, with one page for each letter of the alphabet.

In their Spelling Logs, encourage children to include

• words they have misspelled in their writing assignments or on their spelling tests.

• rhyming words, words that share a spelling pattern, or word families.

• words used often in their writing, such as *some* and *said*, along with pictures or context sentences that help children remember the words' meanings.

See pages T251–T254 for additional information about the Spelling Log.

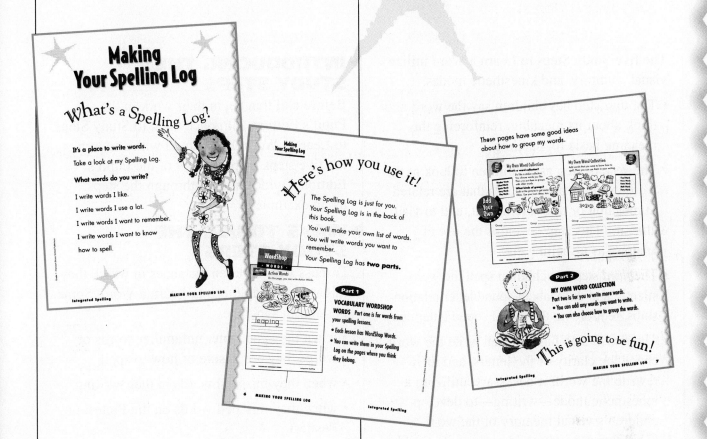

Skill development takes place in the context of reading, writing, listening, and speaking.

Study Steps to Learn a Word

STUDY STEPS TO LEARN A WORD *will help children become successful, independent spellers.*

The five Study Steps to Learn a Word utilize visual, auditory, and kinesthetic modes.

- The *first* step has children say the word and think about its meaning, reinforcing the meaning basis for spelling.

- The *second* step asks children to look at the word, to think about words that are related in meaning or that resemble it, and to visualize it. (This step develops the use of analogy as a spelling cue.)

- The *third* step has children spell the word silently and think about sound/letter relationships, reinforcing the use of sound/letter cues.

- The *fourth* step has children write the word, check the clarity of the letters, and then rewrite the word, if necessary, utilizing a kinesthetic mode—writing—to develop children's visual memory of the word. (This step reminds children to write legibly to avoid spelling errors.)

- The *fifth* step has children cover the word they wrote and check its spelling, strengthening children's visual memory of the word.

▶ INTRODUCING THE STUDY STEPS

Before children begin their work in the Pupil's Edition, introduce them to Study Steps to Learn a Word. Read aloud with children the five steps on pages 8–9 of the Pupil's Edition. Guide children through the steps, using examples.

▶ WAYS TO USE THE STUDY STEPS

Discuss with children instances in which they might use Study Steps to Learn a Word. Some possibilities include

- when they encounter unfamiliar words or words they are unsure of how to spell.

- when they misspell words in their writing.

- when they misspell words on the Pretest or Posttest.

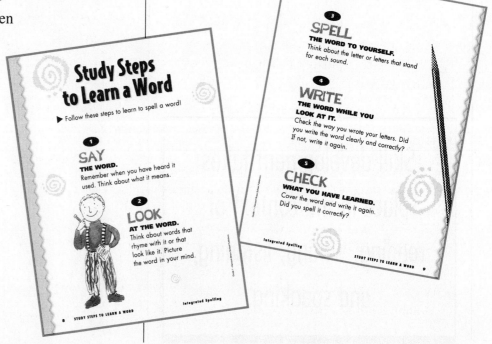

Initial Consonants

OBJECTIVE

To recognize the sounds and spellings of the initial consonants *b, d, h,* and *t*

LESSON PLANNER

See the Assignment Guide on page T11 for a 3-day or 5-day plan.

▶ INFORMAL ASSESSMENT

Have children listen as you identify and pronounce the names of children and classroom items that begin with the consonant *b,* such as *boy, Brian, box,* and *bird.* Emphasize the initial consonant as you say each word. Point out that the words begin with the same sound. Repeat the words. Then ask children what sound they hear at the beginning of all the words (/b/). Lead children to identify the letter that represents the sound (*b*). Encourage children to identify and pronounce the names of other items that have the same initial consonant sound.

Repeat this procedure for words beginning with the consonant *d* (*desk, Darla, Dan, dog*). Then do the same with the consonants *h* (*hair, hall, hand, Harry*) and *t* (*table, tack, tape, Terry*).

You may notice that some children have difficulty recognizing the sounds and spellings of initial consonants. This lesson will help children distinguish between the consonants *b, d, h,* and *t*.

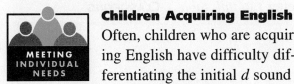

Children Acquiring English
Often, children who are acquiring English have difficulty differentiating the initial *d* sound from the *t* sound. Give children practice in listening to and pronouncing pairs of words with these initial consonant sounds. Provide practice with words such as *dip, tip; dent, tent; dug, tug; dime, time; dill, till;* and *done, ton.* Point out the letter that stands for the initial consonant sound in each word. Then repeat

the words in random order, and ask children to identify the initial consonant in each word.
COMPARING AND CONTRASTING

▶ INITIAL IT

After children complete the first two pages of the lesson, they may enjoy creating a bulletin board featuring words and corresponding pictures of items whose names begin with the consonants *b, d, h,* and *t.* Divide a bulletin board into four sections labeled *b, d, h,* and *t.* In the *b* section, draw a box. In the *d* section, draw a door. In the *h* section, draw a hat. In the *t* section, draw a table. Invite children to draw pictures of things whose names begin with each letter. Have children label their drawings with the letter that represents the initial sound of each picture name. Then have them attach their drawings to the appropriate section of the bulletin board.

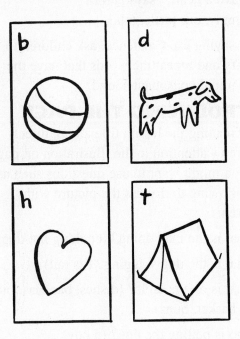

NOTE: Fill in the blanks on the Home Activities Master before sending it home. See the Assignment Guide on page T11.

See page T268 for the Home Activities Master.

►Introduction

WARM-UP Say these sentences, emphasizing the initial consonants *b, d, h,* and *t:*

> <u>B</u>art the <u>B</u>ear is <u>b</u>ig.
>
> <u>D</u>o not <u>d</u>isturb <u>D</u>an the <u>d</u>og.
>
> "<u>H</u>ave a <u>h</u>eart," says <u>H</u>azel.
>
> <u>T</u>ammy, our <u>t</u>urtle, <u>t</u>alks.

After saying each sentence, ask children to identify and repeat the words that have the same initial consonant sound.

INTRODUCING THE PAGE

After reading the lesson title aloud, direct children's attention to the illustration on page 10. You might want to use questions such as the following to discuss the picture with children:

• What is the man doing? (cooking hot dogs)

• What is the dog wagging? (its tail)

• What is on the table? (dishes, bananas, picnic basket, buns)

• Who is petting the dog? (a boy)

Read the directions aloud. Then have children repeat the sounds of the consonants *b, d, h,* and *t* as you point to each letter in the corners of the picture. Ask a volunteer to restate what children are to do on the page.

Either work through the page with children or have them complete it independently. (Children should draw lines from pictures representing the words to the initial consonants: from the letter *b* to *basket, boy, bananas, buns;* from the letter *d* to *dog, dishes;* from the letter *h* to *hot dogs;* and from the letter *t* to *tail, table.*) **CLASSIFYING**

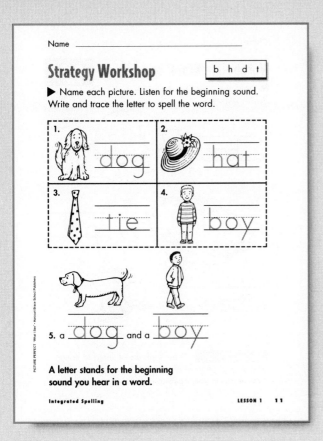

Name _____

Strategy Workshop

`b h d t`

▶ Name each picture. Listen for the beginning sound. Write and trace the letter to spell the word.

1. dog
2. hat
3. tie
4. boy

5. a dog and a boy

A letter stands for the beginning sound you hear in a word.

Integrated Spelling

LESSON 1   11

▶Strategy Workshop

INITIAL CONSONANTS Remind children of the sounds of the initial consonants *b, d, h,* and *t*. Read the directions at the top of page 11 with children.

Help children identify the first picture as a dog. Say the word *dog*. Then have children identify the sound they hear at the beginning of the word (/d/). Point out the letter box at the top of the page, and have a volunteer tell which letter stands for the beginning sound in the word (*d*). Explain to children that they can use this strategy to write words that name the pictures on this page. Then help them identify the remaining pictures as representing the words *hat, tie,* and *boy*.

After children complete the activity, have them share and explain their responses.

APPLYING SPELLING STRATEGIES

SPELLING IN CONTEXT Have
children discuss the picture at the bottom of page 11. Give guidance as needed to help them complete the phrase and read it aloud. (*dog, boy*) **CONCEPT OF WORD**

MEETING INDIVIDUAL NEEDS

Extra Support/Children Acquiring English Children may benefit from a review of the consonant sounds that begin each word on the page. Display pictures or objects whose names begin with /b/, /d/, /h/, and /t/. Ask children to identify the letter that represents the initial sound of each picture or object name.

IN SUMMARY Invite children to tell
what they have discovered about spelling words that begin with /b/, /d/, /h/, and /t/. (These words begin with the consonants *b, d, h,* and *t*.)

Vocabulary WordShop

▶ Write the word from the box that names each thing.

Picnic
· WORDS ·
pie
hat
bee

1. hat

2. pie

3. bee

Plan a Picnic Draw a picture of things to bring on a picnic. Write words to go with your picture. Add these words to your Spelling Log.

12   LESSON 1   Integrated Spelling

▶ Vocabulary WordShop

WORDSHOP WORDS Point out the WordShop Words on page 12, and ask volunteers to read them aloud. Then discuss how the words are alike. (They name things that might be seen at a picnic.)

Direct children's attention to the pictures, and ask volunteers to name the items. Read with children the directions at the top of the page. Explain that they are to label the pictures by writing the words from the box on the lines. After children complete the activity, have them share their responses.

MEETING INDIVIDUAL NEEDS

Children Acquiring English Play a game in which you say each WordShop Word and perform an action that is associated with the word. For example, pretend to put on a hat, eat a piece of pie, and buzz like a bee. Then have children point to the word on the page that is associated with the action.

BUILDING VOCABULARY

PLAN A PICNIC Provide children with paper and painting or drawing materials. Suggest that children paint or draw a picture of items to bring along on a picnic. After their pictures are complete, help children label their work.

EXPLORING PICNIC WORDS

Encourage children to draw on their own picnic experiences as you guide a discussion by asking them to do the following:

• Name some foods to eat at a picnic.
• Describe places to go for a picnic.
• Name some things to do while on a picnic.
• Describe a nice day to have a picnic.

Name _____

Vocabulary Adventures

▶ Write a word from the box that tells what each child sees.

hat
bee
pie

1. pie

2. bee

3. hat

Integrated Spelling   LESSON 1   13

"TEACHERS OF YOUNG CHILDREN *should recognize the important role they can play in contributing to their students' phonemic awareness by spending a few minutes daily engaging their students in oral activities that emphasize the sounds of language.***"**
(Hallie Kay Yopp)

VOCABULARY ADVENTURES

Read aloud the directions at the top of page 13. Then focus children's attention on the art, and ask volunteers to tell what the child in each picture sees. Have children write words from the box to identify the items. After children complete the page, have them share and explain their responses. **USING NAMING WORDS**

 Working Together You may want children to work in pairs to do this activity. Suggest that partners take turns, with one child reading the sentence frame aloud while the other child selects and writes the word in the sentence.

 **Spelling Log** Children may want to write the Picnic Words from this lesson in their Spelling Logs.

Optional Writing Idea

 Patterned Writing: Sentences Write the letters *b, d, h,* and *t* on the board as column heads. Have children look at the illustration on Pupil's Edition page 10 and recall some words that begin with *b, d, h,* and *t.* Write in the corresponding columns the words that are volunteered. Then ask children to name additional words that start with these consonants. Write them in the corresponding columns.

Write these sentence frames on the board, and help children read them aloud:

I see a _____ .
I do not see a _____ .

Have children copy and complete the sentence frames by writing words from the chart on the board.

▶ Lesson Wrap-Up

RETEACH: Learning Differences
Some children may need additional auditory and kinesthetic reinforcement to recognize and spell words beginning with *b*, *d*, *h*, and *t*. Have children make four flash cards, one for each consonant. Say words that begin with these consonants and have children hold up the corresponding flash card after each word is pronounced.

AUDITORY/KINESTHETIC MODALITIES

B—My Name Is Bob

Have children do this activity in small groups. Provide each group with a set of cards with the letters *b*, *d*, *h*, and *t* on them.

Have children lay the cards face down and take turns turning over a card and identifying the letter. Tell children to think of words that name a person, place, and thing that begin with the letter. Then invite children to make up sentences using the words. You might wish to use the following as a model:

B—my name is Bob. I come from Boston. I bring home beans.

LESSON 2
Words with -ap

OBJECTIVE
To recognize the sounds and spelling of the phonogram -ap

LESSON PLANNER
See the Assignment Guide on page T11 for a 3-day or 5-day plan.

▶ INFORMAL ASSESSMENT

Have children listen as you say and act out the following rhyme, emphasizing words with the phonogram -ap:

Use your hands to clap, clap.
Use your feet to tap, tap.
Use your fingers to snap, snap.
It's fun to clap, tap, and snap!

Repeat the rhyme several times, and encourage children to join in. After several repetitions, children should be able to say the rhyme as they perform the actions.

Ask children to identify the words that rhyme. Then have them repeat the words *clap, tap,* and *snap* as they listen for the ending sounds.

You may notice that some children have difficulty recognizing rhyming words ending with the -ap phonogram. This lesson will help children recognize the sounds and spelling of this phonogram.

Children Acquiring English
Frequently, children who are acquiring English have difficulty differentiating the short *a* sound from short *e* and short *u* sounds. Give children practice in listening to and pronouncing pairs of words with these vowel sounds. Provide practice with words such as *cap, cup; sap, sup; rap, rut; nap, nut; pup, pep;* and *hap, hep.* Then repeat the word pairs in random order, and ask children to identify which word in each pair has the same ending sounds as *clap.* **COMPARING AND CONTRASTING**

▶ LIFT THE FLAP

After children complete the first two pages of the lesson, they may enjoy creating a bulletin board featuring words and corresponding pictures of items whose names contain the -ap phonogram. Demonstrate how to fold a sheet of construction paper in half. Then explain to children that on the front of the flap they should draw a picture of an item whose name contains the -ap phonogram. Show children how to lift the flap and write the picture name underneath. Assist children who need help in writing the picture names. Help children display their work so the flaps can be lifted. Invite them to look at one another's pictures, guess the picture names, and then lift the flaps to check their guesses.

HOME ACTIVITIES MASTER: Lesson 2

NOTE: Fill in the blanks on the Home
Activities Master before sending it home.
See the Assignment Guide on page T11.

See page T269 for the Home Activities Master.

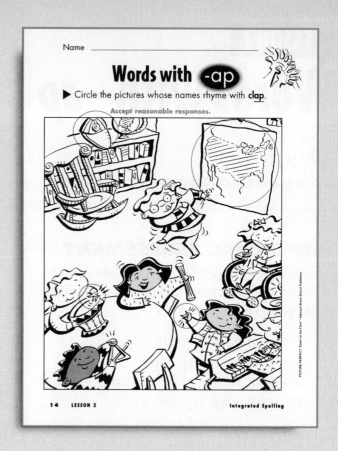

▶ Introduction

WARM-UP
Clap your hands and snap your fingers; then ask children to identify the actions. Have them join you in saying the words *clap* and *snap* as they listen for the ending sounds.

INTRODUCING THE PAGE
Have children turn to page 14 and follow along as you read the lesson title aloud. Direct children's attention to the picture and discuss it with them. You might want to use questions like the following to guide their exploration:

- What are the people doing? (making music)

- What are some ways the children are making music or keeping time to the beat? (playing instruments; snapping, clapping, and tapping)

Invite children to describe other picture details, making sure that the map and the cap are mentioned in the discussion.

Read the directions aloud. Then have children repeat the word *clap* several times as they listen for the ending sounds. Ask a volunteer to restate what children are to do on the page. Point out that they can test for a rhyme by saying *clap* and another word as they listen to determine if the ending sounds are the same—for example, *clap, tap; clap, triangle.*

Either work through the page with children or have them complete it independently. (Children should circle pictures representing the words *tap*ping drum, *snap*ping fingers, *clap*ping hands, *map*, and *cap*.) **CLASSIFYING**

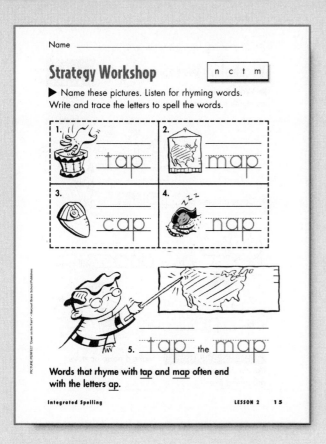

Name _____

Strategy Workshop

| n | c | t | m |

▶ Name these pictures. Listen for rhyming words.
Write and trace the letters to spell the words.

1. *tap*

2. *map*

3. *cap*

4. *nap*

5. *tap* the *map*

Words that rhyme with tap and map often end
with the letters ap.

Integrated Spelling   LESSON 2   15

▶ Strategy Workshop

RHYMING WORDS Help children
recall that rhyming words sound alike except
for their beginning sounds. Explain that
rhyming words are often spelled the same
way except for their beginning letters. Tell
children that they can sometimes figure out
how to spell a word by spelling a rhyming
word and changing the beginning letter.

Help children identify the first picture on
page 15 as fingers tapping a drum. Write the
word *tap* on the board, and have children say
it aloud. Guide them in changing the word *tap*
into the word *lap* by asking the following:

• What letter stands for the beginning sound
of *lap*? (*l*)

• What letters stand for the ending sounds
that you hear in both *tap* and *lap*? (*ap*)

Record children's responses on the board, and
have them read the word *lap* aloud. Explain to
children that they can use this strategy to write
words that name the pictures on this page.

Then help them identify the remaining pictures
as a map, a cap, and someone taking a nap.
APPLYING SPELLING STRATEGIES

SPELLING IN CONTEXT Have
children discuss the picture at the bottom of
page 15. Give guidance as needed to help
them complete the phrase and read it aloud.
(*tap, map*) **CONCEPT OF WORD**

**Extra Support/Children
Acquiring English** Children
may benefit from a review of
the initial consonant sounds
that are blended with the phonogram *-ap* to
form the rhyming picture names. Display pictures whose names begin with /t/, /k/, /m/, and
/n/. Ask children to identify the letter that represents the initial sound of each picture name.

IN SUMMARY Invite children to tell
what they have discovered about spelling
words that rhyme with *tap* and *map*. (These
words often end with the letters *ap*.)

▶ Vocabulary WordShop

WORDSHOP WORDS Point out the WordShop Words on page 16, and ask volunteers to read them aloud. Then discuss with children how these words are alike. (They are all associated with farms.)

Direct children's attention to the pictures, and explain that each person is speaking. Discuss with children what each person might be saying. Read with children the directions at the top of the page. Explain that they are to complete each sentence by writing the words from the box on the lines. Give children assistance in reading the sentences, if necessary. Then have them complete the activity. After children complete the sentences, have them share their responses.

MEETING INDIVIDUAL NEEDS

Children Acquiring English Have children point to the picture of the farm animal as you say its name. Then ask them to point to the picture that shows where the animals live. **BUILDING VOCABULARY**

ACT LIKE AN ANIMAL Assign children to work in groups of three. Then ask children to take turns acting out the noises or movements made by any animal they choose. Other children in the group try to guess the animal. Children may choose the farm animals mentioned on page 16 or other animals they know about.

EXPLORING FARM WORDS

Share the following information to extend children's knowledge about other words associated with farms.

Point out that much of the food we eat is grown or raised on farms. Then work with children to compile a list of vegetables. Explain that other foods come from animals that are raised on farms. Mention that milk comes from cows, eggs from chickens, and beef from cattle.

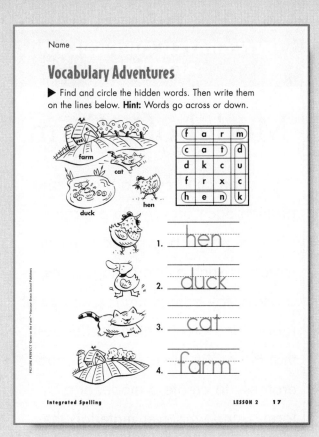

Name _____

Vocabulary Adventures

▶ Find and circle the hidden words. Then write them on the lines below. **Hint:** Words go across or down.

f	a	r	m
c	a	t	d
d	k	c	u
f	r	x	c
h	e	n	k

farm

cat

duck

hen

1. hen

2. duck

3. cat

4. farm

Integrated Spelling   LESSON 2   17

"NOT ONLY DO *beginning readers use their phonics knowledge to enable them to read words they have not seen before, this same knowledge enables them to write.*"
(Patricia M. Cunningham)

VOCABULARY ADVENTURES

Read with children the directions at the top of page 17. Then focus their attention on the large illustration, and read the labels. Explain that this picture shows what words to look for in the puzzle. After the puzzle is finished, have children complete items 1–4 by writing each word they circled next to the correct picture. **USING NAMING WORDS**

MEETING INDIVIDUAL NEEDS

Challenge Suggest that children create similar word-search puzzles, using words in the *-ap* phonogram family. Provide children with grid paper with large squares to record their puzzles. Laminate the finished puzzles or place them in acetate sleeves. Have children use erasable markers to circle their responses.

Farm
★ WORDS ★

Spelling Log Children may want to write the Farm Words from this lesson in their Spelling Logs.

Optional Writing Idea

Shared Writing: Sentences About a Picture

Have children look at the illustration on Pupil's Edition page 14. Ask children to tell what the boys and girls in the classroom are doing. Record their responses on a chart similar to the following:

The boys and girls	
dance	sing
make music	clap
tap a drum	

Have children work cooperatively to write a sentence about the picture. Children can dictate their sentences for you to write, or you may choose to have them use invented spelling to write the sentences themselves.

▶ Lesson Wrap-Up

RETEACH: Learning Differences
Some children may need additional auditory and kinesthetic reinforcement to recognize and spell words containing the *-ap* phonogram. Say pairs of words ending with this phonogram, for example: *tap, snap; sap, rap; nap, map;* and *clap, flap.* Have children chant each pair as they softly clap. After several repetitions, present word pairs that do and do not rhyme, for example: *tap, sap;* and *tap, safe.* Children can signal when the pair rhymes by clapping as they repeat the words.

AUDITORY/KINESTHETIC MODALITIES

Simon Says

Playing the game "Simon Says" is an enjoyable way to reinforce words ending with the phonogram *-ap*. Before starting the game, remind children to perform the specified action only if Simon says so. Then use simple commands such as the following:

Simon says, "Tap your feet."

Simon says, "Clap your hands."

Simon says, "Snap your fingers."

Simon says, "Flap your arms."

LANGUAGE ARTS

Model of a Farm

Assign children to a group, and provide each group with a large piece of poster board and other art materials such as clay, magazines, scissors, toy animal figures, scraps of fabric, and plant materials. Suggest that the group members work cooperatively to create a model of a farm, using whatever materials they like to represent the fields, the animals, the buildings, and the equipment. Have children write farm words on self-stick notes and attach them to their farm models as labels. Display the completed models in the classroom.

ART

Words with -ot

OBJECTIVE
To recognize the sounds and spelling of the phonogram -ot

LESSON PLANNER
See the Assignment Guide on page T11 for a 3-day or 5-day plan.

▶ INFORMAL ASSESSMENT

Have children listen as you recite the following rhyme, emphasizing words with the phonogram -ot:

> What a day!
> It is very h<u>ot</u>.
> I need some ice.
> I need a <u>lot</u>.
> What have you <u>got</u>
> In that <u>pot</u>?
> I have some ice.
> Please take a <u>lot</u>.

Repeat the rhyme several times, encouraging children to act it out by pretending to be hot, pointing to the imaginary pot, and offering the imaginary ice. After several repetitions, children should be able to say the rhyme as they perform the actions.

Ask children to identify the words that rhyme. Then have them repeat the words *hot, lot, got,* and *pot* as they listen for the ending sounds.

You may notice that some children have difficulty recognizing rhyming words ending with the *-ot* phonogram. This lesson will help children recognize the sounds and spelling of this phonogram.

Children Acquiring English
Often, children who are acquiring English have difficulty differentiating the short *o* sound from the short *a* sound. Give children practice in listening to and pronouncing pairs of words with these vowel sounds. For example, use words such as *pot, pat; hot, hat; rot, rat; cot, cat;* and *knot, gnat*. Then repeat the words in random order, and ask children to identify the ones with the short *o* sound.

COMPARING AND CONTRASTING

▶ THE -ot POT

Display a pot labeled "The *-ot* Pot." Provide children with index cards and drawing materials. Then invite them to draw pictures whose names rhyme with the word *pot*. Have children label the pictures before depositing the cards in "The *-ot* Pot."

NOTE: Fill in the blanks on the Home Activities Master before sending it home. See the Assignment Guide on page T11.

See page T270 for the Home Activities Master.

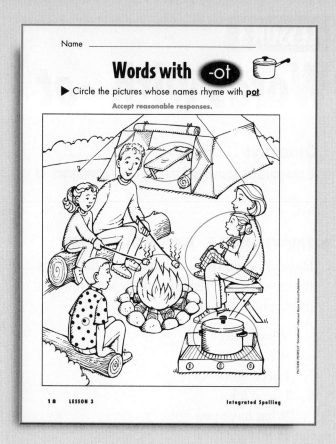

▶ Introduction

WARM-UP
Say this sentence, emphasizing the words *spot, hot,* and *lot*: "This spot got hot a lot." Ask children to repeat the words *spot, hot, got,* and *lot* as they listen for the ending sounds.

INTRODUCING THE PAGE
After reading the lesson title aloud, direct children's attention to the illustration on page 18. You may want to use questions such as the following to discuss the picture with children:

- What is inside the tent?
  (a cot)

- What is on the camp stove?
  (a pot)

- What is on the boy's shirt?
  (dots)

Invite children to describe other picture details, making sure that the tot on the woman's lap and the hot marshmallows and campfire are mentioned in the discussion.

Read the directions aloud. Then have children repeat the word *pot* several times, listening for the ending sounds. Remind children that they can test for a rhyme by saying *pot* and another word as they listen to determine if the ending sounds are the same. Ask a volunteer to restate what children are to do on the page.

Either work through the page with children or have them complete it independently. (Children should circle pictures representing the words *cot, hot, pot, dot,* and *tot*.)

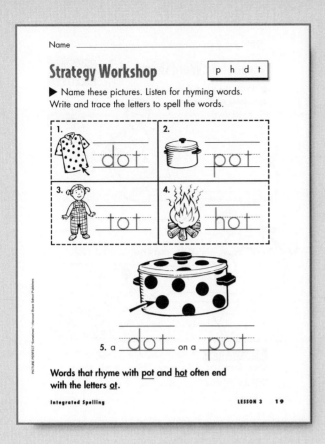

Name _____

Strategy Workshop

| p | h | d | t |

▶ Name these pictures. Listen for rhyming words.
Write and trace the letters to spell the words.

1. dot

2. pot

3. tot

4. hot

5. a ‗dot‗ on a ‗pot‗

Words that rhyme with <u>pot</u> and <u>hot</u> often end
with the letters <u>ot</u>.

Integrated Spelling

LESSON 3   19

▶ Strategy Workshop

RHYMING WORDS Help children recall that rhyming words sound alike except for their beginning sounds. Explain that rhyming words are often spelled the same way except for their beginning letters. Tell children that they can sometimes figure out how to spell a word by spelling a rhyming word and changing the beginning letter.

Help children identify the first picture on page 19 as a dot. Write the word *dot* on the board, and have children say it aloud. Guide them in changing the word *dot* into the word *lot* by asking questions like these:

• What letter stands for the beginning sound of *lot*? *(l)*

• What letters stand for the ending sounds that you hear in both *dot* and *lot*? *(ot)*

Write children's responses on the board, and have them read the word *lot* aloud. Explain to children that they can use this strategy to write words that name the other pictures on

this page. Then help them identify the remaining pictures as representing the words *pot, tot,* and *hot*. **APPLYING SPELLING STRATEGIES**

SPELLING IN CONTEXT Have children discuss the picture at the bottom of page 19. Give guidance as needed to help them complete the phrase and read it aloud. (*dot, pot*) **CONCEPT OF WORD**

MEETING INDIVIDUAL NEEDS **Extra Support/Children Acquiring English** Children may benefit from a review of the initial consonant sounds that are blended with the *-ot* phonogram to form the rhyming picture names. Display pictures whose names begin with /p/, /h/, /d/, and /t/. Have children identify the letter that represents the initial sound of each picture name.

IN SUMMARY Invite children to tell what they have discovered about spelling words that rhyme with *hot* and *pot*. (These words often end with the letters *ot*.)

Vocabulary WordShop

WORDSHOP WORDS Point out the WordShop Words on page 20, and ask volunteers to read them aloud. Then talk with children about how these words are alike. (Each word can be used to refer to a person.)

Direct children's attention to the illustrations, and ask volunteers to describe what they see pictured. Read the directions with children. Explain that they are to complete the sentences the boy is saying by writing the words from the box on the lines. After children complete the activity, have them share their responses.

 Children Acquiring English Play a game in which children make up sentences using the WordShop Words. Explain that when they use the word *I* or *me* they should point to themselves. If they use the word *you*, then they should point to someone else in the group. **BUILDING VOCABULARY**

WHAT I LIKE Provide children with drawing materials. Suggest that children draw a picture of themselves with a favorite possession or doing an activity they enjoy. Encourage children to use the WordShop Words when discussing their work.

EXPLORING PERSON WORDS Extend children's knowledge about the Person Words by asking questions like these:

• Which two WordShop Words can you use to talk about yourself?

• Which WordShop Word can you use to take the place of a person's name?

Name _____

Vocabulary Adventures

▶ Look at the picture. Write words to tell what the children are saying.

| you |
| me |
| I |

1. My dog and ___I___ are happy.

2. Do _you_ see my dog?

3. My dog will come to __me__.

PICTURE PERFECT "Sometimes" • Harcourt Brace School Publishers

Integrated Spelling

LESSON 3   21

> " REAL CHILDREN'S BOOKS, *with their authentic texts, are what children check their invented spellings against.* "
> *(Kenneth S. Goodman)*

VOCABULARY ADVENTURES

Read with children the directions at the top of page 21. Then focus their attention on the large illustration, and explain that looking at the picture will help them complete the activity. Then point out the children's faces next to each sentence, and explain that the children are talking about their dogs. Have children write words from the box to complete the sentences. After children complete the activity, have them share and explain their responses.

USING PERSONAL PRONOUNS

Working Together Point out that each face on page 21 signals who is speaking, and the words next to the face tell what the speaker is saying. Assign partners, and have children read aloud the sentences as a dialogue.

Spelling Log Children may want to write the Person Words from this lesson in their Spelling Logs.

Optional Writing Idea

Patterned Writing: Sentences Direct children's attention to the large picture on Pupil's Edition page 21, and help them identify the setting as a park. Then make a chart with the headings *Sights* and *Sounds*. Have children volunteer words that name sights and sounds associated with a park. Record their responses.

Sights	Sounds
birds	chirping
people	laughing
dogs	barking

Write these sentence frames on the chart, and help children read them aloud:

I see the _____. They are _____.

Invite children to write a word from each column to complete the sentences. Have children share their completed sentences with the class.

▶ Lesson Wrap-Up

RETEACH: Learning Differences

Some children may benefit from additional auditory and kinesthetic reinforcement to recognize and spell words containing the *-ot* phonogram. Say pairs of words, such as *hot, pot; cot, cat; tot, lot;* and *rot, rat*. If both words end with the phonogram *-ot*, have children stand and clap as they repeat the word pair. **AUDITORY/KINESTHETIC MODALITIES**

Pet Books

Children might enjoy making pet books about an imaginary, personal, or classroom pet. Explain to children that a pet book might include a description of their pet, a drawing or photograph, and details about what they like about and do together with their pet. Children can make their own pet books by stapling blank pages between decorated construction paper covers. Then invite them to fill up the book with words, phrases, sentences, stories, or even rhymes that refer to their pets.

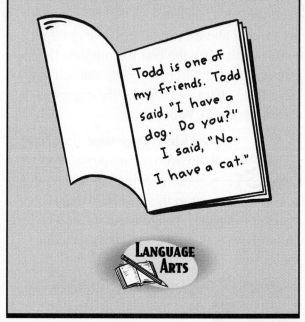

Todd is one of my friends. Todd said, "I have a dog. Do you?" I said, "No. I have a cat."

LANGUAGE ARTS

Words with -an

OBJECTIVE

To recognize the sounds and spelling of the phonogram -an

LESSON PLANNER

See the Assignment Guide on page T11 for a 3-day or 5-day plan.

▶ INFORMAL ASSESSMENT

Have children listen as you read the following traditional rhyme aloud, emphasizing the -an phonogram each time it occurs:

> D<u>an</u>, D<u>an</u>, the butcher m<u>an</u>,
> Washed his face in a frying p<u>an</u>.

Repeat the rhyme several times, encouraging children to chime in as they become familiar with the words. They may enjoy clapping or tapping in rhythm.

Ask children to identify the rhyming words. Then have them repeat the words *Dan, man,* and *pan* as they listen for the ending sounds.

You may notice that some children have difficulty recognizing rhyming words ending with the -*an* phonogram. This lesson will help children recognize the sounds and spelling of this phonogram.

Children Acquiring English
Frequently, children who are acquiring English have difficulty differentiating the short *a* sound from short *e* and short *u* sounds. Give children practice in listening to and pronouncing pairs of words with these vowel sounds. For examples, use words such as *man, men; pan, pen; can, cup; ban, bun; ran, run;* and *fan, fun.* **COMPARING AND CONTRASTING**

▶ THE -an CAN

Label a large, empty can with a plastic lid "The -*an* Can." Cut a slit in the lid so that children can deposit words and pictures in the can. Invite children to look through discarded magazines and newspapers to find pictures whose names rhyme with the word *can.* Have children cut out the pictures, mount them on large index cards, and label the pictures before depositing the cards in the empty can. Encourage children to check the cards to make sure that all the picture names belong in the -*an* family.

NOTE: Fill in the blanks on the Home Activities Master before sending it home. See the Assignment Guide on page T11.

See page T271 for the Home Activities Master.

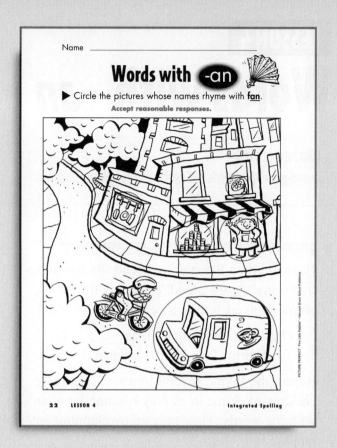

▶Introduction

WARM-UP Fold a piece of paper accordion fashion, and ask a volunteer to show how it can be used as a fan. Have children join you in saying the words *can* and *fan* as they listen for the rhyming sounds.

INTRODUCING THE PAGE

Have children turn to page 22 and follow along as you read the lesson title aloud. Focus children's attention on the picture, and discuss it with them. You might want to use questions like the following to guide their exploration:

• What is the child doing? (riding a bicycle)

• What people and things does the child pass while riding his bicycle? (pans and cans in a shop, a van, a man)

Invite children to describe other picture details. Draw attention to the window fan, and have children compare it with the hand fan shown at the top of the page.

Read the directions aloud. Then have children repeat the word *fan* several times as they listen for the ending sounds. Remind children that they can test for a rhyme by saying *fan* and another word as they listen to determine if the ending sounds are the same.

Either work through the page with children or have them complete it independently. (Children should circle pictures representing the words *pan, can, van, man,* and *fan.*)

CLASSIFYING

Name _____

Strategy Workshop

[v f p m]

▶ Name these pictures. Listen for rhyming words.
Write and trace the letters to spell the words.

1. fan
2. van
3. man
4. pan

5. the man in the van

Words that rhyme with <u>man</u> and <u>van</u> often end
with the letters <u>an</u>.

Integrated Spelling   LESSON 4   23

▶ Strategy Workshop

RHYMING WORDS Remind children that rhyming words sound alike except for their beginning sounds. Explain that rhyming words are often spelled the same way except for their beginning letters. Tell children that they can sometimes figure out how to spell a word by spelling a rhyming word and changing the beginning letter.

Help children identify the first picture on page 23 as a fan. Write the word *fan* on the board, and have children say it aloud. Guide them in changing the word *fan* into the word *tan* by asking questions like these:

- What letter stands for the beginning sound of *tan*? (*t*)

- What letters stand for the ending sounds that you hear in both *fan* and *tan*? (*an*)

Record children's responses on the board, and have them read the word *tan* aloud. Explain to children that they can use this strategy to write words that name the pictures on this page. Then help them identify the remaining pictures as a van, a man, and a pan. **APPLYING SPELLING STRATEGIES**

SPELLING IN CONTEXT Have children discuss the picture at the bottom of page 23. Help children complete the phrase and read it aloud. (*man, van*)

CONCEPT OF WORD

MEETING INDIVIDUAL NEEDS

Extra Support/Children Acquiring English Children may benefit from a review of the initial consonant sounds that are blended with the phonogram *-an* to form the rhyming picture names. Display pictures whose names begin with /f/, /v/, /m/, and /p/. Ask children to identify the letter that represents the initial sound of each picture name.

IN SUMMARY Invite children to tell what they have discovered about spelling words that rhyme with *man* and *van*. (These words often end with the letters *an*.)

Name _____

Vocabulary WordShop

▶ Draw a line to help the cat count the rabbits. Write the word that tells how many rabbits are in each hat.

Number
· WORDS ·

one
two
three

1. three

2. one

3. two

24   LESSON 4   Integrated Spelling

▶Vocabulary WordShop

WORDSHOP WORDS   Point out the WordShop Words on page 24, and ask volunteers to read them aloud. Then discuss with children how the words are alike. (They name numbers).

Point out the maze before reading aloud the directions. If children are unfamiliar with mazes, explain what a maze is and how to move through one. Point out that if a pathway is blocked, a different path should be tried. Read with children the directions at the top of the page. Before children draw a line, suggest that they use a finger to trace a path. Have children complete the maze and then write words from the box to label the pictures. After children complete the page, ask them to share their responses.

 Working Together You might want to have children work with a partner to complete the maze and write the WordShop Words. Suggest that

each child trace the maze with a finger before drawing a line.

EXPLORING NUMBER WORDS   Extend children's knowledge of the WordShop Words through the following activity:

• Make a chart on the board with the headings *one, two,* and *three.*

• Ask children to name things in the classroom of which there is only one. For example, there may be one teacher's desk, one door, or one American flag. List each response under the appropriate heading.

• Ask children to name things that come in twos–for example, two eyes, two ears, two hands, two feet, two socks, two shoes, or two gloves. Record all responses under the appropriate heading.

• Invite children to name classroom items of which they find three. For example, there might be three children named Chris, three pet rabbits, or three pieces of chalk. Write all responses under the heading *three.*

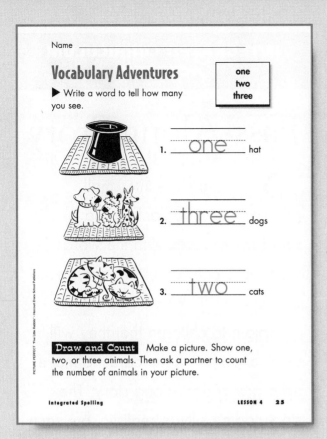

Name _____

Vocabulary Adventures

▶ Write a word to tell how many you see.

| one |
| two |
| three |

1. __one__ hat

2. __three__ dogs

3. __two__ cats

Draw and Count Make a picture. Show one, two, or three animals. Then ask a partner to count the number of animals in your picture.

Integrated Spelling   LESSON 4   25

"**W**HENEVER WE WRITE, *we engage in the process of spelling, the act of transforming our thoughts into a visual record by placing graphic symbols, or graphemes, on a writing surface.*"
(Richard E. Hodges)

VOCABULARY ADVENTURES

Read with children the directions at the top of page 25. Call attention to the first picture, and ask children to tell what they see on the mat. Then ask them to count the number of hats they see. Have children write their responses on the line next to the picture. Guide children through the rest of the activity, or have them complete it independently. **USING NUMBER WORDS**

DRAW AND COUNT

Provide children with drawing materials. After children make and share their pictures, suggest that they label those pictures with a WordShop Word.

Number ★ WORDS ★ **Spelling Log** Children may want to write the Number Words from this lesson in their Spelling Logs.

Optional Writing Idea

Shared Writing: Sentences About a Picture Encourage children to work together to make up sentences about the picture on Pupil's Edition page 22. Help children brainstorm by asking the following questions:

• What do the people in the picture look like? What are they doing?

• Where are the people in the picture?

• What do you think will happen to the people next?

Have children use their ideas to write sentences that might be made into a group story. Children can dictate their sentences for you to write, or they can use invented spelling to write the sentences themselves.

▶ Lesson Wrap-Up

RETEACH: Learning Differences
Some children may benefit from additional auditory and kinesthetic reinforcement to recognize and spell words containing the -an phonogram. Say pairs of words, such as *man, can; fan, fun; tan, van; ran, run; man, men;* and *fan, can.* Have children listen to each word pair and repeat the words after you. If both words end with the phonogram -an, have children stand and clap as they repeat the word pairs. **AUDITORY/ KINESTHETIC MODALITIES**

Pass-Along Story

Divide the class into small groups, and give each group a set of index cards with the words *man, van, can, pan, fan, one, two,* and *three.*

Explain to children that they will use the words on the cards to make up a group pass-along story. The story can be silly or realistic, but each sentence in the story should include one of the words on the cards.

Have children mix up the cards and place them face down. Then begin the story with a sentence such as *One day, Nan went shopping.* Have a child select a card, read the word, and use the word in a story sentence. Continue until all the words are incorporated into the story.

LANGUAGE ARTS

Words with -at

OBJECTIVE

To recognize the sounds and spelling of the phonogram -at

LESSON PLANNER

See the Assignment Guide on page T11 for a 3-day or 5-day plan.

▶ INFORMAL ASSESSMENT

Have children listen as you say the following rhyme, emphasizing words ending with the phonogram -at:

> First, meow like a c<u>at</u>.
> Then, flap your arms like a b<u>at</u>.
> Next, give your head a p<u>at</u>.
> Last, set your hand down fl<u>at</u>.

Repeat the rhyme, one line at a time. Have children say each line with you and then follow its direction. After several repetitions, children should be able to recite the rhyme.

Ask children to identify the words that rhyme. Then have them repeat the words *cat, bat, pat,* and *flat* as they listen for the ending sounds.

You may notice that some children have difficulty recognizing rhyming words ending with the *-at* phonogram. This lesson will help children recognize the sounds and spelling of this phonogram.

MEETING INDIVIDUAL NEEDS

Children Acquiring English Frequently, children who are acquiring English have difficulty differentiating the short *a* sound from the short *e* and short *u* sounds. Give children practice in listening to and pronouncing pairs of words with these vowel sounds. Provide practice with pairs of words such as *cat, cut; bat, bet; bat, but; hat, hut; mat, met; pat, pet;* and *sat, set.* Then repeat the word pairs in random order, and ask children to identify which word in each pair has the same ending sounds as *fat.* **COMPARING AND CONTRASTING**

▶ THE -at HATS

After children complete the first two pages of the lesson, they may enjoy making their own paper hats that they decorate with words that contain the -at phonogram. Distribute a sheet of construction paper and school glue or tape to each child. Model for children how to fold and fasten a sheet of paper to make a hat. Then explain that children should write words that contain the -at phonogram on their hats. They might write words using crayons, paint, or glue and glitter. Later, encourage children to display their hats. Challenge volunteers to locate and read all the -at words on each hat.

NOTE: Fill in the blanks on the Home Activities Master before sending it home. See the Assignment Guide on page T11.

See page T272 for the Home Activities Master.

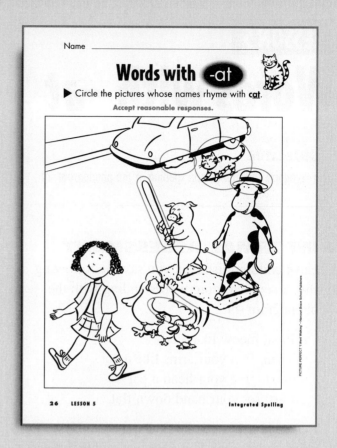

▶Introduction

WARM-UP Display pictures of a cat and a bat. Ask children to identify each animal. Have them repeat the words *cat* and *bat* with you several times as they listen for the ending sounds.

INTRODUCING THE PAGE

Have children turn to page 26 and follow along as you read the lesson title aloud. Direct children's attention to the picture and discuss it with them. You might want to use questions like the following to guide their exploration:

• What are the animals walking across as they follow the girl? (a mat)

• What is the pig carrying? (a baseball bat)

• What is the mother duck doing to her ducklings? (patting them)

• What is the cow wearing? (a hat)

• What animal is near the car? (a cat)

Invite children to describe other picture details, making sure that the flat tire is mentioned in the discussion.

Read the directions aloud. Then have children repeat the word *cat* several times as they listen for the ending sounds. Ask a volunteer to restate what children are to do on the page. Point out that they can test for a rhyme by saying *cat* and another word as they listen to determine if the ending sounds are the same—for example, *cat, hat; cat, tire*.

Either work through the page with children or have them complete it independently, identifying the rhyming words. (Children should circle pictures representing the words *bat, hat, mat, pat, cat* and *flat*.). **CLASSIFYING**

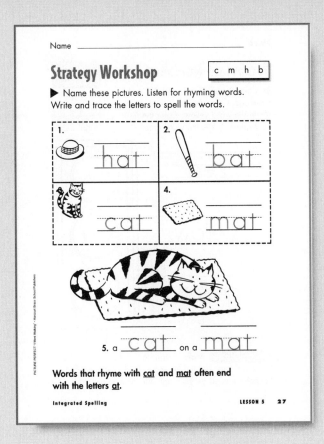

Name _____

Strategy Workshop

| c | m | h | b |

▶ Name these pictures. Listen for rhyming words.
Write and trace the letters to spell the words.

1. hat

2. bat

3. cat

4. mat

5. a cat on a mat

Words that rhyme with <u>cat</u> and <u>mat</u> often end
with the letters <u>at</u>.

Integrated Spelling   LESSON 5   27

▶Strategy Workshop

RHYMING WORDS Help children
recall that rhyming words sound alike except
for their beginning sounds. Explain that
rhyming words are often spelled the same
way except for their beginning letters. Tell
children that they can sometimes figure out
how to spell a word by spelling a rhyming
word and changing the beginning letter.

Help children identify the first picture on
page 27 as a hat. Write the word *hat* on the
board, and have children say it aloud. Guide
them by changing the word *hat* into the word
fat by asking the following:

• What letter stands for the beginning sound
  of *fat*? (*f*)

• What letters stand for the ending sounds that
  you hear in both *hat* and *fat*? (*at*)

Record children's responses on the board, and
have them read the word *fat* aloud. Explain to
children that they can use this strategy to
write words that name the pictures on this
page. Then help them identify the remaining
pictures as a bat, cat, and mat. **APPLYING
SPELLING STRATEGIES**

SPELLING IN CONTEXT Have
children discuss the picture at the bottom of
page 27. Give guidance as needed to help
them complete the phrase and read it aloud.
(*cat, mat*). **CONCEPT OF WORD**

**Extra Support/Children
Acquiring English** Children
may benefit from a review of
the initial consonant sounds
that are blended with the phonogram -*at* to
form the rhyming picture words. Display pictures whose names begin with /h/, /b/, /k/, and
/m/. Ask children to identify the letter that
represents the initial sound of each picture
name.

IN SUMMARY Invite children to tell
what they have discovered about spelling
words that rhyme with *cat* and *mat*. (These
words often end with the letters *at*.)

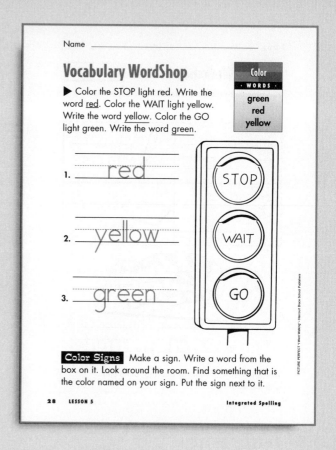

▶ Vocabulary WordShop

WORDSHOP WORDS Point out the WordShop Words on page 28, and ask volunteers to read them aloud. Then discuss with children how the words are alike. (They all name colors.)

Direct children's attention to the picture of the traffic light. Discuss the illustration, and ask children to read the word that appears on each light. Provide children with red, yellow, and green crayons or markers. Then read with children the directions at the top of the page. Explain that they are to color each light and to label the picture by writing the words from the box on the lines. After children complete the activity, have them discuss their responses.

Children Acquiring English
Play a game in which children move around the room. Write each WordShop Word on a sign. Explain to children that you will hold up a sign with a WordShop Word on it. If the word is *green*, they are to go for a walk around the room. If the word is *yellow*, they are to sit and wait for the next direction. If the word is *red*, they are to stop walking or "freeze" in their position. **BUILDING VOCABULARY**

COLOR SIGNS Provide children with construction paper on which they can write Color Words to make their signs. After children complete the activity, they can use their signs to begin a color words category on a word wall.

EXPLORING COLOR WORDS
Invite children to name food items that are either red, yellow, or green, for example:

• Red: tomato, strawberry, cherry, apple

• Yellow: banana, corn, squash, butter, lemon

• Green: lettuce, pea, cucumber, celery, pear

Encourage children to draw or paint pictures of foods they have named and to label each food with the name of its color.

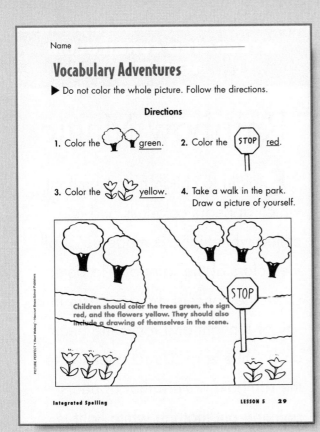

Vocabulary Adventures

▶ Do not color the whole picture. Follow the directions.

Directions

1. Color the 🌳🌳 green.   2. Color the (STOP) red.

3. Color the 🌷🌷 yellow.   4. Take a walk in the park. Draw a picture of yourself.

Children should color the trees green, the sign red, and the flowers yellow. They should also include a drawing of themselves in the scene.

Name _____

Integrated Spelling   LESSON 5   29

> ❝**F**INALLY, THE KEY *to an effective spelling program is the establishment of a strong classroom writing program.*❞
> (Darrell Morris)

VOCABULARY ADVENTURES

Read aloud the directions at the top of page 29. Then direct children's attention to the illustration, and have volunteers identify the trees, the stop sign, and the flowers in the scene. Provide children with red, green, and yellow crayons or markers, and help them read the individual instructions. Have children complete the page independently, providing help as necessary. **USING COLOR WORDS**

 Working Together This activity lends itself to having children work in pairs. Partners can take turns, with one child reading aloud one step in the directions while the other does the coloring task.

 Spelling Log Children may want to write the Color Words from this lesson in their Spelling Logs.

Optional Writing Idea

 Shared Writing: Safety Rules Ask children to look at the picture of the traffic light on Pupil's Edition page 28. Encourage them to make up a list of safety rules to follow when crossing a street. Help children generate ideas by asking these questions:

• Where should you stand while waiting to cross a street?

• Where should you look before going into a street?

Have children use their ideas to write sentences that may be turned into a set of rules. Children can dictate their sentences for you to write, or you may choose to have them use invented spelling to write the sentences themselves.

▶Lesson Wrap-Up

RETEACH: Learning Differences

Provide children with finger paints and paper. Then write the following words with the -at phonogram on the board: *bat, hat, mat, cat, flat, fat, sat, rat.* Randomly point to each word, read it aloud, and have children repeat it with you. Then have children copy the word, using the finger paints. After the paint is dry, have children show their words to a partner and have the partner spell and read aloud each word.

AUDITORY/KINESTHETIC MODALITIES

Rainbow Magic

Explain to children that sunlight, which appears colorless and is called white light, is made up of all the colors of the rainbow. To demonstrate the concept, hold a prism in a ray of sunlight and focus the beam on a white card. Direct attention to the rainbow pattern that appears, pointing out that the white light is separated into the colors that make it up. (If a prism is unavailable, fill a shallow pan with water and rest a mirror against the inside of the pan. Place the dish so that sunlight falls on the mirror and projects the rainbow onto the card.)

Help children identify the colors of the rainbow. Encourage children to draw or paint rainbow pictures.

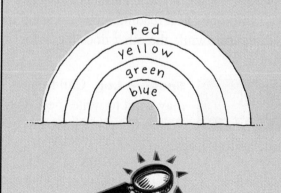

SCIENCE

Words with -op

OBJECTIVE

To recognize the sounds and spelling of the phonogram -op

LESSON PLANNER

See the Assignment Guide on page T11 for a 3-day or 5-day plan.

▶ INFORMAL ASSESSMENT

Have children carry out the actions indicated in parentheses as you read the following rhyme aloud. Emphasize words ending with the phonogram -op:

Everyone h<u>op</u>, h<u>op</u>, h<u>op</u>!
(*Children hop in place.*)
Everyone dr<u>op</u>, dr<u>op</u>, dr<u>op</u>!
(*Children stoop and touch the floor.*)
Everyone cl<u>op</u>, cl<u>op</u>, cl<u>op</u>!
(*Children march in place.*)
Everyone fl<u>op</u>, fl<u>op</u>, fl<u>op</u>!
(*Children bend over at waist.*)
Everyone st<u>op</u>, st<u>op</u>, st<u>op</u>!
(*Children slowly sink to the floor and stop moving.*)

Invite several children to help you lead the rhyme as you repeat it several times. As the words become familiar, encourage children to chime in as they perform the actions.

Ask children to identify the words that rhyme. Then have them repeat the words *hop, drop, clop, flop*, and *stop* as they listen for the ending sounds.

You may notice that some children have difficulty recognizing rhyming words ending with the -op phonogram. This lesson will help children recognize the sounds and spelling of this phonogram.

Children Acquiring English
The short *o* sound in words such as *hop* and *stop* may present difficulties for children who speak Spanish, Tagalog, Thai, Vietnamese, and Chinese. These children may confuse the short *o* sound with the vowel sounds they hear in *hut, road*, or *taught*. To assist children, give them practice in listening to and pronouncing pairs of words with these vowel sounds. For example, use words such as *hop, hope; pop, pup;* and *sop, soap*. **COMPARING AND CONTRASTING**

▶ WORD STORE

After children complete the first two pages of the lesson, they may enjoy setting up a display for a store called "The -op Shop" that features words ending with the -op phonogram. Provide children with construction paper labels and a number of clean and empty food cans and packages. Have children write words ending with the phonogram -op on the labels. After children attach the labels to the containers, have them arrange a display of the "merchandise."

Encourage children to browse in "The -op Shop." Suggest that partners take turns selecting a container, reading the word on the label, and then using the word in a sentence.

NOTE: Fill in the blanks on the Home Activities Master before sending it home. See the Assignment Guide on page T11.

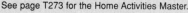

See page T273 for the Home Activities Master.

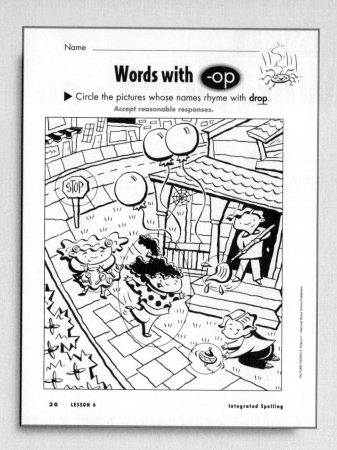

Introduction

WARM-UP Ask a volunteer to spin around like a top. Then ask the child to stop. Have children repeat the words *top* and *stop* as they listen for the rhyming sounds.

INTRODUCING THE PAGE

Have children follow along as you read the lesson title on page 30. Focus children's attention on activities and items illustrated in the picture. Guide a discussion by asking the following:

• What is the boy using to clean the steps? (a mop)

• What are the children doing to have fun? (doing a hop; playing with a top)

• What sign tells people in cars what to do when they reach the street corner? (a stop sign)

Invite children to name other picture details, making sure that the lollipop design on the girl's dress is mentioned in the discussion.

Read the directions aloud. Then have children repeat the word *drop* several times as they listen for the ending sounds. Ask a volunteer to restate what children are to do on the page. Remind children that they can test for a rhyme by saying *drop* and another word as they listen to determine if the ending sounds are the same–for example, *drop, crop* and *drop, rope.*

Either work through the page with children or have them complete it independently. (Children should circle pictures representing the words *mop*, a child doing a *hop, top, stop* sign, and the lolli*pop* design.) **CLASSIFYING**

Name _____

Strategy Workshop

| m | t | p | h |

▶ Name these pictures. Listen for rhyming words. Write and trace the letters to spell the words.

1. pop
2. hop
3. mop
4. top

5. the top of the mop

Words that rhyme with top and mop often end with the letters op.

Integrated Spelling   LESSON 6   31

▶ Strategy Workshop

RHYMING WORDS Help children recall that rhyming words sound alike except for their beginning sounds. Explain that rhyming words are often spelled the same way except for their beginning letters. Tell children that they can sometimes figure out how to spell a word by spelling a rhyming word and changing the beginning letter.

Help children identify the first picture on page 31 as a popping balloon. Write the word *pop* on the board, and have children say it aloud. Guide them in changing the word *pop* into the word *top* by asking the following:

- What letter stands for the beginning sound of *top*? (*t*)
- What letters stand for the ending sounds that you hear in both *pop* and *top*? (*op*)

Record children's responses on the board, and have them read the word *top* aloud. Explain to children that they can use this strategy to write words that name the pictures on this page. Then help them identify the remaining pictures as representing the words *hop, mop,* and *top*. **APPLYING SPELLING STRATEGIES**

SPELLING IN CONTEXT Have children discuss the picture at the bottom of page 31. Help children complete the phrase and read it aloud. (*top, mop*) **CONCEPT OF WORD**

MEETING INDIVIDUAL NEEDS

Extra Support/Children Acquiring English Children may benefit from a review of the initial consonant sounds that are blended with the phonogram *-op* to form the rhyming picture names. Display pictures whose names begin with /p/, /h/, /m/, and /t/. Ask children to identify the letter that represents the initial sound of each picture name.

IN SUMMARY Invite children to tell what they have discovered about spelling words that rhyme with *mop* and *top*. (These words often end with the letters *op*.)

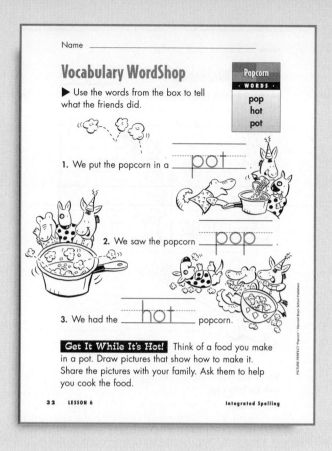

Name _____

Vocabulary WordShop

▶ Use the words from the box to tell what the friends did.

Popcorn
• WORDS •

pop
hot
pot

1. We put the popcorn in a _pot_.

2. We saw the popcorn _pop_.

3. We had the _hot_ popcorn.

Get It While It's Hot! Think of a food you make in a pot. Draw pictures that show how to make it. Share the pictures with your family. Ask them to help you cook the food.

32   LESSON 6   Integrated Spelling

▶Vocabulary WordShop

WORDSHOP WORDS Point out the WordShop Words on page 32, and ask volunteers to read them aloud. Then discuss with children how the words are alike. (They all have something to do with popcorn.)

Read with children the directions at the top of the page. Then direct children's attention to the pictures. Explain that each picture and sentence tells something about what the friends did together. Assist children in reading the sentences, if necessary. Then have them complete the sentences by writing words from the box.

MEETING INDIVIDUAL NEEDS

Children Acquiring English
Have children look at the first picture. Ask them to identify the popcorn and the pot. Then have children explain what happens to the popcorn in the pot before it is eaten. **BUILDING VOCABULARY**

GET IT WHILE IT'S HOT!

Before children begin to draw, talk with them about different foods that are prepared in a pot, such as soup, stew, or hot dogs. Invite children who have watched or helped an adult make such foods share details about the experience. Encourage children to share their completed pictures with their families.

EXPLORING POPCORN WORDS Extend children's knowledge about the WordShop Words and the process of making popcorn by asking the following:

• How does popcorn look, feel, and taste before it is cooked?

• How does popcorn change after it is popped? Tell how it looks, feels, and tastes.

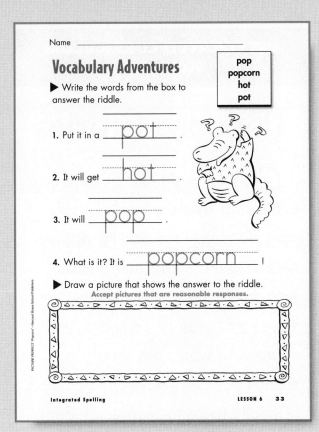

Name _____

Vocabulary Adventures

| pop |
| popcorn |
| hot |
| pot |

▶ Write the words from the box to answer the riddle.

1. Put it in a _pot_ .

2. It will get _hot_ .

3. It will _pop_ .

4. What is it? It is _popcorn_ !

▶ Draw a picture that shows the answer to the riddle.
Accept pictures that are reasonable responses.

Integrated Spelling

LESSON 6   33

PICTURE PERFECT "Popcorn" • Harcourt Brace School Publishers

" **T**HE ENGLISH LANGUAGE *is besieged with patterns . . . . Spelling patterns should be taught and practiced by the child.* **"** (Robert McCracken and Marlene McCracken)

VOCABULARY ADVENTURES

Read with children the directions for the first activity at the top of page 33. Remind children to write words from the box to complete the sentences. Afterward, have them share and explain their responses.

Read the directions for the second activity with children. Before children begin to draw, point out that they wrote the answer to the riddle in sentence 4. Have a volunteer give the answer to the riddle. **USING NAMING, DESCRIBING, AND ACTION WORDS**

★ WORDS ★

Spelling Log Children may want to write the Popcorn Words from this lesson in their Spelling Logs.

Optional Writing Idea

Patterned Writing: Sentences Create a word web about foods cooked in a pot by drawing a picture of a large pot with eight lines extending from it on chart paper. Ask volunteers to name foods they would mix together in a pot to make something to eat. Write each response next to a line.

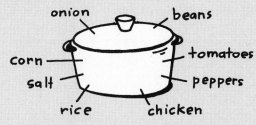

Write this sentence frame on the board, and help children read it aloud:

Put ___ and ___ in the pot.

Have children copy and complete the sentence frame by writing words from the word web.

Lesson 6   **T55**

►Lesson Wrap-Up

RETEACH: Learning Differences

Distribute index cards on which you have pasted a sandpaper rectangle with the letters *op* written with a black marker. Then say words such as *hop, pop, plop, stop, bop, shop,* and *top.* As you pronounce each word, emphasize the *-op* phonogram. Have children say the word as they trace the letters *op* on the sandpaper. **AUDITORY/KINESTHETIC MODALITIES**

Popcorn Stories

Children might enjoy creating comic-strip style stories about popcorn. To initiate the activity, display several comic strips, and discuss how the pictures as well as the words tell the story. Point out that the characters' words are shown in speech balloons. Have children work in small groups to brainstorm ideas for their stories. After children brainstorm, suggest that they divide the jobs of drawing and writing. Provide a place where children can display their finished stories.

LANGUAGE ARTS

LESSON 7

Words with -et

OBJECTIVE

To recognize the sounds and spelling of the phonogram -et

LESSON PLANNER

See the Assignment Guide on page T11 for a 3-day or 5-day plan.

▶ INFORMAL ASSESSMENT

Before reading the following rhyme, ask children to stand and imagine that they are standing on the edge of a pool, ready to dive or jump in. As you read, emphasize words with the -et phonogram.

> G<u>et</u> ready!
> G<u>et</u> s<u>et</u>!
> It's time to <u>get</u> w<u>et</u>!

Repeat the rhyme several times, and encourage children to join in. After several repetitions, children should be able to recite the rhyme.

Ask children to identify the words that rhyme. Then have them repeat the words *get*, *set*, and *wet* as they listen for the ending sounds.

You may notice that some children have difficulty recognizing rhyming words ending with the -et phonogram. This lesson will help children recognize the sounds and spelling of this phonogram.

Children Acquiring English
Frequently, children who are acquiring English have problems distinguishing between the sounds of short *e* and short *a*. These children may benefit from practice in listening to and repeating pairs of words with these vowel sounds. Provide practice with words such as *bet, bat; vet, vat; pet, pat; set, sat;* and *met, mat*.

In addition, speakers of Spanish, Vietnamese, and Tagalog may find it difficult to distinguish the sound of short *e* from the sound of long *a*. These children may benefit from practice with word pairs such as *wet,*

wait; let, late; get, gate; met, mate; and *bet, bait*. **COMPARING AND CONTRASTING**

JET SET

▶ Distribute simple cutout shapes of jets, and invite children to write on each shape a word that belongs to the -et family. Have children add this set of words to the classroom word wall or use them to create a bulletin board.

NOTE: Fill in the blanks on the Home Activities Master before sending it home. See the Assignment Guide on page T11.

See page T274 for the Home Activities Master.

Name _____

Words with -et ✈

▶ Circle the pictures whose names rhyme with **jet**.

Accept reasonable responses.

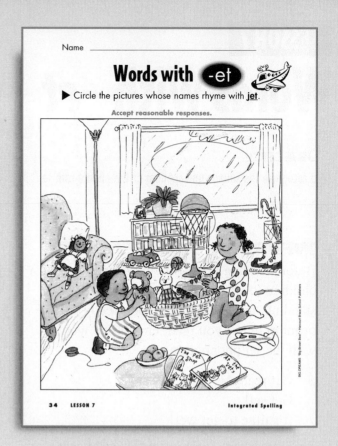

34   LESSON 7   Integrated Spelling

▶Introduction

WARM-UP Have children repeat the phrase *get set* several times as they listen for rhyming sounds.

INTRODUCING THE PAGE

Have children turn to page 34 and follow along as you read the lesson title. Focus children's attention on the picture, and discuss it with them. You might want to use questions like the following to guide their exploration:

• What are the children doing? (putting away toys)

• What toys do you see? (stuffed animals, basketball, yo-yo, jump rope, car, doll, basketball net, jet) If necessary, direct children's attention to the basketball net and the jet.

• Look at the book covers and titles. What do you think these books are about? (pets, a vet) If children are unfamiliar with the role of a veterinarian (vet), you may want to discuss it briefly.

Invite children to describe other picture details. If necessary, call attention to the wet rain on the window.

Read the directions aloud. Then have children repeat the word *jet* several times as they listen for the ending sounds. Ask a volunteer to restate what children are to do on the page. Remind children that they can test for a rhyme by saying *jet* and another word as they listen to determine if the ending sounds are the same.

Either work through the page with children or have them complete it independently. (Children should circle pictures representing the words *jet, net, pet, vet,* and *wet*.)

CLASSIFYING

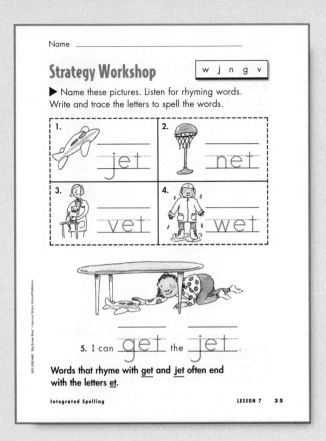

Name _____

Strategy Workshop

| w | j | n | g | v |

▶ Name these pictures. Listen for rhyming words.
Write and trace the letters to spell the words.

1. jet
2. net
3. vet
4. wet

5. I can get the jet .

Words that rhyme with get and jet often end
with the letters et.

Integrated Spelling   LESSON 7   35

▶ Strategy Workshop

RHYMING WORDS Help children
recall that rhyming words sound alike except
for their beginning sounds. Explain that
rhyming words are often spelled the same
way except for their beginning letters. Tell
children that they can sometimes figure out
how to spell a word by spelling a rhyming
word and changing the beginning letter.

Help children identify the first picture on
page 35 as a toy jet. Write the word *jet* on the
board, and have children say it aloud. Guide
them in changing the word *jet* into the word
pet by asking questions such as these:

• What letter stands for the beginning sound
  of *pet*? (*p*)

• What letters stand for the ending sounds
  that you hear in both *jet* and *pet*? (*et*)

Write children's responses on the board, and
have them read the word *pet* aloud. Explain to
children that they can use this strategy to
write words that name the pictures on this
page. Then help them identify the remaining
pictures as a net, a vet, and a child who is
wet. **APPLYING SPELLING STRATEGIES**

SPELLING IN CONTEXT Have
children look at and discuss the picture at the
bottom of page 35. Help children complete
the sentence and read it aloud. (*get, jet*)
CONCEPT OF WORD

MEETING INDIVIDUAL NEEDS **Extra Support/Children
Acquiring English** Children
may benefit from a review of
the initial consonant sounds that
are blended with the phonogram *-et* to form the
rhyming picture names. Display pictures whose
names begin with /j/, /n/, /v/, /w/, and /g/. Ask
children to identify the letter that represents the
initial sound of each picture name.

IN SUMMARY Invite children to tell
what they have discovered about spelling
words that rhyme with *get* and *jet*. (These
words often end with the letters *et*.)

Name _____

Vocabulary WordShop

▶ Paint the sky blue. Write the word <u>blue</u>. Paint the bear brown. Write the word <u>brown</u>. Use a word from the box to tell what the bear likes to do.

Painting
· WORDS ·
brown
paint
blue

1. blue

2. brown

3. paint

Paint a Picture Paint a picture. Use blue, brown, and other colors. Then write the words that name the colors you used. Add these words to your Spelling Log.

36   LESSON 7   Integrated Spelling

▶Vocabulary WordShop

WORDSHOP WORDS Point out the WordShop Words on page 36, and ask volunteers to read them aloud. Distribute paints to each child. As you read each Painting Word, have children hold up the item or items that correspond to the word.

Focus children's attention on the illustration, and have them name some picture details. Then read aloud the first two lines of the directions. Have children paint the sky blue and write the word *blue*. Help children read aloud the next two direction lines. Pause after each line, allowing time for children to paint a section and write the Painting Word. Help children read aloud the last two direction lines. Explain that they will write a word that tells what the bear is doing.

MEETING INDIVIDUAL NEEDS

Children Acquiring English Paint sample patches of blue and brown on art paper. Ask children to share the words for these colors and for the word *paint* in their primary languages. Record these words on the art paper. Play a game in which volunteers say the words in their primary languages. Have the rest of the group respond with the corresponding English words. **REINFORCING SELF-ESTEEM**

PAINT A PICTURE Provide children with paint materials. After children complete the activity, they can display their paintings on a word wall labeled "Painting Words."

EXPLORING PAINTING WORDS Explore with children how a word can be used as both a naming word and an action word. Write the word *paint* on the board. Then illustrate the concept by holding up a jar of paint and saying, "The *paint* is (blue)." Point out that *paint* is used as a naming word. Next, pantomime dipping a brush into the paint and painting a classroom wall surface. As you do, say "Watch me *paint* this wall." Point out that *paint* is used as an action word.

Name _____

Vocabulary Adventures

▶ Follow the directions for each picture.

1. Draw a circle around the animals that like to <u>paint</u>.

2. Color the big animal <u>brown</u>. **Children should color the bigger bear brown.**

3. Color the little animal's hat <u>blue</u>. **Children should color the littler bear's hat blue.**

Integrated Spelling   LESSON 7   37

BIG DREAMS "Big Brown Bear" • Harcourt Brace School Publishers

> " INVENTED SPELLERS' ERRORS *don't interfere with their learning to spell correctly later. Like early attempts to walk, talk, and draw, initial attempts to spell do not produce habits to be overcome.* " *(Susan Sowers)*

VOCABULARY ADVENTURES

Help children read aloud the directions at the top of page 37. Then distribute brown and blue markers or crayons. Point out the first picture, and help children identify what each set of bears is doing. Have children follow along as you read the directions for item 1. Allow time for them to circle the bears that are painting. Then help children read the coloring instructions for the next two items. Have children complete the activity independently, providing help as needed. **USING NAMING AND ACTION WORDS**

 Working Together If you decide to have children work together in pairs or independently to complete the page, you may want to suggest that children who finish first offer to help others.

 **Spelling Log** Children may want to write the Painting Words from this lesson in their Spelling Logs.

Optional Writing Idea

 Shared Writing: Story Encourage children to make up a story based on the picture on Pupil's Edition page 34. Help children focus on the picture details by asking the following:

• Who do you see in the picture? Where are the children?

• What are the children doing now? What will the children do next?

Organize children's responses in a chart similar to the following:

People	Place	Actions
children	living room	(Now) playing with toys
		(Next) eat lunch, go outside to play

Have children use their responses to write sentences that might be turned into a group story.

▶ Lesson Wrap-Up

RETEACH: Learning Differences

You will want to do this "wet word" activity on the sidewalk or the playground. Give each child a squeeze bottle filled with water. Then say words that end with the *-et* phonogram, such as *wet, get, set, met, jet, pet,* and *let.* Have children use their squeeze bottles to write each word as you lead the group in saying the letters aloud. Have children check their "wet" words by pointing to the letters as you spell the word aloud.

AUDITORY/KINESTHETIC MODALITIES

Job Riddles

Talk with children about community helpers and their work. Invite children to make up a simple oral riddle describing each job. Have children take turns posing their riddles for others to guess. To help children get started, share the following riddles or make up ones of your own.

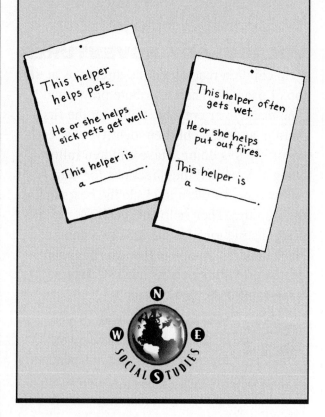

This helper helps pets.

He or she helps sick pets get well.

This helper is a _____.

This helper often gets wet.

He or she helps put out fires.

This helper is a _____.

N
W E
S
SOCIAL STUDIES

Words with -ell

OBJECTIVE
To recognize the sounds and spelling of the phonogram -ell

LESSON PLANNER
See the Assignment Guide on page T11 for a 3-day or 5-day plan.

▶ INFORMAL ASSESSMENT

Read aloud the following rhyming tongue twister, emphasizing words with the phonogram -ell. You might want to ring a bell to focus attention on the sounds of this phonogram.

Little N<u>ell</u> rings a b<u>ell</u> to s<u>ell</u> a sh<u>ell</u>.

Repeat the rhyme several times, and invite children to join in.

Ask children to identify the words that rhyme. Then have them repeat the words *Nell, bell, sell*, and *shell* as they listen for the ending sounds.

You may notice that some children have difficulty recognizing rhyming words ending with the -ell phonogram. This lesson will help children recognize the sounds and spelling of this phonogram.

Children Acquiring English
Short vowel sounds often present a great deal of difficulty for children who are acquiring English. Many children have problems distinguishing between the short *e* and short *i* sounds. Provide practice by asking children to listen to and repeat these word pairs: *bell, bill; tell, till; well, will; fell, fill;* and *sell, sill.*

In addition, speakers of Spanish, Tagalog, and Vietnamese may find it difficult to distinguish the short *e* sound from the long *a* sound. To assist these children in differentiating between these sounds, use word pairs such as *bell, bail; tell, tale; well, wail; fell, fail; sell, sale;* and *shell, shale.* **COMPARING AND CONTRASTING**

▶ BELLS, BELLS, BELLS

After children complete the first two pages of the lesson, they may enjoy creating a display of pictures and words that contain the -ell phonogram. Distribute large bells cut from construction paper. Ask children to either write words or draw pictures on the bells of items whose names end with the phonogram -ell. Stretch string in a zigzag pattern across a bulletin board, and help children attach their -ell bells to the string with paper clips or staples.

HOME ACTIVITIES MASTER: Lesson 8

NOTE: Fill in the blanks on the Home Activities Master before sending it home. See the Assignment Guide on page T11.

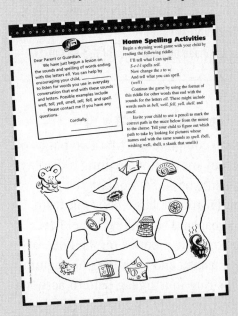

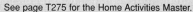

See page T275 for the Home Activities Master.

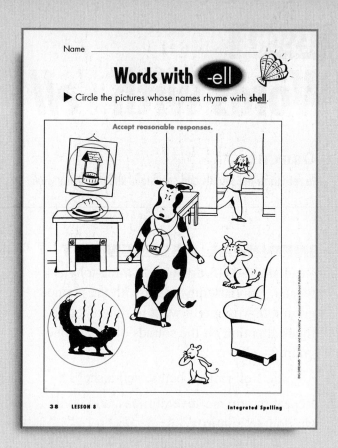

▶ Introduction

WARM-UP
Sprinkle a few drops of scent on a tissue and wave it about. Then ask children to tell what they smell. Have children join you in repeating the words *smell* and *tell* as they listen for the ending sounds.

INTRODUCING THE PAGE
Have children turn to page 38 and follow along as you read the lesson title aloud. Direct attention to the picture and discuss it with children. You might want to use questions like the following to guide their exploration:

• How do you think the animals and the person in this picture are feeling? (They seem very upset.)

• Why do you think they are feeling this way? (because the skunk has a bad smell)

• Imagine you are in the room. What sounds might you hear? (Children should mention the girl's yell and the cow's bell.)

Invite children to describe other picture details, making sure that the wishing well and the shell on the mantel are mentioned.

Read the directions aloud. Have children repeat the word *shell* several times as they listen for the ending sounds. Then ask a volunteer to restate what the children are to do on the page. Remind children that they can test for a rhyme by saying *shell* and another word as they listen to determine whether the ending sounds are the same—for example, *shell, yell* and *shell, shall*.

Either work through the page with children or have them complete it independently. (Children should circle pictures representing the words *shell, well, bell, smell,* and *yell.*)
CLASSIFYING

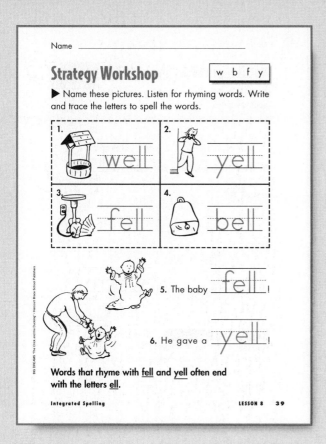

Name _____

Strategy Workshop

| w | b | f | y |

▶ Name these pictures. Listen for rhyming words. Write and trace the letters to spell the words.

1. well

2. yell

3. fell

4. bell

5. The baby fell !

6. He gave a yell !

Words that rhyme with <u>fell</u> and <u>yell</u> often end with the letters <u>ell</u>.

Integrated Spelling   LESSON 8   39

▶ Strategy Workshop

RHYMING WORDS Help children recall that rhyming words sound alike except for their beginning sounds. Explain that rhyming words are often spelled the same way except for their beginning letters. Tell children that they can sometimes figure out how to spell a word by spelling a rhyming word and changing the beginning letter.

Help children identify the first picture on page 39 as a wishing well. Write the word *well* on the board, and have children say it aloud. Guide them in changing the word *well* into the word *bell* by asking the following questions:

• What letter stands for the beginning sound of *bell*? (*b*)

• What letters stand for the ending sounds that you hear in both *well* and *bell*? (*ell*)

Record children's responses on the board and have them read the word *bell* aloud. Explain to children that they can use this strategy to write words that name the pictures on this page. Then help them identify the remaining pictures as representing the words *yell, fell,* and *bell.* **APPLYING SPELLING STRATEGIES**

SPELLING IN CONTEXT Have children discuss the picture at the bottom of page 39. Give guidance as needed to help them complete the sentences and read them aloud. (*fell, yell*) **CONCEPT OF WORD**

Extra Support/Children Acquiring English Children may benefit from a review of the initial consonant sounds that are blended with the phonogram -*ell* to form the picture names. Display pictures whose names begin with /w/, /y/, /f/, and /b/. Ask children to identify the letter that represents the initial sound of each picture name.

IN SUMMARY Invite children to tell what they have discovered about spelling words that rhyme with *fell* and *yell.* (These words often end with the letters *ell.*)

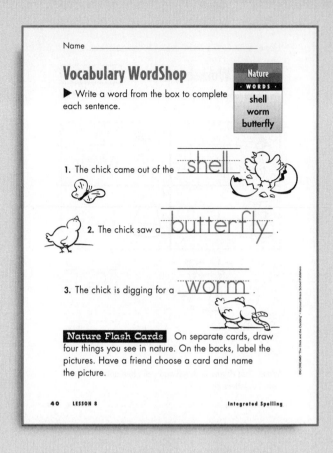

▶ Vocabulary WordShop

WORDSHOP WORDS

Point out the WordShop Words on page 40, and ask volunteers to read them aloud. Then discuss with children how these words are alike. (They all relate to things seen in nature.) Ask volunteers to describe the items and tell where they have seen them.

Direct children's attention to the pictures, and ask volunteers to describe what they see in each scene. Read with children the directions at the top of the page. Explain that they are to write a word from the box to complete each sentence. Give children assistance in reading the sentences, if necessary. After children complete the activity, have them share their responses.

Children Acquiring English

Display labeled picture cards of a shell, a worm, and a butterfly. Have children select a card, name the pictured item, and then use the word in an oral sentence. **BUILDING VOCABULARY**

NATURE FLASH CARDS

Provide children with drawing materials. Before children begin their drawings, discuss things children might see in nature. Using the Nature Words as inspiration, ask questions such as these: Where do you see butterflies? Where would you find a shell? Where do worms live?

EXPLORING NATURE WORDS

Share with children the following information about butterflies:

• Butterflies are flying insects. They have two pairs of wings. The wings are various colors—including blue, green, black, and yellow. Butterflies are seen during the day because that is the time they fly. The insects can be found throughout the world.

• Before a butterfly turns into an adult it goes through a stage when it is a caterpillar. A caterpillar looks somewhat like a worm.

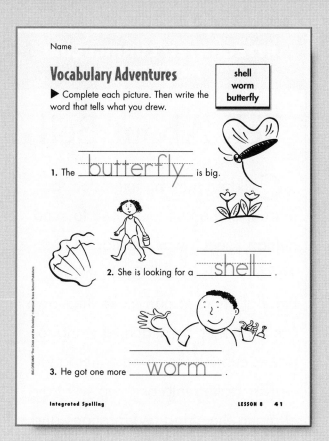

Name _____

Vocabulary Adventures

| shell |
| worm |
| **butterfly** |

▶ Complete each picture. Then write the word that tells what you drew.

1. The <u>butterfly</u> is big.

2. She is looking for a <u>shell</u>.

3. He got one more <u>worm</u>.

BIG DREAMS "The Chick and the Duckling" • Harcourt Brace School Publishers

---

> IN ORDER FOR CHILDREN TO *tune in to the meaning and spelling of new words, they need to develop a genuine interest in words.* *(Debbie Powell and David Hornsby)*

VOCABULARY ADVENTURES

After you read aloud the direction line at the top of page 41, provide children with crayons or markers. Have children complete the pictures and then complete each sentence by writing the word that describes what they drew in each picture. After children have completed the page, invite them to share their drawings and sentences. **USING NAMING WORDS**

Spelling Log Children may want to write the Nature Words from this lesson in their Spelling Logs.

Optional Writing Idea

Shared Writing: Asking and Telling Sentences
Children might enjoy writing questions and answers based on the flash cards they made in the activity on Pupil's Edition page 40. Have children suggest asking and telling sentences that might be written about the items shown on their flash cards.

Asking Sentences	Telling Sentences
Where would you find a shell?	You would find a shell at the beach.
Where does a worm dig?	A worm digs in the dirt.

Then assign each child a partner, and have them use their flash cards and asking and telling sentences to play a game of "Nature Trivia." Suggest partners take turns asking and answering the questions.

►Lesson Wrap-Up

RETEACH: Learning Differences
Some children may need additional visual and kinesthetic reinforcement to spell words containing the *-ell* phonogram. Invite children to work at the board. Write one of the following words for each child: *bell, yell, tell, fell, sell, well*. Have children read the words aloud. Then have them trace the words by using colored chalk. After children trace the words, have them write the words on the board. Ask children to erase the words and write the words again from memory. If the words are not correct, have children repeat the activity.

VISUAL/KINESTHETIC MODALITIES

INTEGRATED CURRICULUM ACTIVITY

Tell About Bell

Children may be interested to learn that the first telephone to send human speech was developed in 1876 by Alexander Graham Bell. Pairs of children can make their own "cell" phones by attaching string to paper cups. If the string is held taut, words spoken into one cup will travel along the string as vibrations and will be heard in the other cup. As children speak to their partners, encourage them to use words such as *bell, fell, well, shell,* and *tell* in their conversations.

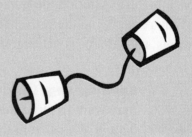

SCIENCE

LESSON 9

Words with -en

OBJECTIVE
To recognize the sounds and spelling of the phonogram -en

LESSON PLANNER
See the Assignment Guide on page T11 for a 3-day or 5-day plan.

▶ INFORMAL ASSESSMENT

Have children listen as you recite this traditional rhyme, emphasizing words with the phonogram -en:

> Little Boy B<u>en</u>, who lives in the g<u>len</u>,
> Has a blue cat and one blue h<u>en</u>,
> Which lays blue eggs, a score and t<u>en</u>.
> Where shall I find the little Boy B<u>en</u>?

Repeat the rhyme several times, and encourage children to join in as they become familiar with the words.

Ask children to identify the words that rhyme. Then have them repeat the words *Ben, glen, hen,* and *ten,* as they listen for the ending sounds.

You may notice that some children have difficulty recognizing rhyming words ending with the *-en* phonogram. This lesson will help children recognize the sounds and spelling of this phonogram.

MEETING INDIVIDUAL NEEDS

Children Acquiring English
Frequently, children who are acquiring English have difficulty distinguishing between the sounds of short *e* and short *a*. They may need practice in listening to and repeating pairs of words such as *pen, pan; Ben, ban; ten, tan; men, man; den, Dan; Jen, Jan,* and *Ken, can.*

In addition, speakers of Spanish, Tagalog, and Vietnamese may find it difficult to distinguish the short *e* sound from the long *a* sound. Provide these children with listening practice by saying word pairs such as *pen, pain; men, main; den, Dane; Jen, Jane;* and *Ken, cane.* Then repeat these pairs of words in random order, and ask children to identify the word in each pair that has the same ending sounds as *pen.* **COMPARING AND CONTRASTING**

▶ THE -en PEN

Write as a label "The *-en* Pen" on a large tag, and attach it to a felt-tip pen. Display the pen, and tell children that the pen may be used only to write words that end with the letters *en.* Attach the pen with a length of string to a bulletin board covered with newsprint. Then invite children to use the pen to write words on the board that belong in the same word family as *pen.*

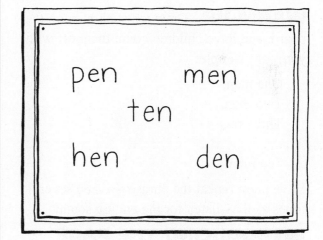

NOTE: Fill in the blanks on the Home Activities Master before sending it home. See the Assignment Guide on page T11.

See page T276 for the Home Activities Master.

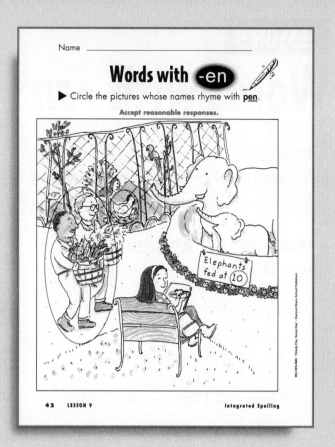

▶ Introduction

WARM-UP Draw ten stick men on the board, and have children count them off with you; for example:

One man,
Two men,
Three men,
. . .
Ten men!

Have them repeat the phrase *ten men* several times as they listen for the ending sounds.

INTRODUCING THE PAGE

Have children turn to page 42 and follow along as you read the lesson title aloud. Direct attention to the picture and discuss it with children. You might want to use questions such as the following to guide their discussion:

• What place do you see in the picture? (a zoo)

• What animals live here? (elephants, a hen, birds, chicks)

• What are the people doing? (feeding elephants and drawing pictures of them)

• At what time do the elephants get fed? (at ten)

Invite children to describe other picture details, making sure that the pen is mentioned.

Read the directions aloud. Have children repeat the word *pen* several times as they listen for the ending sounds. Remind children that they can test for a rhyme by saying *pen* and another word as they listen to determine if the ending sounds are the same.

Either work through the page with children or have them complete it independently. (Children should circle the pictures representing the words *men, pen, hen,* and the numeral *ten.*) **CLASSIFYING**

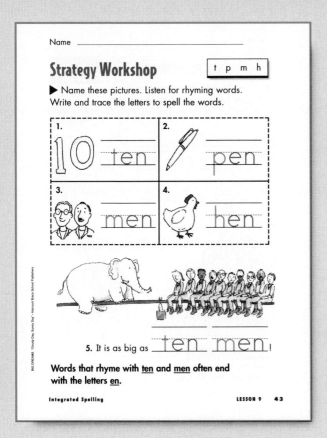

Name _____

Strategy Workshop

| t | p | m | h |

▶ Name these pictures. Listen for rhyming words.
Write and trace the letters to spell the words.

1. ten

2. pen

3. men

4. hen

5. It is as big as ten men!

**Words that rhyme with ten and men often end
with the letters en.**

Integrated Spelling   LESSON 9   43

▶ Strategy Workshop

RHYMING WORDS Help children
recall that rhyming words sound alike except
for their beginning sounds. Explain that
rhyming words are often spelled the same
way except for their beginning letters. Tell
children that they can sometimes figure out
how to spell a word by spelling a rhyming
word and changing the beginning letter.

Help children identify the first picture on
page 43 as the numeral ten. Write the word
ten on the board, and have children say it
aloud. Guide them in changing the word *ten*
into the word *den* by asking the following:

• What letter stands for the beginning sound
of *den*? (*d*)

• What letters stand for the ending sounds that
you hear in both *ten* and *den*? (*en*)

Record children's responses on the board, and
have them read the word *den* aloud. Explain
to children that they can use this strategy to
write words that name the pictures on this
page. Then help them identify the remaining
pictures as a pen, two men, and a hen.

APPLYING SPELLING STRATEGIES

SPELLING IN CONTEXT Have
children discuss the picture at the bottom of
page 43. You may want to suggest that they
count the men. Help children complete the
sentence and read it aloud. (*ten, men*)

CONCEPT OF WORD

MEETING INDIVIDUAL NEEDS

**Extra Support/Children
Acquiring English** Children
may benefit from a review of
the initial consonant sounds
that are blended with the phonogram *-en* to
form the picture names. Display pictures
whose names begin with /t/, /p/, /m/, and /h/.
Ask children to identify the letter that represents the initial sound of each picture name.

IN SUMMARY Invite children to tell
what they have discovered about spelling
words that rhyme with *ten* and *men*. (These
words often end with the letters *en*.)

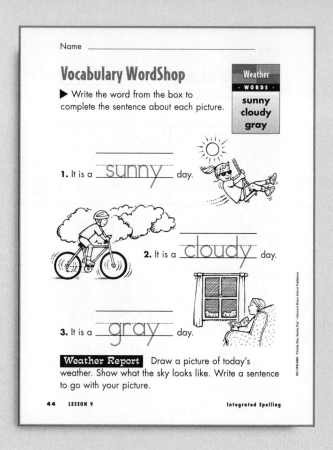

►Vocabulary WordShop

WORDSHOP WORDS Point out the WordShop Words on page 44, and ask volunteers to read them aloud. Then talk with children about how these words are alike. (They all have something to do with the weather.)

Direct children's attention to the illustrations, and ask volunteers to name some items that they see pictured. Read with children the directions at the top of the page. Ask children to describe what the sky looks like in each picture. Explain that they will write a Weather Word to complete each sentence that tells about the pictures. After children complete the activity, have them share and discuss their responses.

MEETING INDIVIDUAL NEEDS

Children Acquiring English
Check children's pronunciation of each WordShop Word. Point out that the sound at the end of *cloudy* and *sunny* is the long *e* sound.

Mention that the sound at the end of *gray* is the long *a* sound. **PRACTICING PRONUNCIATION**

WEATHER REPORT Call on volunteers to give their observations of the day's weather. Then provide children with drawing materials. Suggest that after children draw their pictures and write their sentences, they share their work with classroom friends.

EXPLORING WEATHER WORDS Extend children's knowledge about other words related to weather by working with children to create a word web. Write *Weather Words* in the center of a web, and add words suggested by children that tell about kinds of weather that they have observed.

```
        showers   lightning
  hail                        windy
cold      ( Weather Words )    hot
  rainy
      snowy   humid   thunder
```

Worksheet (page 45)

Name _____

Vocabulary Adventures

▶ Read and follow the directions.

1. Draw a picture of a <u>sunny</u> day.

> Accept reasonable responses.

2. Draw a picture of a <u>cloudy</u> day.

> Accept reasonable responses.

3. Draw a picture. Show what you like to do on a <u>gray</u> day.

> Accept reasonable responses.

4. Write a sentence to go with one of your pictures.

_____

Sentences will vary.

_____

_____

Integrated Spelling   LESSON 9   45

VOCABULARY ADVENTURES

Read the directions at the top of page 45 with children. Provide children with crayons and markers. Then read aloud the directions for item 1, and have children draw a picture that shows a sunny day. Repeat this procedure for items 2 and 3. Then read aloud the directions for item 4, and explain to children that they are to write a sentence about one of their pictures. After children complete the page, have them share and explain their responses. **USING DESCRIBING WORDS**

 Working Together You may want to have children work with a partner to complete the activity. Encourage children to discuss and agree on what they will draw and write about.

 **Spelling Log** Children may want to write the Weather Words from this lesson in their Spelling Logs.

Optional Writing Idea

 Patterned Writing: Sentences Ask children to name activities that they like to do on sunny and cloudy days. Write their responses in a chart similar to the following:

Sunny Days	Cloudy Days
swim	draw
hike	cook

Write these sentence frames on the board, and help children read them aloud:

It is _____. I _____.

Provide children with two sheets of drawing paper and crayons. Tell them to draw two pictures, one showing what they like to do on sunny days and the other showing what they like to do on cloudy days. Have children copy the sentence frames under their pictures, completing them with the headings and the chart entries.

Lesson Wrap-Up

RETEACH: Learning Differences

Write the following words on index cards: *pen, ten, hen, men, den*. Use one color to write the initial consonant and a second color to write the *-en* phonogram. Provide each child with a set of prepared word cards, two colors of felt-tip pens, and a set of blank index cards. Direct children to copy each word, using one color to write the first letter and the other color to write the middle and ending letters. **VISUAL/KINESTHETIC MODALITIES**

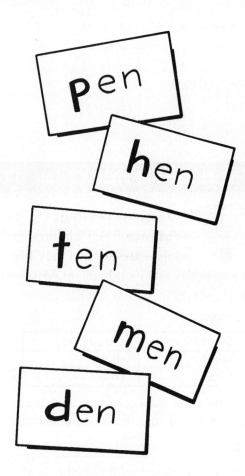

Sunny Side Up

Point out to children that we have sunny days because of the sun. Explain that the sun is a star made of burning gases. Ask children why the sun is important to living things. Elicit the following facts, and write them on the board:

The sun gives us light.
The sun gives us heat.
The sun helps plants grow.

Help children conclude that plants, animals, and people need the sun to live.

Invite children to cut out suns from construction paper. On one side, have them draw a picture or write a sentence telling why they like the sun. On the other side, have them draw a smiling face.

SCIENCE

LESSON 10
Words with *-ick*

OBJECTIVE
To recognize the sounds and spelling of the phonogram *-ick*

LESSON PLANNER
See the Assignment Guide on page T11 for a 3-day or 5-day plan.

▶ INFORMAL ASSESSMENT

Have children listen as you say the words that accompany the following finger play, emphasizing words with the phonogram *-ick*:

> One day a ch<u>ick</u>
> Built a house of sticks.
> (*Interlace fingers.*)
> Another ch<u>ick</u>
> Built a house made of br<u>ick</u>.
> (*Place fists one on top of the other.*)
> When the wind blew qu<u>ick</u>,
> (*Blow on interlaced fingers.*)
> Each st<u>ick</u> proved sl<u>ick</u>!
> (*Wave fingers in the air.*)
> But the th<u>ick</u> bricks
> (*Place fists one on top of the other.*)
> Did the tr<u>ick</u>!

Repeat the finger play several times, and encourage children to join in on the words and the motions.

Ask children to identify the words that rhyme. Then have them repeat the words *chick, brick, quick, stick, slick, thick*, and *trick*, listening for the ending sounds.

You may notice that some children have difficulty recognizing rhyming words ending with the *-ick* phonogram. This lesson will help children recognize the sounds and spelling of this phonogram.

MEETING INDIVIDUAL NEEDS

Children Acquiring English
Frequently, Spanish-speaking children replace the short *i* sound with the long *e* sound. To help them differentiate between these sounds, provide practice in listening to and pronouncing word pairs such as *chick, cheek; lick, leak; sick, seek; wick, week; slick, sleek;* and *pick, peek*. Then repeat the word pairs in random order, and have children identify the words that rhyme with *chick*. Children who speak Vietnamese, Chinese, Tagalog, and other languages may encounter similar difficulties. They can also benefit from this type of discrimination practice. **COMPARING AND CONTRASTING**

▶ BRICK WORD WALL

After children complete the first two pages of the lesson, involve them in creating a brick word wall that features words ending with the *-ick* phonogram. Give children brick shapes cut out of red construction paper. On each brick, have them write a word belonging to the *-ick* family. Then have them use the bricks to "build" a word wall.

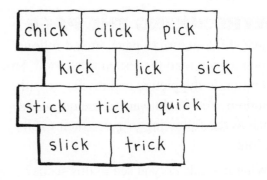

NOTE: Fill in blanks on the Home Activities Master before sending it home. See the Assignment Guide on page T11.

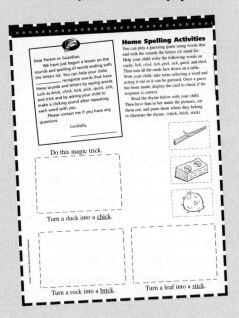

Dear Parent or Guardian,
We have just begun a lesson on the sounds and spelling of words ending with the letters *ick*. You can help your child, _____, recognize words that have these sounds and letters by saying words such as *brick, chick, kick, pick, quick, sick,* and *trick* and by asking your child to make a clicking sound after repeating each word with you.
Please contact me if you have any questions.

Cordially,
_____

Home Spelling Activities
You can play a guessing game using words that end with the sounds the letters *ick* stand for. Help your child write the following words on cards: *lick, chick, tick, pick, quick,* and *thick.* Then turn all the cards face down on a table. With your child, take turns selecting a word and acting it out so it can be guessed. Once a guess has been made, display the card to check if the response is correct.
Read the rhyme below with your child. Then have him or her name the pictures, cut them out, and paste them where they belong to illustrate the rhyme. (chick, brick, stick)

Do this magic trick.

Turn a duck into a <u>chick</u>.

Turn a rock into a <u>brick</u>.   Turn a leaf into a <u>stick</u>.

See page T277 for the Home Activities Master.

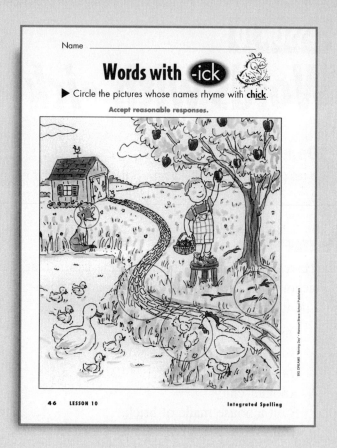

Words with -ick

▶ Circle the pictures whose names rhyme with **chick**.

Accept reasonable responses.

46   LESSON 10   Integrated Spelling

▶Introduction

WARM-UP Chant the nursery rhyme "One, Two, Buckle My Shoe." Then repeat the line *Five, six, pick up sticks*. Have children join you in saying the words *pick* and *stick* several times as they listen for the ending sounds.

INTRODUCING THE PAGE

Have children turn to page 46 and follow along as you read the lesson title aloud. Direct attention to the picture and discuss it with children. You might want to use questions such as the following to guide their exploration:

• What animals do you see in this scene? (fox, duck, ducklings, hen, chicks)

• What is the fox doing? (licking his chops)

• What is the child doing? (picking apples)

Invite children to describe other picture details, making sure the sticks and bricks are mentioned.

Read the directions aloud. Then have children repeat the word *chick* several times, listening for the ending sounds. Remind them that they can test for a rhyme by saying *chick* and another word as they listen to determine if the ending sounds are the same–for example, *chick, chop* and *chick, chap*.

Either work through the page with children or have them complete it independently. (Children should circle pictures representing the words *brick*, fox *lick*ing its chops, *chick, stick,* and the child *pick*ing fruit.) **CLASSIFYING**

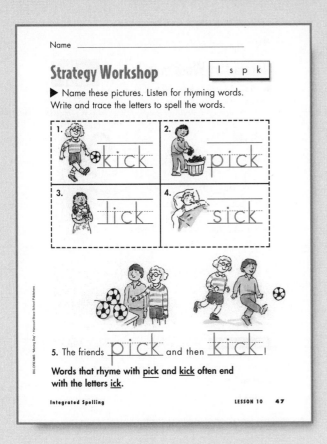

Strategy Workshop

RHYMING WORDS Help children recall that rhyming words sound alike except for their beginning sounds. Explain that rhyming words are often spelled the same way except for their beginning letters. Tell children that they can sometimes figure out how to spell a word by spelling a rhyming word and changing the beginning letter.

Help children identify the first picture on page 47 as a girl kicking a ball. Write the word *kick* on the board, and have children say it aloud. Guide them in changing the word *kick* into the word *tick* by asking questions like these:

• What letter stands for the beginning sound of *tick*? (*t*)

• What letters stand for the ending sounds that you hear in both *kick* and *tick*? (*ick*)

Write children's responses on the board, and have them read the word *tick* aloud. Explain to children that they can use this strategy to write words that name the pictures on this page. Then help them identify the remaining pictures as representing the words *pick, lick*, and *sick*. **APPLYING SPELLING STRATEGIES**

SPELLING IN CONTEXT Have children discuss the pictures at the bottom of page 47. Make the point that the children are picking out or choosing a ball. Help children complete the sentence and read it aloud. (*pick, kick*) **CONCEPT OF WORD**

Extra Support/Children Acquiring English Children may benefit from a review of the initial consonant sounds that are blended with the phonogram *-ick* to form the picture names. Display pictures whose names begin with /k/, /p/, /l/, and /s/. Ask children to identify the letter that represents the initial sound of each picture name.

IN SUMMARY Invite children to tell what they have discovered about spelling words that rhyme with *pick* and *kick*. (These words often end with the letters *ick*.)

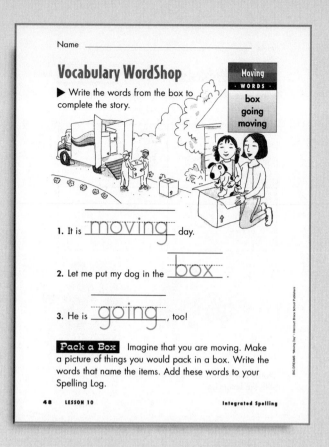

Name _____

Vocabulary WordShop

▶ Write the words from the box to complete the story.

Moving
• WORDS •
box
going
moving

1. It is _moving_ day.

2. Let me put my dog in the _box_ .

3. He is _going_ , too!

Pack a Box Imagine that you are moving. Make a picture of things you would pack in a box. Write the words that name the items. Add these words to your Spelling Log.

48 LESSON 10   Integrated Spelling

▶ Vocabulary WordShop

WORDSHOP WORDS Point out the WordShop Words on page 48, and ask volunteers to read them aloud. Then talk with children about how these words are alike. (They are about moving.)

Direct children's attention to the illustration. Invite volunteers to talk about the main idea of the picture and to discuss some of the picture details. Then help children read the directions aloud. After children write a Moving Word to finish each sentence, have them share and explain their responses.

MEETING INDIVIDUAL NEEDS

Children Acquiring English Talk about the difference between the words *moving* and *going*. Explain that both words refer to traveling from one place to another, but that *moving* can mean a permanent change from one home to another.

UNDERSTANDING WORD MEANINGS

PACK A BOX Provide children with drawing materials. Ask volunteers to suggest items that they would pack. Create a list of the responses on the board. After children draw and label their pictures, encourage them to share their work.

EXPLORING MOVING WORDS Use this opportunity to compare the spelling of action words that end with *-ing*. Write the base forms of *going* and *moving* on the board: *go, move*. Point out that *go* does not end with the letter *e*. Then write *going* next to its base form. Explain that the spelling of *go* does not change when the ending *-ing* is added. Point out that *move* ends with the letter *e*. Then write *moving* next to its base form. Ask children to tell what letter is dropped before the ending *-ing* is added (*e*). You may want to repeat this procedure using the words *give, giving* and *talk, talking* as examples.

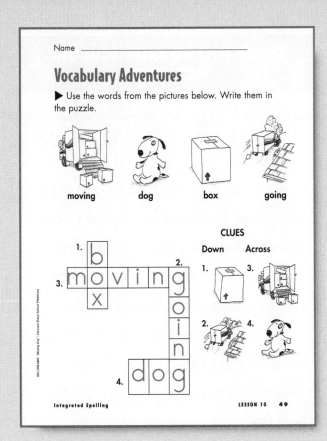

Name _____

Vocabulary Adventures

▶ Use the words from the pictures below. Write them in the puzzle.

moving   dog   box   going

CLUES

Down   **Across**

Integrated Spelling   LESSON 10   49

"TEACHING WORDS TOGETHER as families has a number of advantages. If the most frequent word in the family is known, this knowledge builds a bridge from familiar to new." (Robert J. Marzano and Jana S. Marzano)

VOCABULARY ADVENTURES

Read with children the directions at the top of page 49. Direct their attention to the illustrations at the top of the page, and help them read the labels. You may want to have children work together as a group to complete the puzzle, or you may prefer to guide them through a few puzzle clues. Then have children complete the activity. **USING NAMING AND ACTION WORDS**

Spelling Log Children may want to write the Moving Words from this lesson in their Spelling Logs.

Optional Writing Idea

Independent Writing: Journal Entry Ask children to look at the picture on Pupil's Edition page 48. Invite them to write a journal entry about a real or imaginary time they moved from one home to another. Before children begin to write, suggest that they organize their ideas by writing answers to these questions:

• Where did you move from? Where did you move to?

• How did you feel before you moved? How did you feel after you moved?

• What problems did you have in your new home? How did you solve them?

Have children use their ideas to write sentences for a journal entry. Children can dictate sentences for you to write, or you may choose to have them use invented spelling to write the sentences themselves.

▶Lesson Wrap-Up

RETEACH: Learning Differences

Give pairs of children word cards with the following words: *pick, kick, lick, sick, tick, brick, trick, bell, fell, sell, tell, well,* and *yell.* Have partners place the cards face down and mix them up. Then have children take turns turning over a card and reading the word aloud. Have them separate the words into two piles—those that end with the phonogram *-ick*, and those that end with the phonogram *-ell.* VISUAL/AUDITORY MODALITIES

INTEGRATED CURRICULUM ACTIVITY

Pick-Up Sticks

Have children write words ending with the *-ick* phonogram on craft sticks. Then have groups of children use the sticks to play the game "Pick-Up Sticks." Demonstrate how the game is played, and explain that in order to keep a stick, the player must read the word on it. Tell children that if another stick is moved while they are removing a stick from the pile, the turn passes to the next player. Have children continue the game until all the sticks have been picked up.

INTEGRATED CURRICULUM ACTIVITY

Map Adventures

Remind children that before they can move to a new home, they need to know how to get there. Display a simple local map. First, help children locate where the school is on the map. Then invite volunteers to take turns naming other local places or streets that they know. Help children find the routes that connect their school location with the new locations mentioned. Have them take turns tracing their fingers along the roadways that a moving van would follow to get to a new destination. Help children understand whether they are traveling north, south, east, or west as they move their fingers.

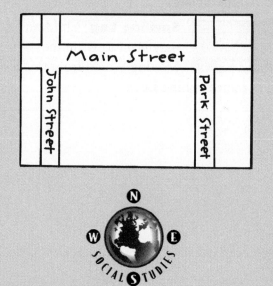

Words with -ip

OBJECTIVE
To recognize the sounds and spelling of the phonogram -ip

LESSON PLANNER
See the Assignment Guide on page T11 for a 3-day or 5-day plan.

▶ INFORMAL ASSESSMENT

Have children listen as you read the following rhyme aloud, emphasizing words with the -ip phonogram:

> Touch your nose
> Right on the t<u>ip</u>.
> Stand up tall,
> Then hop and sk<u>ip</u>.
> Pour some juice,
> Then take a s<u>ip</u>.
> Wipe up any
> Messy dr<u>ip</u>.

Repeat the rhyme several times, and have children make appropriate motions as they say the words with you.

Ask children to identify the words that rhyme. Then have them repeat the words *tip, skip, sip,* and *drip* as they listen for the ending sounds.

You may notice that some children have difficulty recognizing rhyming words ending with the -ip phonogram. This lesson will help children recognize the sounds and spelling of this phonogram.

Children Acquiring English

Check to see if any Spanish-speaking children are replacing the short *i* sound with the long *e* sound. If they are, provide them with practice in listening to and pronouncing word pairs such as *slip, sleep; whip, weep; sip, seep; lip, leap; rip, reap; hip, heap; dip, deep;* and *chip, cheep.* Then repeat these word pairs in random order, and ask children to identify the word in each pair that has the same ending sounds as *flip.* Children who speak Chinese, Vietnamese, Tagalog, and other languages may have similar difficulties and can benefit from the same kind of practice. **COMPARING AND CONTRASTING**

▶ MISSING CHIPS

After children complete the first two pages of the lesson, they may enjoy working together to create a bulletin board display that features words ending with the -ip phonogram. Staple a giant-size paper cookie to a bulletin board, and explain to children that the baker forgot to add the chocolate chips to the cookie dough. Distribute large chip cutouts, and have children write words that end with the -ip phonogram on them. Have children tape or staple their "word chips" on the cookie to create a word wall.

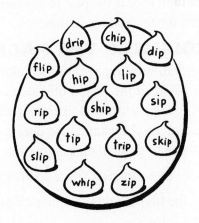

NOTE: Fill in the blanks on the Home Activities Master before sending it home. See the Assignment Guide on page T11.

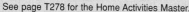

See page T278 for the Home Activities Master.

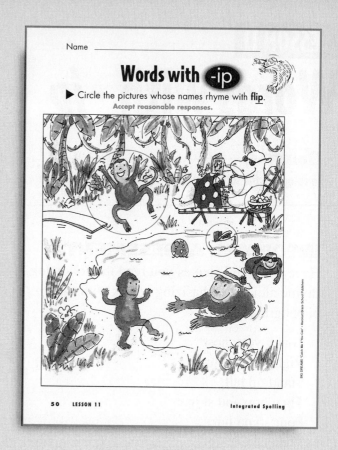

Name _____

Words with -ip

▶ Circle the pictures whose names rhyme with **flip**.
Accept reasonable responses.

50   LESSON 11   Integrated Spelling

▶Introduction

WARM-UP Ask children to observe and describe your actions as you purse your lips together and then use your hand to "zip" them shut. Explain that you are "zipping your lips." Have children repeat the phrase *zip your lip* as they listen for the ending sounds.

INTRODUCING THE PAGE

Have children turn to page 50 and follow along as you read the lesson title aloud. Direct attention to the picture and discuss it with children. You might want to use questions such as these to guide their exploration:

• Where are these animals? (at a pond or a lake)

• What is the hippo doing? (eating chips and sipping a drink)

• What is the monkey doing? (a flip)

• What is the little gorilla doing? (dipping its toes in the water)

Invite children to describe other picture details, making sure that they mention the toy ship in the discussion.

Read the directions aloud. Have children repeat the word *flip* several times, listening for the ending sounds. Remind them that they can test for a rhyme by saying *flip* and another word as they listen to determine if the ending sounds are the same.

Either work through the page with children or have them complete the activity independently. (Children should circle pictures representing the words *flip*, *chip*, *sip*, *dip*, and *ship*.) **CLASSIFYING**

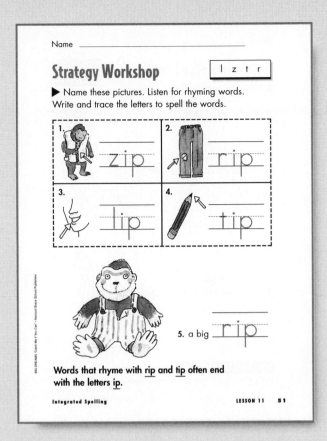

Name _____

Strategy Workshop

[l   z   t   r]

▶ Name these pictures. Listen for rhyming words.
Write and trace the letters to spell the words.

1. zip
2. rip
3. lip
4. tip

5. a big rip

Words that rhyme with rip and tip often end
with the letters ip.

Integrated Spelling

LESSON 11   51

▶Strategy Workshop

RHYMING WORDS Help children recall that rhyming words sound alike except for their beginning sounds. Explain that rhyming words are often spelled the same way except for their beginning letters. Tell children that they can sometimes figure out how to spell a word by spelling a rhyming word and changing the beginning letter.

Help children identify the first picture on page 51 as an illustration that represents the word *zip*. Write the word *zip* on the board, and have children say it aloud. Guide them in changing the word *zip* into the word *dip* by asking questions like these:

• What letter stands for the beginning sound of *dip*? (*d*)

• What letters stand for the ending sounds that you hear in both *zip* and *dip*? (*ip*)

Record children's responses on the board, and have them read the word *dip* aloud. Explain to children that they can use this strategy to write words that name the pictures on this page. Then help them identify the remaining pictures as a rip, a lip, and the tip of a pencil.

APPLYING SPELLING STRATEGIES

SPELLING IN CONTEXT Have children discuss the picture at the bottom of page 51. Help children complete the phrase and read it aloud. (*rip*) **CONCEPT OF WORD**

MEETING INDIVIDUAL NEEDS **Extra Support/Children Acquiring English** Children may benefit from a review of the initial consonant sounds that are blended with the phonogram -*ip* to form the picture names. Display pictures whose names begin with /z/, /r/, /l/, and /t/. Ask children to identify the letter that represents the initial sound of each picture name.

IN SUMMARY Invite children to tell what they have discovered about spelling words that rhyme with *rip* and *tip*. (These words often end with the letters *ip*.)

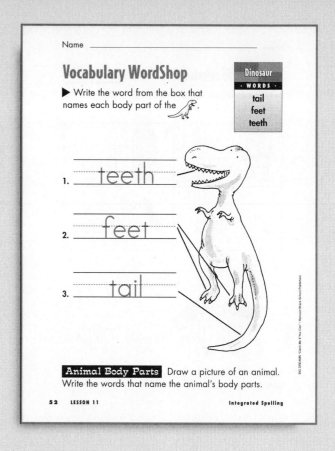

Name _____

Vocabulary WordShop

▶ Write the word from the box that names each body part of the 🦕.

Dinosaur
· WORDS ·
tail
feet
teeth

1. teeth

2. feet

3. tail

Animal Body Parts Draw a picture of an animal. Write the words that name the animal's body parts.

52   LESSON 11   Integrated Spelling

▶ Vocabulary WordShop

WORDSHOP WORDS Point out the WordShop Words on page 52, and ask volunteers to read them aloud. Then discuss with children how the words are alike. (They name dinosaur body parts.) Lead children to the understanding that the words name the body parts of other animals as well.

Direct children's attention to the picture of the dinosaur. Discuss the illustration, and ask children to name some body parts that they see pictured. Read the directions at the top of the page with children. Explain that they are to label the picture by writing the words from the box on the lines. After children complete the activity, have them share their responses.

MEETING INDIVIDUAL NEEDS

Children Acquiring English Play a game in which children pretend to be dinosaurs. You say each WordShop Word as children point to the corresponding part on their dinosaur bodies. **BUILDING VOCABULARY**

ANIMAL BODY PARTS Provide children with drawing or painting materials and paper. Before children begin, talk about other animals that have tails, feet, and teeth, such as dogs, cats, and horses. After their pictures are complete, encourage them to use the WordShop Words to label their work.

EXPLORING DINOSAUR WORDS Extend children's knowledge of words that name animal body parts by explaining that the feet of some real dinosaurs had claws. Ask:

• What other animals do you know of that have claws on their feet? (Possible responses: cats, dogs, bears, kangaroos)

• What do claws look and feel like? (Possible responses: sharp, pointed, hooked)

Conclude the discussion by mentioning that many animals use their claws for protection to dig, tear, and scratch. Bears, for example, fight against enemies with their sharp claws. Cats use their claws to climb up trees to get away from enemies.

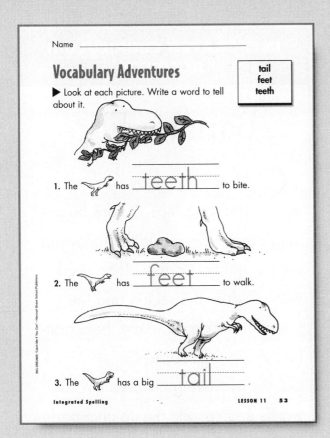

Name _____

Vocabulary Adventures

tail
feet
teeth

▶ Look at each picture. Write a word to tell about it.

1. The 🦕 has __teeth__ to bite.

2. The 🦕 has __feet__ to walk.

3. The 🦕 has a big __tail__ .

Integrated Spelling　　　　　　　LESSON 11　**53**

"REMEMBER: CHILDREN LEARN *to spell pattern by pattern, not word by word. Humans are naturally attuned to perceiving and making use of patterns in all the information they take in and process.*"
(J. Richard Gentry and Jean Wallace Gillet)

VOCABULARY ADVENTURES

Read with children the directions at the top of page 53. Then focus their attention on the art, and ask volunteers to tell which body part the dinosaur is using in each picture. Have children write words from the box so that the sentences tell about the pictures. Help children read the sentences, if necessary. After children complete the sentences, have them share and explain their responses. **USING NAMING WORDS**

Working Together You may want children to work in pairs to do this activity. Suggest that partners take turns, with one child reading the sentence frame aloud and the other child selecting and writing the word to complete the sentence.

Spelling Log Children may want to write the Dinosaur Words from this lesson in their Spelling Logs.

Optional Writing Idea

Patterned Writing: Sentences Have children name action words that have the -ip phonogram, such as *flip, dip, nip,* and *trip*. Record their responses on chart paper under the heading *Action Words*. Next, have children name the three Dinosaur Words, and list their responses on the chart under the heading *Naming Words*. Then write this sentence frame on the board, and help children read it aloud:

A dinosaur will _____ with its _____.

Invite children to complete the sentence by using the action and naming word entries from the chart. You might want to share this example with children: A dinosaur will *flip* with its *tail*. Encourage children to share their completed sentences with the class.

▶ Lesson Wrap-Up

RETEACH: Learning Differences

Provide children with plastic trays filled with sand or salt. Say a word in the *-ip* family, emphasizing the sounds of the phonogram. Then dictate the spelling as each child uses a fingertip to write the word in the tray. Have children spell the word aloud with you as they write it again. Finally, have children smooth out the mixture in their trays and spell the word aloud as they write it from memory. **AUDITORY/KINESTHETIC MODALITIES**

Banana Flip

Children may enjoy creating and sipping banana flips. Before beginning the activity, write the following recipe on chart paper. Then read with children the recipe and the steps for making it. Next, help partners make the recipe. Conclude the activity by having children circle words ending with the *-ip* phonogram that appear in the recipe.

BANANA FLIP

What you need:

1

2 ◻ ◻

3/4 cup

What you do:

1. Peel the .

2. Break the into little bits.

3. Put the in a .

4. Whip on high for 3 minutes.

5. Pour into a glass, and sip your flip.

MATH
1+2=3
4+1=5 3+2=5

LESSON 12
Words with -ad

OBJECTIVE
To recognize the sounds and spelling of the phonogram *-ad*

LESSON PLANNER
See the Assignment Guide on page T11 for a 3-day or 5-day plan.

▶ INFORMAL ASSESSMENT

Have children listen as you read the following rhyme aloud, emphasizing words with the *-ad* phonogram:

> T<u>ad</u> is almost always gl<u>ad</u>.
> He rarely gets s<u>ad</u>,
> So he never feels b<u>ad</u>.

Repeat the rhyme several times, and encourage children to join you. After several repetitions, children should be able to recite the rhyme.

Ask children to identify the words that rhyme. Then have them repeat the words *Tad*, *glad*, *sad*, and *bad* as they listen for the ending sounds.

You may notice that some children have difficulty recognizing rhyming words with the *-ad* phonogram. This lesson will help children recognize the sounds and spelling of this phonogram.

MEETING INDIVIDUAL NEEDS

Children Acquiring English
Frequently, children who are acquiring English have difficulty differentiating the short *a* sound from the short *e* and short *u* sounds. Give children practice in listening to and pronouncing pairs of words with these vowel sounds. Provide practice with words such as *mad, mud; bad, bed; bad, bud; sad, said; had, head*; and *lad, led*. Then repeat the word pairs in random order, and ask children to identify which word in each pair has the same ending sounds as *dad*. **COMPARING AND CONTRASTING**

▶ MOOD PAD

After children complete the first two pages of the lesson, they may enjoy creating "Mood Pads" that feature words that contain the *-ad* phonogram and their corresponding pictures. Distribute a set of crayons or markers and four sheets of paper to each child. Explain that on one sheet of paper, children should draw the face of someone (real or imaginary) who is glad, and write the word *glad* underneath. On another sheet of paper, they should draw the same person with a sad face and write *sad*. Another sheet of paper should show the same person with a mad face and the word *mad*. Then have children create a cover sheet with a title. Assist children in stapling their pages together to make their "Mood Pads" complete.

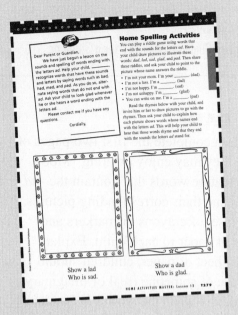

HOME ACTIVITIES MASTER: Lesson 12

NOTE: Fill in the blanks on the Home Activities Master before sending it home. See the Assignment Guide on page T11.

See page T279 for the Home Activities Master.

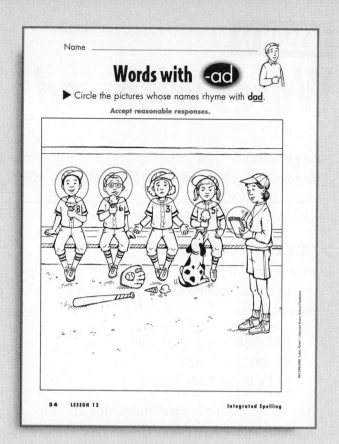

Name _____

Words with -ad

▶ Circle the pictures whose names rhyme with **dad**.

Accept reasonable responses.

54   LESSON 12   Integrated Spelling

▶ Introduction

WARM-UP Make a sad face and a glad face; then ask children to identify each face. Have them join you in saying the words *sad* and *glad* as they listen for the ending sounds.

INTRODUCING THE PAGE

Have children turn to page 54 and follow along as you read the lesson title aloud. Direct children's attention to the picture and discuss it with them. You might want to use questions like the following to guide their exploration:

• What are the children doing? (eating ice cream)

• How does the girl look whose ice cream has fallen on the ground? (sad)

• A dog is trying to lick one girl's ice cream cone. How does she look? (mad)

• One boy looks upset. How do you think his ice cream tastes? (bad)

Invite children to describe other picture details, making sure that the glad face and the note pad are mentioned in the discussion.

Read the directions aloud. Then have children repeat the word *dad* several times as they listen for the ending sounds. Ask a volunteer to restate what children are to do on the page. Point out that they can test for a rhyme by saying *dad* and another word as they listen to determine if the ending sounds are the same—for example, *dad, pad; dad, dog.*

Either work through the page with children or have them complete it independently. (Children should circle pictures representing the words *glad, sad, mad, bad,* and *pad.*)

CLASSIFYING

Strategy Workshop

m s p d

▶ Name these pictures. Listen for rhyming words. Write and trace the letters to spell the words.

1. pad
2. mad
3. dad
4. sad

5. This **dad** has a **pad**.

Words that rhyme with <u>dad</u> and <u>pad</u> often end with the letters <u>ad</u>.

Integrated Spelling   LESSON 12   55

▶ Strategy Workshop

RHYMING WORDS Help children recall that rhyming words sound alike except for their beginning sounds. Explain that rhyming words are often spelled the same way except for their beginning letters. Tell children that they can sometimes figure out how to spell a word by spelling a rhyming word and changing the beginning letter.

Help children identify the first picture on page 55 as a pad. Write the word *pad* on the board, and have children say it aloud. Guide them in changing the word *pad* into the word *mad* by asking the following:

- What letter stands for the beginning sound of *mad*? (*m*)

- What letters stand for the ending sounds that you hear in both *pad* and *mad*? (*ad*)

Record children's responses on the board, and have them read the word *mad* aloud. Explain to children that they can use this strategy to write words that name the pictures on this page. Then help them identify the remaining pictures as representing the words *mad*, *dad*, and *sad*. **APPLYING SPELLING STRATEGIES**

SPELLING IN CONTEXT Have children discuss the picture at the bottom of page 55. Give guidance as needed to help them complete the sentence and read it aloud. (*dad, pad*) **CONCEPT OF WORD**

MEETING INDIVIDUAL NEEDS

Extra Support/Children Acquiring English Children may benefit from a review of the initial consonant sounds that are blended with the phonogram *-ad* to form the rhyming picture names. Display pictures whose names begin with /p/, /m/, /d/, and /s/. Ask children to identify the letter that represents the initial sound of each picture name.

IN SUMMARY Invite children to tell what they have discovered about spelling words that rhyme with *dad* and *pad*. (These words often end with the letters *ad*.)

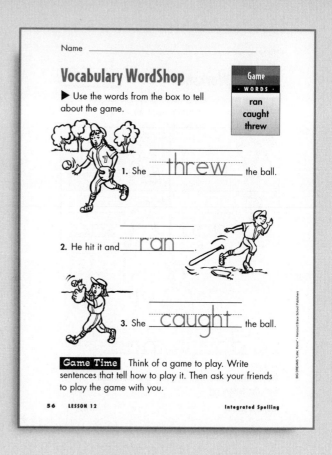

▶ Use the words from the box to tell about the game.

Game
• WORDS •
ran
caught
threw

1. She _threw_ the ball.

2. He hit it and _ran_.

3. She _caught_ the ball.

Game Time Think of a game to play. Write sentences that tell how to play it. Then ask your friends to play the game with you.

56   LESSON 12   Integrated Spelling

▶Vocabulary WordShop

WORDSHOP WORDS
Point out the WordShop Words on page 56, and ask volunteers to read them aloud. Then talk to children about how these words are alike. (All the words name actions in a game.)

Read the directions with children, and call their attention to the illustrations. Explain that they will write a word from the box to describe what the person did in each picture and to complete each sentence. After children complete the activity, encourage them to share their answers.

Children Acquiring English
You may want to consider doing this activity in the gym or on the playground. Have children work in groups of three. Give each group a ball, and tell two of the children to play a game of tossing a ball and running to catch it. The third child can act as a sports announcer, describing the action in the game after it occurs. **UNDERSTANDING WORD MEANINGS**

GAME TIME
Have volunteers suggest names of games they like to play. Before children begin to write their sentences, suggest they make lists of the most important directions for their games. You may want to conclude this activity in the gym or on the playground.

EXPLORING GAME WORDS
Explain to children that many action words change from present to past time by adding -ed. Write these examples on the board:

walk + ed = walked   play + ed = played

Point out that the WordShop Words do not change from present to past by adding -ed. Instead, each word has a special spelling. Write the present and past time of each WordShop Word on the board. Then ask:

- What letter changes when *run* becomes *ran*?
- What letter changes when *throw* becomes *threw*?
- What letters change when *catch* becomes *caught*?

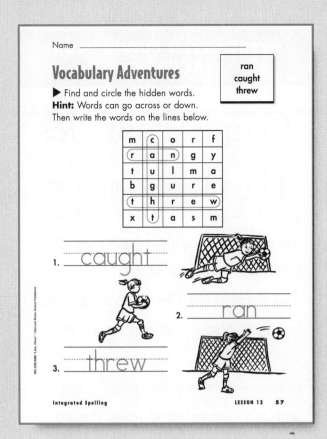

Name _____

Vocabulary Adventures

ran
caught
threw

▶ Find and circle the hidden words.
Hint: Words can go across or down.
Then write the words on the lines below.

m	c	o	r	f
r	a	n	g	y
t	u	l	m	a
b	g	u	r	e
t	h	r	e	w
x	t	a	s	m

1. caught

2. ran

3. threw

Integrated Spelling   LESSON 12   57

> ". . . WE SEE THE SOCIAL
> CONSTRUCTION *of word families*
> *as a powerful tool in spelling*
> *instruction.*"
> *(J. O'Flahavan and R. Blassberg)*

VOCABULARY ADVENTURES

Read the directions at the top of page 57 with children. Ask children to read the words in the box aloud. Explain that these three words are the ones to look for in the puzzle. After the puzzle is finished, have children complete items 1–3 by writing the words they circled next to the correct pictures. **USING ACTION WORDS**

MEETING INDIVIDUAL NEEDS

Challenge Suggest that children create similar word-search puzzles, using words in the *-ad* phonogram family. Provide children with grid paper that has large squares to record their puzzles. Laminate the finished puzzles or place them in acetate sleeves, and have children use erasable markers to circle their responses.

Game ★ WORDS ★

Spelling Log Children may want to write the Game Words from this lesson in their Spelling Logs.

►Lesson Wrap-Up

RETEACH: Learning Differences

Provide children with sandpaper cutouts of the letters *a, d, d, s, m, b, h,* and *p.* Say a word in the *-ad* family, such as *dad,* emphasizing the sound of the phonogram. Then dictate the spelling as each child puts the letters together and then uses a fingertip to trace each cutout. Have children spell the word aloud with you as they trace it again. Finally, have children close their eyes and spell the word aloud from memory.

AUDITORY/KINESTHETIC MODALITIES

INTEGRATED CURRICULUM ACTIVITY

Game Charades

Have children work in pairs or groups to prepare a charade that shows them playing a game, such as football, tennis, or soccer. Point out that each of the Game Words in the lesson is also an action word. Work with children to generate a list of action words that are associated with the games, or display the list that was created for the Optional Writing Idea on page T91. Then invite children to perform their charades, pantomiming the actions related to the game.

After a charade is complete, invite other classmates to guess the game that was acted out. Encourage children to describe what actions they observed. Have children identify any Game Words they hear speakers use in their descriptions.

LANGUAGE ARTS

LESSON 13

Words with -in

OBJECTIVE

To recognize the sounds and spelling of the phonogram -in

LESSON PLANNER

See the Assignment Guide on page T11 for a 3-day or 5-day plan.

▶ INFORMAL ASSESSMENT

Have children listen as you read the following rhyme, emphasizing words with the phonogram -in. You might want to tap the table with a ruler to focus attention on the sounds of this phonogram.

> Find a pickle in the b*in*.
> Eat it fast and you will w*in*.
> For your prize you'll get a p*in*
> Made of silver, not of t*in*.

Repeat the rhyme several times, and invite children to join in as they become familiar with the words.

Ask children to identify the words that rhyme. Then have them repeat the words *bin, win, pin,* and *tin* as they listen for the ending sounds.

You may notice that some children have difficulty recognizing rhyming words ending with the -*in* phonogram. This lesson will help children recognize the sounds and spelling of this phonogram.

Children Acquiring English

Short vowel sounds often present the greatest difficulty for children who are acquiring English. Many children have problems distinguishing between the short *i* and short *e* sounds. Provide practice by asking children to listen to and repeat these word pairs: *bin, Ben; kin, Ken; din, den; pin, pen; tin, ten;* and *win, when.*

In addition, children who speak Spanish, Chinese, Vietnamese, and Tagalog often replace the short *i* vowel sound with the long

e sound. Have children listen to and pronounce the following word pairs: *bin, bean; kin, keen; din, dean;* and *tin, teen.* Pronounce the word pairs again in random order, and have children identify the word in each pair that contains the -*in* phonogram. **COMPARING AND CONTRASTING**

▶ SPIN AN -in

After children complete the first two pages of the lesson, they may enjoy creating a large spinner featuring words that contain the -*in* phonogram. Draw four concentric circles on a piece of tagboard. Then divide the circles into four equal parts by drawing two perpendicular diameters, leaving the center circle uncut. In the center circle, write the word *in* and attach a spinner with a brad. On the twelve parts of the spinner, have children write words that are spelled with the -*in* phonogram. Possible words include *bin, din, fin, kin, pin, shin, spin, tin, win, grin, twin,* and *thin.* Display the spinner on a table. Provide time for children to take turns spinning it. Challenge children to read the word in the outside circle of the section the spinner lands on and to use the word in a sentence. Have children follow the same procedure for the words in the second and third circles.

NOTE: Fill in the blanks on the Home Activities Master before sending it home. See the Assignment Guide on page T11.

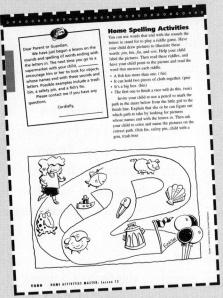

See page T280 for the Home Activities Master.

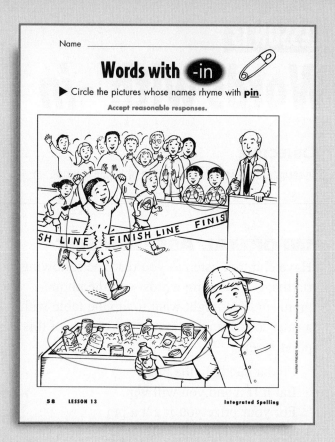

Name _____

Words with -in

▶ Circle the pictures whose names rhyme with **pin**.

Accept reasonable responses.

58   LESSON 13   Integrated Spelling

▶ Introduction

WARM-UP
Choose one child to stand with you before the group. Point to the child as you say, "This is my twin. We like to spin," emphasizing the words *twin* and *spin*. Then have the child spin around with you once, like a ballet dancer. Invite pairs of children to follow your example, repeating the rhyme as they spin and listen for the rhyming sounds.

INTRODUCING THE PAGE
Have children turn to page 58 and follow along as you read the lesson title aloud. Direct attention to the picture and discuss it with children. You might want to use questions like the following to guide the discussion:

• Where are the people in this picture? (at a race)

• What are the runners trying to do? (win)

• Find the two children who look exactly alike. What is each one called? (twin)

• Look at the cans of juice. What do you call the container that they are in? (bin)

Invite children to describe other picture details, making sure that the shirt with a picture of a fish fin and a person's grin are mentioned.

Read the directions aloud. Have children repeat the word *pin* several times as they listen for the ending sounds. Remind children that they can test for a rhyme by saying *pin* and another word as they listen to determine if the ending sounds are the same.

Either work through the page with children or have them complete the page independently. (Children should circle pictures representing the words *win*, *twin*, *fin*, *bin*, and *grin*.) **CLASSIFYING**

Name _____

Strategy Workshop

| b | p | w | f |

▶ Name these pictures. Listen for rhyming words.
Write and trace the letters to spell the words.

1. fin

2. bin

3. win

4. pin

5. If you __win__ , you get a __pin__ .

Words that rhyme with <u>win</u> and <u>pin</u> often end with the letters <u>in</u>.

Integrated Spelling   LESSON 13   59

▶ Strategy Workshop

RHYMING WORDS Help children recall that rhyming words sound alike except for their beginning sounds. Explain that rhyming words are often spelled the same way except for their beginning letters. Tell children that they can sometimes figure out how to spell a word by spelling a rhyming word and changing the beginning letter.

Ask children to turn to page 59, and help them identify the first picture as a fin. Write the word *fin* on the board, and have children say it aloud. Guide them in changing the word *fin* to *pin* by asking the following questions:

• What letter stands for the beginning sound of *pin*? (*p*)

• What letters stand for the ending sounds that you hear in both *fin* and *pin*? (*in*)

Record children's responses on the board, and have them read the word *pin* aloud. Explain to children that they can use this strategy to write words that name the pictures on this page. Then help them identify the remaining pictures as representing the words *bin*, *win*, and *pin*. **APPLYING SPELLING STRATEGIES**

SPELLING IN CONTEXT Have children discuss the picture at the bottom of page 59. Give guidance as needed to help them complete the sentence and read it aloud. (*pin*, *win*) **CONCEPT OF WORD**

MEETING INDIVIDUAL NEEDS

Extra Support/Children Acquiring English Children may benefit from a review of the initial consonant sounds that are blended with the phonogram *-in* to form the picture names. Display pictures whose names begin with /b/, /p/, /w/, and /f/. Ask children to identify the letter that represents the initial sound of each picture name.

IN SUMMARY Invite children to tell what they have discovered about spelling words that rhyme with *win* and *pin*. (These words often end with the letters *in*.)

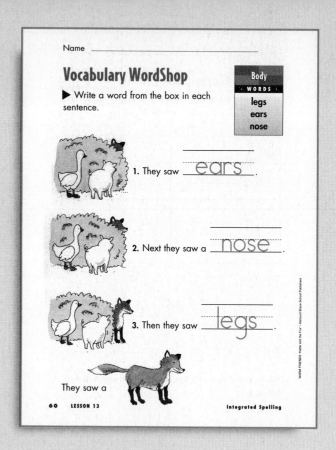

Name _____

Vocabulary WordShop

▶ Write a word from the box in each sentence.

Body
• WORDS •
legs
ears
nose

1. They saw ___ears___.

2. Next they saw a ___nose___.

3. Then they saw ___legs___.

They saw a

Integrated Spelling

▶ Vocabulary WordShop

WORDSHOP WORDS Point out the WordShop Words on page 60, and ask volunteers to read them aloud. Then talk with children about how these words are alike. (They name parts of the body.) Explain that the words name parts of a person's body as well as an animal's body.

Focus attention on the illustrations, and ask children to name the body part that the goose and pig are looking at in each picture. Then read the directions at the top of the page with children. After children complete the page, have them share their responses.

MEETING INDIVIDUAL NEEDS

Children Acquiring English
Play a game in which you say each WordShop Word as children point to the corresponding part on their bodies. **BUILDING VOCABULARY**

EXPLORING BODY WORDS

You can use the Body Words to explore the concept of singular and plural naming words with children.

• Ask children to identify the two Body Words that name more than one body part. *(ears, legs)* Mention that words that name more than one are called plurals. Point out that some naming words are made plural by adding an -*s* to the end of the word. Write the words *ear* and *ears* on the board to illustrate. Ask children to suggest other body words that name more than one. (Possible responses: arms, eyes, hands, fingers)

• Focus attention on the word *nose*, and explain that it is a singular naming word. Point out that singular words name only one. Ask children to suggest other body words that name only one. (Possible responses: mouth, head)

Name _____

Vocabulary Adventures

▶ Use words from the box to tell about the picture.

| legs |
| nose |
| ears |

1. nose   2. ears

3. legs

Favorite Animals Make a picture of your favorite animal. Write the WordShop Words and other words to label your picture. Add these words to your Spelling Log.

Integrated Spelling   LESSON 13   61

"WORD STUDY *is a general term that applies to a wide variety of word activities and games. The most basic technique involves comparison and contrast, using word cards containing particular features of words.* "

(Janet W. Bloodgood)

VOCABULARY ADVENTURES

Direct children's attention to the picture of the fox on page 61. Discuss the illustration, and ask children to name some body parts that they see pictured. Read with children the directions at the top of the page. Explain that they are to label the picture by writing words from the box on the lines. After children complete the activity, have them share their responses. **USING NAMING WORDS**

FAVORITE ANIMALS

Provide children with drawing materials. Then read the directions with children. Ask children to volunteer other body words that they can use to label their pictures. Create a list on the board. Suggest children refer to the list when they label their pictures.

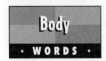

Spelling Log Children may want to write the Body Words from this lesson in their Spelling Logs.

Optional Writing Idea

Shared Writing: Story Ask children to look at the picture on Pupil's Edition page 58. Encourage them to make up a story based on the picture. Help children generate story ideas by asking the following:

• Where are the people in the picture?

• What are the children doing?

• How do the children feel?

• Who will win the race? What will the winner do next?

Have children use their ideas to write sentences that might be turned into a group story. Children can dictate their sentences for you to write, or you may choose to have them use invented spelling to write the sentences themselves.

►Lesson Wrap-Up

RETEACH: Learning Differences
Some children may need additional auditory reinforcement to spell words containing the *-in* phonogram. Allow these children to listen to your voice on tape, slowly saying and then spelling the words *pin, tin, fin, bin,* and *win*. After children have listened to each word pronounced and spelled on the tape, have them turn off the machine and write the word. After they write all five words, have them rewind the tape and listen once more to check their spelling of each word. **AUDITORY MODALITY**

Word Hunt

Organize children into teams of three. Provide children with scissors, and discarded magazines, newspapers, and other print material. Have each team find and cut out two pictures of items whose names end with phonogram *-in*. After the pictures are found, have team members work together to spell the names of the items as you list the words on the board.

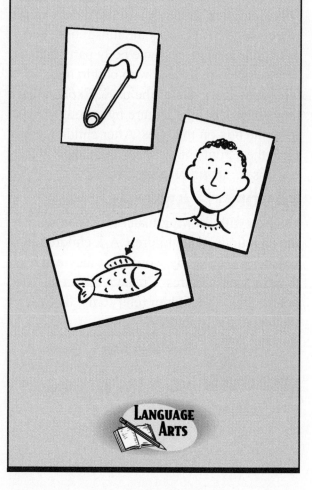

LANGUAGE ARTS

LESSON 14

Words with -ill

OBJECTIVE
To recognize the sounds and spelling of the phonogram -ill

LESSON PLANNER
See the Assignment Guide on page T11 for a 3-day or 5-day plan.

▶ INFORMAL ASSESSMENT

Have children listen as you read the following rhyming tongue twister aloud, emphasizing words with the phonogram -ill:

Bill and Jill sit still on the hill.

Repeat the rhyme several times, and invite children to join in.

Ask children to identify the words that rhyme. Then have them repeat the words *Bill*, *Jill*, *still*, and *hill* as they listen for the ending sounds.

You may notice that some children have difficulty recognizing rhyming words ending with the -ill phonogram. This lesson will help children recognize the sounds and spelling of this phonogram.

Children Acquiring English
Short vowel sounds often present the greatest difficulty for children who are acquiring English. Many children have problems distinguishing between the short *i* and short *e* sounds. Provide practice by asking children to listen to and repeat these word pairs: *bill, bell; fill, fell; dill, dell; sill, sell; till, tell;* and *will, well*.

In addition, children who speak Spanish, Chinese, Vietnamese, and Tagalog often replace the short *i* vowel sound with the long *e* sound. Have children listen to and pronounce the following word pairs: *ill, eel; fill, feel; sill, seal; till, teal; dill, deal; hill, heal; mill, meal;* and *pill, peal*. Pronounce the word pairs again in random order, and have children identify the word in each pair that contains the -ill phonogram. **COMPARING AND**

▶ CONTRASTING

FILL THE HILL

After children complete the first two pages of the lesson, they may enjoy creating a display of pictures and words that contain the -ill phonogram. Distribute simple cutout shapes of fir trees and markers or crayons to children. Invite children either to write words whose names end with the phonogram -ill or to draw pictures representing the words on the shapes. Draw a big hill on a bulletin board. Stretch string in a zigzag pattern across the hill, and help children attach their -ill trees to the string with paper clips or staples.

NOTE: Fill in the blanks on the Home Activities Master before sending it home. See the Assignment Guide on page T11.

See page T281 for the Home Activities Master.

▶ Introduction

WARM-UP Draw a hill on the chalkboard and walk your fingers up the hill as you say, "Bill and Jill went up a hill." Have children join you in repeating the sentence as they listen for the rhyming sounds.

INTRODUCING THE PAGE

Have children turn to page 62 and follow along as you read the lesson title aloud. Direct attention to the picture and discuss it with children. You might want to use questions like the following to guide their exploration:

• Where are the people in this picture? (nurse's office)

• What is the nurse doing? (filling a glass with water)

• What is on the nurse's desk? (pills)

• What do you see in the pictures on the wall? (a hill, a windmill)

Invite children to describe other picture details, making sure that they mention the window sill.

Read the directions aloud. Have children repeat the word *hill* several times as they listen for the ending sounds. Remind children that they can test for a rhyme by saying *hill* and another word as they listen to determine if the ending sounds are the same.

Either work through the page with children or have them complete the page independently. (Children should circle pictures representing the words *fill*, *pill*, *windmill*, *hill*, and *sill*.) **CLASSIFYING**

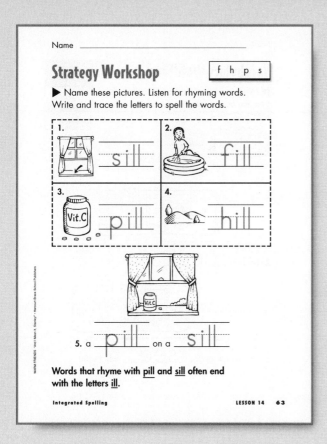

Name _____

Strategy Workshop

`f  h  p  s`

▶ Name these pictures. Listen for rhyming words.
Write and trace the letters to spell the words.

1. s i l l
2. f i l l
3. p i l l
4. h i l l

5. a p i l l on a s i l l

**Words that rhyme with <u>pill</u> and <u>sill</u> often end
with the letters <u>ill</u>.**

Integrated Spelling   LESSON 14   63

▶Strategy Workshop

RHYMING WORDS Help children recall that rhyming words sound alike except for their beginning sounds. Explain that rhyming words are often spelled the same way except for their beginning letters. Tell children that they can sometimes figure out how to spell a word by spelling a rhyming word and changing the beginning letter.

Ask children to turn to page 63, and help them identify the first picture as a sill. Write the word *sill* on the board, and have children say it aloud. Guide them in changing the word *sill* to *dill* by asking the following questions:

• What letter stands for the beginning sound of *dill*? (*d*)

• What letters stand for the ending sounds that you hear in both *sill* and *dill*? (*ill*)

Record children's responses on the board, and have them read the word *dill* aloud. Explain to children that they can use this strategy to write words that name the pictures on this page. Then help them identify the remaining pictures as illustrating the words *fill*, *pill*, and *hill*. **APPLYING SPELLING STRATEGIES**

SPELLING IN CONTEXT Have children discuss the picture at the bottom of page 63. Give guidance as needed to help them complete the phrase and read it aloud. (*pill, sill*) **CONCEPT OF WORD**

MEETING INDIVIDUAL NEEDS

Extra Support/Children Acquiring English Children may benefit from a review of the initial consonant sounds that are blended with the phonogram *-ill* to form the picture names. Display pictures whose names begin with /f/, /h/, /p/, and /s/. Ask children to identify the letter that represents the initial sound of each picture name.

IN SUMMARY Invite children to tell what they have discovered about spelling words that rhyme with *pill* and *sill*. (These words often end with the letters *ill*.)

Name _____

Vocabulary WordShop

▶ What is the boy saying? Write words from the box to complete the sentences.

> **Sense**
> · WORDS ·
> see
> peek
> listen

1. I want you to __listen__ to me.

2. Do not __peek__.

3. Come now and __see__ what I did.

64   LESSON 14   Integrated Spelling

▶Vocabulary WordShop

WORDSHOP WORDS Point out the WordShop Words on page 64, and ask volunteers to read them aloud. Explain that people use their senses to learn about the world. Sight, hearing, touch, smell, and taste are senses. Then discuss with children how these words are alike. (They all have something to do with a person's senses.) Discuss the word *peek*, making sure that children understand that it means "to look quickly or secretly."

Read the directions aloud with children. Discuss the illustrations, and have children tell what the child and dog are doing in each picture. Explain that they will write a Sense Word in each sentence to tell what the boy is saying. Have children complete the page, giving help where needed. After children finish the activity, encourage them to share and explain their answers.

MEETING INDIVIDUAL NEEDS

Children Acquiring English
Encourage children to say the Sense Words aloud as they pantomime the actions with a partner. **PRACTICING PRONUNCIATION**

EXPLORING SENSE WORDS

Use the word pair *see* and *sea* to introduce and explore the concept of homophones. Write this sentence on the board, and help children read it aloud:

I <u>see</u> the deep blue <u>sea</u>.

Focus children's attention on the underlined words, and have them read the words with you. Lead children to conclude that these words sound the same, but they are not spelled the same, nor do they have the same meaning. Discuss the meaning and spelling of each word. Guide children to the generalization that in order to figure out which spelling should be used, it is important to know how a homophone is used in a sentence.

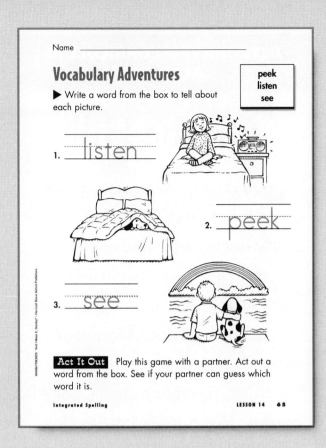

Name _____

Vocabulary Adventures

▶ Write a word from the box to tell about each picture.

| peek |
| listen |
| see |

1. listen

2. peek

3. see

Act It Out Play this game with a partner. Act out a word from the box. See if your partner can guess which word it is.

Integrated Spelling   LESSON 14   65

> *"CHILDREN ARE ABLE to compose when they know about six consonants . . . Consonants are more reliable than vowels and become the foundation on which words are made."*
> (Donald Graves)

VOCABULARY ADVENTURES
Read the directions at the top of page 65 with children. Point out the words in the box, and ask volunteers to read them aloud. Explain that they will write a word from the box to tell about each picture. After children label their pictures, have them share their responses. **USING ACTION WORDS**

ACT IT OUT
Read the directions aloud. Then have each child work with a partner to complete this activity.

 **Spelling Log** Children may want to write the Sense Words from this lesson in their Spelling Logs.

Optional Writing Idea

 **Independent Writing: A Description** Have children write about a favorite place. Before they begin, encourage them to make a list of sensory details that they might use in their descriptions. Help children organize their details by having them complete a chart similar to the one below:

My Favorite Place: The Beach	
Sights I See	**Sounds I Listen To**
waves	seagulls crying
fish	waves crashing
shells	splashing noises
sand	

Then have children write their descriptions. Some may also wish to illustrate their descriptions. Encourage children to share their finished work with partners or in a small group.

▶ Lesson Wrap-Up

RETEACH: Learning Differences

Make flash cards with sketches or cutout pictures of a hill, a dill pickle, a bill, and a window sill. At the bottom of each card, write the word that corresponds to the picture. Cover the initial consonant with a self-stick note. Have children look at a picture, say the picture name, and write on another sheet of paper the word that names the picture. Tell children to remove the self-stick note to check their spelling of the word. **VISUAL MODALITY**

INTEGRATED CURRICULUM ACTIVITY

On the Hill

Invite children to create a model of a hill. Before children begin, briefly discuss what kinds of plant and animal life are seen in hilly areas in your state or near your community. Then provide children with materials such as poster board, tissue paper, newspaper, paint, paintbrushes, glue, sand, modeling clay, and animal figurines. In addition, provide labels on which children can write about what they can do and see on a hill. For example, *climb a tree, smell a flower, take a hike, see a deer, hear a bird, play with a dog,* and *ride a bike.*

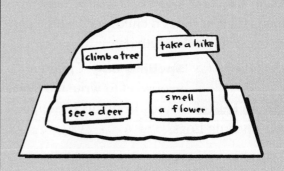

Words with -ug

OBJECTIVE
To recognize the sounds and spelling of the phonogram *-ug*

LESSON PLANNER
See the Assignment Guide on page T11 for a 3-day or 5-day plan.

▶ INFORMAL ASSESSMENT

Have children listen as you read the following rhyme aloud, emphasizing words with the phonogram *-ug:*

> A cute little bug
> Sat snug on a rug.
> She got a milk jug,
> And filled up a mug,
> Then sipped,
>> Glug,
>> Glug,
>> Glug!

Recite the rhyme several times, and encourage children to join in after they have become familiar with the words. After several repetitions, children should be able to say the rhyme as they pantomime the bug's actions.

Ask children to identify the words that rhyme. Then have them repeat the words *bug, snug, rug, jug, mug,* and *glug* as they listen for the ending sounds.

You may notice that some children have difficulty recognizing rhyming words ending with the *-ug* phonogram. This lesson will help children recognize the sounds and spelling of this phonogram.

Children Acquiring English
One of the most difficult sounds for children who are acquiring English to learn is the short *u* sound. This sound is challenging because there are many languages in which this sound does not exist. You may find that many children have difficulty distinguishing this sound from short *a* and short *e* sounds.

Give children practice in listening to and pronouncing words such as *bug, bag, beg; lug, lag, leg; hug, hag; rug, rag; mug, Meg;* and *tug, tag.*

In addition, children whose primary language is Spanish, Vietnamese, Chinese, Tagalog, and Thai may confuse short *u* and short *o* sounds. Have them listen to and repeat word pairs such as *hug, hog; bug, bog; dug, dog; jug, jog;* and *lug, log.* Then repeat these pairs of words in random order, and ask children to identify the word in each pair that has the same ending sounds as *hug.* **COMPARING AND CONTRASTING**

▶ BUGGY ABOUT WORDS

After children complete the first two pages of the lesson, they may enjoy creating a bulletin board featuring words that contain the *-ug* phonogram. Give children drawing paper, pencils, and crayons, and ask them to write several words that rhyme with the word *bug.* Possible words include *mug, tug, hug, dug, plug, jug,* and *snug.* After children have written their words, invite them to use crayons to draw a cute bug around each word. Display these "bug families" on a bulletin board.

NOTE: Fill in the blanks on the Home Activities Master before sending it home. See the Assignment Guide on page T11.

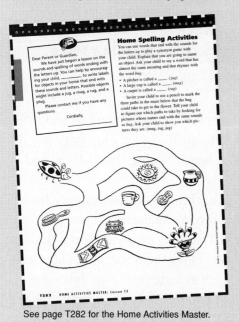

See page T282 for the Home Activities Master.

Name _____

Words with -ug

► Circle the pictures whose names rhyme with **hug**.
Accept reasonable responses.

66   LESSON 15   Integrated Spelling

►Introduction

WARM-UP Say this sentence, emphasizing the words *snug, bug,* and *rug*: "I'm as snug as a bug in a rug." Ask children to repeat the words *snug, bug,* and *rug* as they listen for the ending sounds.

INTRODUCING THE PAGE

After reading the lesson title aloud, direct children's attention to the illustration on page 66. You may want to use questions such as the following to discuss the picture with children:

• What are the people in this illustration doing? (They are posing for a picture.)

• What are the girls showing off in their drawings? (a bug and a tug)

• What are some of the things that you see in this room? (Among the objects, children should mention the rug, the mugs, and the plug.)

Read the directions aloud. Have children repeat the word *hug* several times as they listen for the ending sounds. Remind children that they can test for a rhyme by saying *hug* and another word as they listen to determine if the ending sounds are the same—for example, *hug, bug* and *hug, but*.

Either work through the page with children or have them complete it independently. (Children should circle pictures representing the words *bug, tug, rug, plug,* and *mug*.)
CLASSIFYING

Name _____

Strategy Workshop

| m | b | t | r |

▶ Name these pictures. Listen for rhyming words.
Write and trace the letters to spell the words.

1. rug
2. tug
3. mug
4. bug

5. The bug is on the rug.

Words that rhyme with bug and rug often end
with the letters ug.

Integrated Spelling   LESSON 15   67

▶ Strategy Workshop

RHYMING WORDS Help children recall that rhyming words sound alike except for their beginning sounds. Explain that rhyming words are often spelled the same way except for their beginning letters. Tell children that they can sometimes figure out how to spell a word by spelling a rhyming word and changing the beginning letter.

Help children identify the first picture on page 67 as a rug. Write the word *rug* on the board, and have children say it aloud. Guide them in changing the word *rug* into the word *tug* by asking questions like the following:

• What letter stands for the beginning sound of *tug*? (*t*)

• What letters stand for the ending sounds that you hear in both *rug* and *tug*? (*ug*)

Record children's responses on the board, and have them read the word *tug* aloud. Explain to children that they can use this strategy to write words that name the pictures on this page. Then help them identify the remaining pictures as representing the words *tug, mug,* and *bug*. **APPLYING SPELLING STRATEGIES**

SPELLING IN CONTEXT Have children discuss the picture at the bottom of page 67. Give guidance as needed to help them complete the sentence and read it aloud. (*bug, rug*) **CONCEPT OF WORD**

Extra Support/Children Acquiring English Children may benefit from a review of the initial consonant sounds that are blended with the phonogram *-ug* to form the picture names. Display pictures whose names begin with /r/, /t/, /m/, and /b/. Ask children to identify the letter that represents the initial sound of each picture name.

IN SUMMARY Invite children to tell what they have discovered about spelling words that rhyme with *bug* and *rug*. (These words often end with the letters *ug*.)

Name _____

Vocabulary WordShop

▶ Write a word from the box to complete each sentence.

Do-with-a-Friend · WORDS ·
paint
ride
swim

1. The friends ___swim___.

2. The friends ___ride___.

3. The friends ___paint___.

Friends Together Work with a friend. Make up sentences using the WordShop Words. Act out your sentences.

68 LESSON 15 Integrated Spelling

▶Vocabulary WordShop

WORDSHOP WORDS Point out the WordShop Words on page 68, and ask volunteers to read them aloud. Then talk with children about why they think the words are grouped together. (They name activities that friends do together.) Invite children to tell about activities they do with their friends.

Read the directions with children, and call their attention to the illustrations. Explain that they will write a word from the box to tell what the friends are doing in each picture. After children complete the activity, have them share their responses.

Children Acquiring English Encourage children to say the Do-with-a-Friend Words aloud as they point to each picture on Pupil's Edition page 68. **PRACTICING PRONUNCIATION**

FRIENDS TOGETHER Encourage children to think about their friendship experiences as they create and act out their sentences.

EXPLORING DO-WITH-A-FRIEND WORDS You might want to explore several meanings of the word *ride* by asking questions like these:

• What other word can we use to describe a drive in a car?

• What do you call the equipment that you go on for fun at an amusement park?

• What do you do when you use your bicycle?

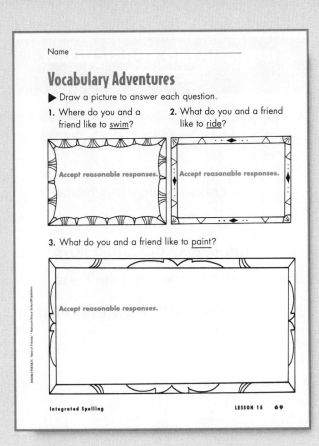

Vocabulary Adventures

▶ Draw a picture to answer each question.

1. Where do you and a friend like to <u>swim</u>?

2. What do you and a friend like to <u>ride</u>?

Accept reasonable responses.

Accept reasonable responses.

3. What do you and a friend like to <u>paint</u>?

Accept reasonable responses.

Integrated Spelling

LESSON 15 69

"**K**IDS GROW AS SPELLERS
*when teachers support them as
readers and writers.*"
(Judie Bartch)

VOCABULARY ADVENTURES

Read the directions at the top of page 69 with children. Provide children with crayons or markers. Then read the question for the first item and have children draw a picture that shows where they like to swim. Repeat this procedure for the remaining items on the page. After children complete the activity, have them share and discuss their drawings.

USING ACTION WORDS

 Working Together You may want to have children work with a partner to complete the activity. Encourage partners to discuss and agree on what to draw in each box.

 **Spelling Log** Children may want to write the Do-with-a-Friend Words from this lesson in their Spelling Logs.

Optional Writing Idea

 Independent Writing: Sentences for Pictures
Have children look at the pictures they drew as responses to the activity on Pupil's Edition page 69. Have them work with their responses to write picture captions. You may want to explain that if a child drew a picture of friends swimming together at a lake, the caption might be something like this:

We swim at the lake.

Have children share both their pictures and the captions with the class.

We swim at the lake.

▶ Lesson Wrap-Up

RETEACH: Learning Differences

Have children use their senses of touch and hearing to reinforce the spelling of words in the *-ug* family. Say one of these words aloud, emphasizing the phonogram sounds: *bug, hug, rug, mug, jug.* Then dictate the word, and have children write it. Ask children to join you in spelling the word aloud as they write it. Have children trace the word for additional reinforcement. Then have children spell the word aloud as they write it from memory. Repeat these steps with each of the words you wish to reteach. **AUDITORY/ KINESTHETIC MODALITIES**

Silly Sentences

Have children play this game in small groups. Provide each group with large index cards, and have them work together to write these words on the cards: *bug, hug, mug, rug,* and *plug.*

Have children shuffle the cards and lay them face down. Tell children to take turns turning over a card and reading the word. Then have them use the word in a silly sentence. For example:

Raisins rained on the round, red *rug*!

Words with -ig

▶ INFORMAL ASSESSMENT

Have children listen as you recite the following rhyme, emphasizing words with the phonogram -ig:

> There was a pig
> Who saw a fig
> On a big twig.

Repeat the rhyme several times and encourage children to join in. After several repetitions, children should be able to say the entire rhyme.

Ask children to identify the words that rhyme. Then have them repeat the words *pig*, *fig*, *big*, and *twig* as they listen for the ending sounds.

You may notice that some children have difficulty recognizing rhyming words ending with the -ig phonogram. This lesson will help children recognize the sounds and spelling of this phonogram.

Children Acquiring English
Children may have difficulty differentiating the short *i* sound from the short *a* sound. Provide children with practice in listening to and pronouncing words such as *big, bag; jig, jag; rig, rag;* and *wig, wag.* **COMPARING AND CONTRASTING**

▶ THE BIG TWIG

After children complete the first two pages of the lesson, they may enjoy creating a bulletin board featuring words that contain the -ig phonogram. On chart paper, draw a long tree branch with many twigs. Provide children with brown and green construction paper, scissors, and markers. Then have children cut out paper leaves. Invite them to write a word that contains the -ig phonogram on each leaf. Possible words include *big, dig, fig, pig, twig,* and *wig*. Have children attach each leaf to one of the twigs on the branch.

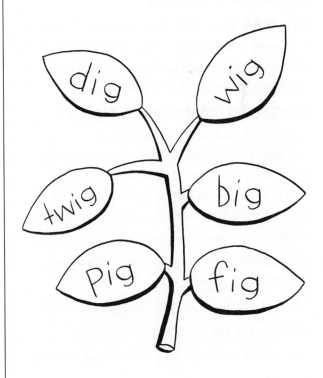

NOTE: Fill in the blanks on the Home Activities Master before sending it home. See the Assignment Guide on page T11.

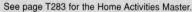

See page T283 for the Home Activities Master.

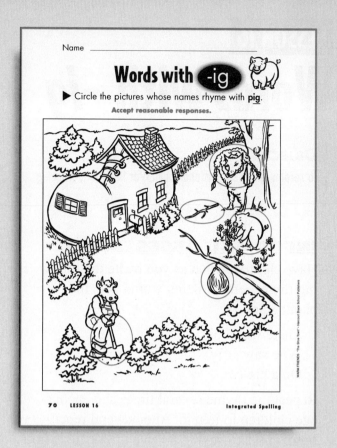

▶ Introduction

WARM-UP Display a picture of a large pig, point to it, and say, "big pig." Then point to the picture several more times, and have children repeat the phrase each time.

INTRODUCING THE PAGE

Have children listen as you read the lesson title aloud. Then direct their attention to the illustration on page 70. Discuss the picture with children. You might want to use questions like the following to guide their exploration:

• What place do you see in the picture? (a house and a yard)

• Who is picking a flower? (a pig)

• What is the farmer doing? (digging)

• What is the wolf putting on its head? (a wig)

Also direct children's attention to the twig on the ground, as well as the branch with the fig.

Read the directions aloud. Have children repeat the word *pig* several times, listening for the ending sounds. Ask a volunteer to restate what children are to do on the page. Remind children that they can test for a rhyme by saying *pig* and another word as they listen to determine if the ending sounds are the same.

Either work through the page with children or have them complete it independently. (Children should circle pictures representing the words *pig*, *dig*, *twig*, *fig*, and *wig*.)

CLASSIFYING

Strategy Workshop

RHYMING WORDS Help children recall that rhyming words sound alike except for their beginning sounds. Explain that rhyming words are often spelled the same way except for their beginning letters. Tell children that they can sometimes figure out how to spell a word by spelling a rhyming word and changing the beginning letter.

Help children identify the first picture on page 71 as a pig. Write the word *pig* on the board, and have children say it aloud. Guide them in changing the word *pig* into the word *big* by asking questions like these:

• What letter stands for the beginning sound of *big*? (*b*)

• What letters stand for the ending sounds that you hear in both *pig* and *big*? (*ig*)

Record children's responses on the board, and have them read the word *big* aloud. Explain to children that they can use this strategy to write words that name the pictures on this page. Then help them identify the remaining pictures as representing the words *dig*, *fig*, and *wig*. **APPLYING SPELLING STRATEGIES**

SPELLING IN CONTEXT Have children discuss the picture at the bottom of page 71. Then have children complete the sentence and read it aloud. (*pig, wig*)
CONCEPT OF WORD

 Extra Support/Children Acquiring English Children may benefit from a review of the initial consonant sounds that are blended with the phonogram *-ig* to form the rhyming picture names. Display pictures whose names begin with /p/, /d/, /f/, and /w/. Ask children to identify the letter that represents the initial sound of each picture name.

IN SUMMARY Invite children to tell what they have discovered about spelling words that rhyme with *pig* and *wig*. (These words often end with the letters *ig*.)

Name _____

Vocabulary WordShop

▶ Write words from the box to tell about the pictures.

Describing WORDS
happy
little
long

1. She has a _____little_____ house.

2. They will take a _____long_____ walk.

3. She is a _____happy_____ hen.

72   LESSON 16   Integrated Spelling

▶ Vocabulary WordShop

WORDSHOP WORDS Point out the WordShop Words on page 72, and ask volunteers to read them aloud. Then talk with children about how these words are alike. (The words tell how something or someone looks or feels.)

Focus children's attention on the animals in each picture. Have volunteers describe other picture details. Then read aloud the directions. Tell children that each sentence tells about a picture. Explain that they are to complete each sentence by writing a word from the box. After children complete the activity, have them share and discuss their answers.

MEETING INDIVIDUAL NEEDS

Children Acquiring English Play a game in which you say each Describing Word and have children identify an object or person in the room that fits the description. **UNDERSTANDING WORD MEANINGS**

EXPLORING DESCRIBING WORDS Introduce the comparative forms of two of the Describing Words, *little* and *long*. Display a small item, and ask children to use one of the Describing Words to tell about the item. (*little*) Then place a smaller item next to the first one, and ask children which of the two items is littler. As you point to each item, have children repeat the following sentences with you:

This (name of item) is *little*.
This (name of item) is *littler*.

To introduce the comparative form *longer*, display a used pencil, and elicit that the Describing Word *long* could be used to tell about the pencil. Then display an unused pencil that is longer, and have children repeat these sentences:

This pencil is *long*.
This pencil is *longer*.

Name _____

Vocabulary Adventures

▶ Read the word below each picture. Write the word that has the opposite meaning.

little
long
happy

sad

1. happy

big

2. little

short

3. long

Describe Something Draw a picture of a person, place, or thing. Write words that describe what you drew. Add these words to your Spelling Log.

Integrated Spelling   LESSON 16   73

"CHILDREN LEARN TO SPEAK *by speaking, making mistakes, and refining their language as they communicate. So they learn how to spell by writing, inventing spellings, and refining their understanding of print.*" (J. Richard Gentry)

VOCABULARY ADVENTURES

Read the directions at the top of page 73 with children. You may want to talk briefly about the concept of words that are opposites, giving examples such as *on* and *off*, and *soft* and *loud*.

Discuss each illustration, and have volunteers read the word below each picture. Have children write the word that has the opposite meaning of the word below each picture. After children complete the activity, have them share and explain their responses. **USING DESCRIBING WORDS**

DESCRIBING SOMETHING

Provide children with drawing materials. Ask children to name the people, places, or things they would like to draw. Create a list on the board. After children complete their pictures, work with them to help them label their pictures with descriptive words.

Spelling Log Children may want to write the Describing Words from this lesson in their Spelling Logs.

Optional Writing Idea

Independent Writing: Sentences For a Picture
Provide children with crayons and drawing paper that is folded into thirds. In the first section, have children draw a picture showing what they looked like when they were little. In the second section, have them draw a picture showing what they look like now that they are big. In the third section, have them draw a picture showing what they look like when they are happy. Have children write sentences about their pictures.

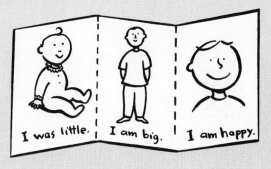

I was little.   I am big.   I am happy.

▶Lesson Wrap-Up

RETEACH: Learning Differences

Some children may need additional auditory and kinesthetic reinforcement to spell words containing the *-ig* phonogram. Give pairs of children large index cards, school glue in a squeeze bottle, and a small container of sand. Suggest that children cover their work surfaces with newspaper. Spell aloud words containing the *-ig* phonogram, such as *big*, *dig*, *fig*, *pig*, and *wig*. Have children take turns using the glue to write each word. Before the glue dries, have them sprinkle the words with sand and shake off any excess. After the glue dries, have partners take turns pronouncing the words and tracing the letters with a finger while spelling the words aloud. **AUDITORY/KINESTHETIC MODALITIES**

The Big Picture

Provide children with discarded magazines, scissors, glue or paste, and large sheets of paper. Ask children to look through the magazines and to cut out pictures of things that are big, such as a big animal like an elephant, a big building like a skyscraper, or a big vehicle like a bus. Have children create collages of their "big" pictures. Later, display all the collages. Invite children to identify each item in their collage, preceding it with the descriptive word *big* (for example, *a big park*).

LESSON 17
Words with -un

OBJECTIVE
To recognize the sounds and spelling of the phonogram -un

LESSON PLANNER
See the Assignment Guide on page T11 for a 3-day or 5-day plan.

▶ INFORMAL ASSESSMENT

Have children listen as you read the following rhyme, emphasizing words with the phonogram -un:

> Let's have some f<u>un</u>!
> We can go for a r<u>un</u>.
> We can sit in the s<u>un</u>.
> We can each eat a raisin b<u>un</u>!

Reread the rhyme several times, and invite children to join in as they become familiar with the words.

Ask children to identify the words that rhyme. Then have them repeat the words *fun, run, sun,* and *bun* as they listen for the ending sounds.

You may notice that some children have difficulty recognizing rhyming words ending with the -un phonogram. This lesson will help children recognize the sounds and spelling of this phonogram.

Children Acquiring English
The short *u* sound is often one of the most difficult sounds for children who are acquiring English to learn. Often, children have difficulty distinguishing this sound from short *a* and short *e* sounds. Give children practice listening to and pronouncing pairs of words with these vowel sounds. For examples, use words such as the following: *fun, fan; run, ran; bun, ban; pun, pan; begun, began; spun, span; bun, Ben;* and *pun, pen.* Then repeat the word pairs in random order, and ask children to identify which word in each pair has the same ending sounds as *sun.* **COMPARING AND CONTRASTING**

▶ FUN IN THE SUN

After children complete the first two pages of the lesson, they may enjoy creating a bulletin board featuring pictures and words that contain the -un phonogram. Display a cutout of a large yellow sun, and attach it to a bulletin board. On large index cards, have children draw pictures and write words ending with the -un phonogram. Help children display their words and pictures around the sun cutout. Suggest that they use lengths of yellow yarn or ribbon as "sun rays" to connect their work to the sun.

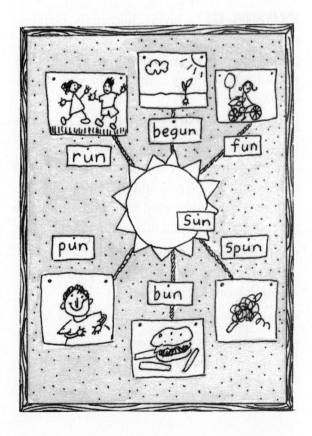

NOTE: Fill in the blanks on the Home Activities Master before sending it home. See the Assignment Guide on page T11.

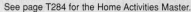

See page T284 for the Home Activities Master.

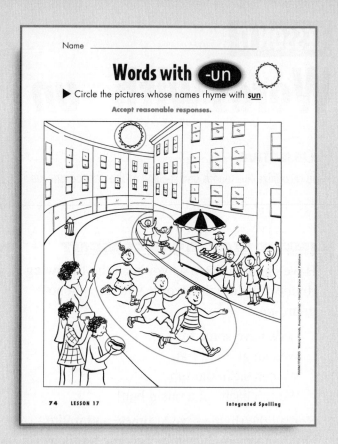

▶Introduction

WARM-UP
Invite children to stand by their desks and jog in place as they chant the phrase *fun run*. Have them repeat the phrase several times as they listen for the ending sounds.

INTRODUCING THE PAGE
Have children turn to page 74 and follow along as you read the lesson title aloud. Direct attention to the picture and discuss it with children. You might want to use questions like the following to guide their exploration:

• What are the children in the middle of the street doing? (running, racing) What is another word for a race? (run)

• What do you see in the sky? (the sun)

• One of the girls who is watching the race is eating. What is she eating? (a hot dog on a bun)

Invite children to describe other picture details. Lead children to conclude that the children who are watching the runners are having fun.

Read the directions aloud. Have children repeat the word *sun* several times as they listen for the ending sounds. Then ask a volunteer to restate what the children are to do on the page. Remind children that they can test for a rhyme by saying *sun* and another word as they listen to determine if the ending sounds are the same—for example, *sun, fun* and *sun, fan.*

Either work through the page with children or have them complete it independently. (Children should circle pictures representing the words *sun, bun, fun,* and *run.*)

CLASSIFYING

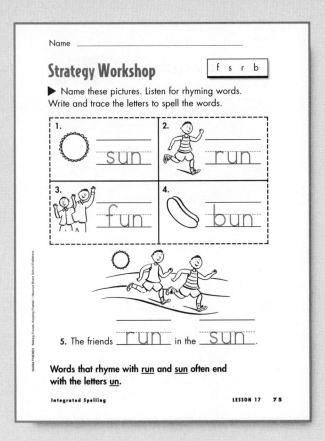

Name _____

Strategy Workshop

| f | s | r | b |

▶ Name these pictures. Listen for rhyming words.
Write and trace the letters to spell the words.

1. sun
2. run
3. fun
4. bun

5. The friends run in the sun.

Words that rhyme with run and sun often end with the letters un.

Integrated Spelling   LESSON 17   75

Strategy Workshop

RHYMING WORDS Help children recall that rhyming words sound alike except for their beginning sounds. Explain that rhyming words are often spelled the same way except for their beginning letters. Tell children that they can sometimes figure out how to spell a word by spelling a rhyming word and changing the beginning letter.

Help children identify the first picture on page 75 as the sun. Write the word *sun* on the board, and have children say it aloud. Guide them in changing the word *sun* into the word *bun* by asking questions like the following:

• What letter stands for the beginning sound of *bun*? (*b*)

• What letters stand for the ending sounds that you hear in both *sun* and *bun*? (*un*)

Record children's responses on the board, and have them read the word *bun* aloud. Explain to children that they can use this strategy to write words that name the pictures on this page. Then help them identify the remaining pictures as representing the words *run, fun,* and *bun.* **APPLYING SPELLING STRATEGIES**

SPELLING IN CONTEXT Have children discuss the picture at the bottom of page 75. Give guidance as needed to help them complete the sentence and read it aloud. (*run, sun*) **CONCEPT OF WORD**

Extra Support/Children Acquiring English Children may benefit from a review of the initial consonant sounds that are blended with the phonogram *-un* to form the picture names. Display pictures whose names begin with /s/, /r/, /f/, and /b/. Ask children to identify the letter that represents the initial sound of each picture name.

IN SUMMARY Invite children to tell what they have discovered about spelling words that rhyme with *run* and *sun.* (These words often end with the letters *un.*)

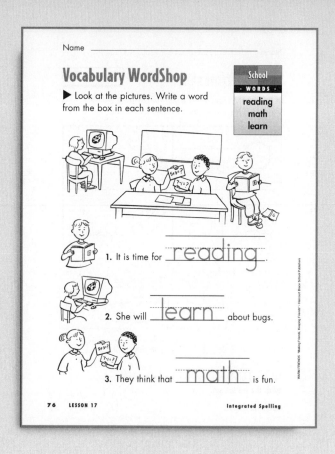

Name _____

Vocabulary WordShop

▶ Look at the pictures. Write a word from the box in each sentence.

School
• WORDS •
reading
math
learn

1. It is time for _reading_.

2. She will _learn_ about bugs.

3. They think that _math_ is fun.

▶ Vocabulary WordShop

WORDSHOP WORDS Point out the WordShop Words on page 76, and ask volunteers to read them aloud. Then talk with children about how these words are alike. (They name school activities and subjects.)

Direct children's attention to the large illustration, and ask volunteers to tell what activities and school subjects the children in the classroom are engaged in. Read with children the directions at the top of the page. Point out the pictures next to the sentences. Explain that they are to complete each sentence by writing the word from the box that tells about the children or child in the picture. After children complete the page, have them share their responses.

Children Acquiring English
Make word cards for the WordShop Words *reading* and *math*. Also, prepare a sentence strip with the sentence frame

I like_____. Have children take turns completing the sentence with one of the word cards and reading the sentence aloud.

PRACTICING PRONUNCIATION

EXPLORING SCHOOL WORDS

Briefly discuss with children the meaning of *learn*, helping them conclude that the word means "to get knowledge." Have volunteers give examples of what they have learned this year. Then informally explore with children what happens to the word *learn* when the suffix *-er* is added. Write *learner* on the board, and explain that adding the word part *-er* to a word can add the meaning "someone who." For example, a *learner* is "someone who learns." Challenge children to similarly define other words related to school. For example, *teach*, *read*, *help*, and *listen*.

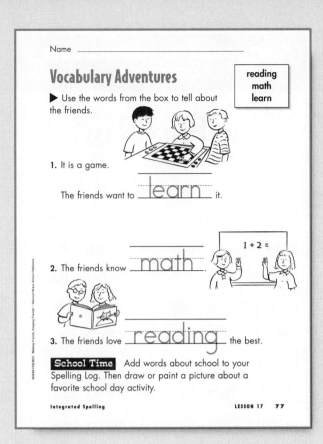

Name _____

Vocabulary Adventures

> Use the words from the box to tell about the friends.

| reading |
| math |
| learn |

1. It is a game.

The friends want to **learn** it.

2. The friends know **math**.

1 + 2 =

3. The friends love **reading** the best.

School Time Add words about school to your Spelling Log. Then draw or paint a picture about a favorite school day activity.

Integrated Spelling

LESSON 17   77

---

*T*HE WORD *RUN* ORIGINALLY *had the meaning "to move quickly or freely." Over the years, it has acquired more than 100 meanings, including the meanings in phrases such as "run the show," "run out of gas," "run aground," "run into trouble," "in the long run," and "a home run."*

VOCABULARY ADVENTURES

Read with children the directions at the top of page 77. Then focus their attention on the pictures, and explain that looking at the pictures will help them complete the activity. Have children write words from the box to complete the sentences. After children complete the sentences, have them share and explain their responses. **USING NAMING AND ACTION WORDS**

SCHOOL TIME
Read the directions with children. Then provide children with drawing materials. Before children begin to draw, ask volunteers to tell about school day activities, such as subjects studied, routine events, and special activities. Write their responses on the board. Encourage children to refer to the responses when they label their pictures.

Spelling Log Children may want to write the School Words from this lesson in their Spelling Logs.

Optional Writing Idea

Independent Writing: Journal Entry Direct children's attention to the pictures on Pupil's Edition page 77. Point out that the pictures show what friends do together. Invite children to tell what activities they do with their friends, either at school or at home. Record their responses in a list on the board:

My friend and I . . .
read stories
play games
draw and paint pictures
write poems

Then have children use the responses to write journal entries about activities they do with friends. Some may wish to illustrate their entries. Encourage children to share their finished work with partners or in a small group.

▶Lesson Wrap-Up

RETEACH: Learning Differences

Help children focus on the sounds and spellings of words that end with the *-un* phonogram by playing this "Echo Game." Display a word card with one of these words: *sun, fun, run,* or *bun*. Read the word *sun* aloud, and have children echo you. Point to each letter, voice the letter sounds, and have children echo you. Then spell the word aloud while pointing to each letter, and have children echo you. Say the word once more, and have children echo you. Repeat this procedure with the rest of the word cards.

AUDITORY MODALITY

A Fun Run

You may wish to do this activity in an open area. To prepare for the activity, use chalk to mark on the ground or floor a circular path large enough for a group of children to run around. Begin the activity by having children stand around the circle. Tell them that they are to run around the circle in a clockwise direction while you say some words. Explain they are to change to a counterclockwise direction when they hear a word that ends with the phonogram *-un*. Also, mention that they are to begin and stop running when they hear a bell (or a whistle). Say the following words at ten-to-fifteen-second intervals: *begun, bell, shell, stick, spun, lick, wick, had, run, tip, nip, trip, sun, get, jet, wet, fun, can, tan, man, van, bun, cap, nap, tap, lap, map,* and *pun*.

P.E./ HEALTH

LESSON 18
Words with -ack

OBJECTIVE
To recognize the sounds and spelling of the phonogram -ack

LESSON PLANNER
See the Assignment Guide on page T11 for a 3-day or 5-day plan.

▶ INFORMAL ASSESSMENT

Have children listen as you recite the following rhyme, emphasizing words with the phonogram -ack:

> Two little ducks
> Named M<u>ack</u> and J<u>ack</u>,
> All they do is
> Qu<u>ack</u>, qu<u>ack</u>, qu<u>ack</u>!

Repeat the rhyme several times, and encourage children to make waddling duck motions. After several repetitions, children should be able to say the rhyme as they perform the actions.

Ask children to identify the words that rhyme. Then have them repeat the words *Mack, Jack*, and *quack* as they listen for the ending sounds.

You may notice that some children have difficulty recognizing rhyming words ending with the *-ack* phonogram. This lesson will help children recognize the sounds and spelling of this phonogram.

Children Acquiring English
Many children who are acquiring English have difficulty distinguishing the short *a* sound from short *u* and sometimes short *e* as well. Give children practice listening to and pronouncing pairs of words with these vowel sounds. For example, use words such as *back, buck; pack, peck; tack, tuck; lack, luck;* and *sack, suck.* **COMPARING AND CONTRASTING**

▶ THE -ack SACK

Display a shopping bag labeled "The *-ack* Sack." Invite children to look through discarded magazines and advertising circulars to find pictures whose names rhyme with the word *sack*. Have children cut out the pictures, mount them on index cards, and label the pictures before depositing the cards in "The *-ack* Sack."

HOME ACTIVITIES MASTER: Lesson 18

NOTE: Fill in the blanks on the Home Activities Master before sending it home. See the Assignment Guide on page T11.

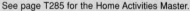

See page T285 for the Home Activities Master.

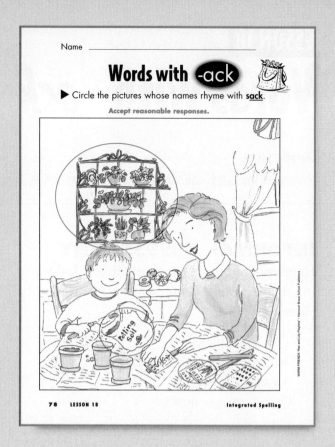

▶ Introduction

WARM-UP Display a backpack or a picture of one, and have children identify it. Have them repeat the word *backpack* as they listen to the two rhyming words that form this word.

INTRODUCING THE PAGE

Have children turn to page 78 and follow along as you read the lesson title aloud. Focus children's attention on the picture, and discuss it with them. You might want to use questions like the following to guide the discussion:

• What are the people in the picture doing? (planting seeds)

• Look on the table. What are the people using to help them plant? (a sack of soil, seed packs, tacks)

• What toys are on the counter? (yo-yo, ball, top, jack) If children do not mention the jack, point out the toy and explain or demonstrate how the game of jacks is played.

Invite children to describe other picture details, making sure that they mention the rack on which plants are displayed.

Read the directions aloud. Then have children say *sack* several times as they listen for the ending sounds. Remind them that they can test for a rhyme by saying *sack* and another word as they listen to determine if the ending sounds are the same.

Either work through the page with children or have them complete it independently. (Children should circle pictures representing the words *pack, sack, tack, rack,* and *jack.*)
CLASSIFYING

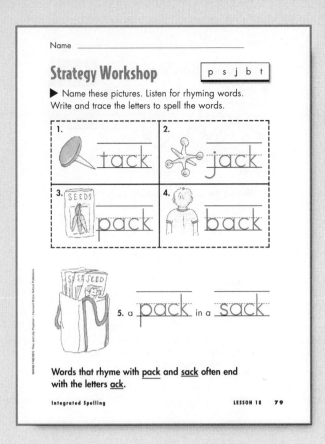

Name _____

Strategy Workshop

p s j b t

▶ Name these pictures. Listen for rhyming words. Write and trace the letters to spell the words.

1. tack
2. jack
3. pack
4. back

5. a pack in a sack

Words that rhyme with <u>pack</u> and <u>sack</u> often end with the letters <u>ack</u>.

▶ Strategy Workshop

RHYMING WORDS Help children recall that rhyming words sound alike except for their beginning sounds. Explain that rhyming words are often spelled the same way except for their beginning letters. Tell children that they can sometimes figure out how to spell a word by spelling a rhyming word and changing the beginning letter.

Help children identify the first picture on page 79 as a tack. Write the word *tack* on the board, and have children say it aloud. Guide them in changing the word *tack* into the word *rack* by asking questions such as these:

• What letter stands for the beginning sound of *rack*? (*r*)

• What letters stand for the ending sounds that you hear in both *tack* and *rack*? (*ack*)

Record children's responses on the board, and have them read the word *rack* aloud. Explain to children that they can use this strategy to write words that name the pictures on this page. Then help them identify the remaining pictures as a jack, a pack, and a person's back. **APPLYING SPELLING STRATEGIES**

SPELLING IN CONTEXT Have children discuss the picture at the bottom of page 79. Give guidance as needed to help them complete the phrase and read it aloud. (*pack, sack*) **CONCEPT OF WORD**

 MEETING INDIVIDUAL NEEDS

Extra Support/Children Acquiring English Children may benefit from a review of the initial consonant sounds that are blended with the phonogram -*ack* to form the rhyming picture names. Display pictures whose names begin with /t/, /j/, /p/, /s/, and /b/. Ask children to identify the letter that represents the initial sound of each picture name.

IN SUMMARY Invite children to tell what they have discovered about spelling words that rhyme with *pack* and *sack*. (These words often end with the letters *ack*.)

Name _____

Vocabulary WordShop

▶ Write a word from the box to complete each sentence.

Dancing
• WORDS •
step
dance
music

1. We hear the ___music___ .

2. We take a big ___step___ .

3. We ___dance___ all day.

80   LESSON 18   Integrated Spelling

▶ Vocabulary WordShop

WORDSHOP WORDS Help children read aloud the WordShop Words on page 80, and discuss how these words are alike. (All the words are associated with dancing.)

Read the directions with children, and call their attention to the illustrations. Invite volunteers to describe picture details and to tell what the dinosaurs are doing in each picture. Help children read the sentences, if necessary. After children complete the activity, have them share their responses with partners or the group.

Children Acquiring English
Play some background music. Then model a simple dance for children. Invite children to follow your lead. Encourage them to say the appropriate Dancing Words aloud as they imitate your steps and the dance. **PRACTICING PRONUNCIATION**

EXPLORING DANCING WORDS
Extend children's knowledge of Dancing Words by explaining that there are many types of dance. Focus children's attention on the third picture of the dinosaurs on page 80. Explain that the animals are doing a particular dance called a *waltz*. Work with children to develop a chart that lists types of dances. You may also wish to elicit the names of dances that are associated with other cultures.

Types of Dances	
ballet	polka
tap	jig
jazz	hula
waltz	conga
square dance	

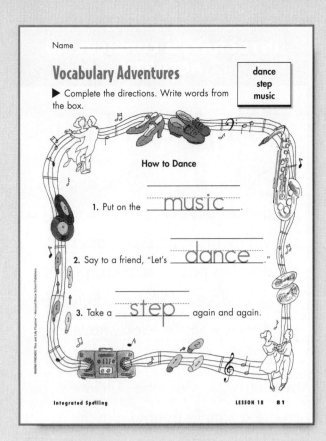

Name _____

Vocabulary Adventures

▶ Complete the directions. Write words from the box.

| dance |
| step |
| music |

How to Dance

1. Put on the _____music_____.

2. Say to a friend, "Let's _____dance_____."

3. Take a _____step_____ again and again.

Integrated Spelling

LESSON 18   81

LEARNING TO SPELL makes a contribution to reading acquisition among children who are just learning to read . . . spelling instruction promotes word reading skill in beginning readers, not by enabling readers to sound out and blend, but rather by helping readers to store words in memory using letter-sound association. *(Linnea C. Ehri and Lee S. Wilce)*

VOCABULARY ADVENTURES

Read with children the directions at the top of page 81. Focus attention on the words in the box, and have them read aloud. Point out the list of sentences, and explain that the list is a set of directions. Help children read the title of the directions aloud. Then explain that they are to complete each sentence, using the best word from the box. After children complete the page, invite them to share their answers.

USING NAMING AND ACTION WORDS

 Working Together You may want to have children work with partners to complete this activity. Encourage partners to discuss each sentence and agree on the word to complete it before writing the word in the blank.

 **Spelling Log** Children may want to write the Dancing Words from this lesson in their Spelling Logs.

Optional Writing Idea

 Patterned Writing: Directions Explain to children that a dance is made up of different kinds of steps. Ask children what other dance movements they know besides *step*. Record their responses on chart paper. For example:

Dance Steps			
step	slide	glide	leap
turn	twist	skip	kick
hop	bend	stretch	dip

Write these sentence frames on the board, and invite children to make up dances by writing dance step words in the blanks.

First _____ and then _____.
Next _____ and then _____.
Last _____ and then _____.

Suggest children exchange directions with partners and demonstrate each other's dances.

Lesson 18   T127

▶ Lesson Wrap-Up

RETEACH: Learning Differences

Begin this activity by distributing cards on which you have printed the *-ack* phonogram with a wide-tipped marker. Have children say the letters of the phonogram aloud as they trace the letters with their fingers. Then say the following words, and have children hold up their cards each time they hear a word in the *-ack* family: *sack, sad, jam, jack, rock, rack, back, bag, taste, tack, pal,* and *pack.* **AUDITORY/KINESTHETIC MODALITIES**

Puppet Play

Children may enjoy making simple dancer puppets and presenting a show. Provide craft sticks, markers, construction paper, scissors, paste, string, and tape. After children create dancers on the sticks, have them attach a piece of string to one end of each stick with tape. Children can create a simple puppet play to demonstrate how dancers move to music. If children completed the Optional Writing Idea described on page T127, they can also use their puppets to act out the dances that they created.

LANGUAGE ARTS

Words with Short *e*

OBJECTIVE
To spell words with short *e*

LESSON PLANNER
Assign words based on the children's developmental levels. See the Assignment Guide on page T11.

▶ INFORMAL ASSESSMENT
Children's writing may show that they have difficulty distinguishing between short *e* and other vowel sounds.

▼ model

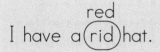

Use this lesson to introduce the spelling of words with a medial short *e* vowel sound. Encourage children to apply what they have learned to help them spell other words with the short *e* sound. After children complete this lesson, have them proofread their writing and correct errors they may have made spelling words in which the letter *e* stands for the medial short *e* sound.

▶ LEARNING DIFFERENCES
Use the following suggestion and the ideas on page T134 to customize learning activities.

Children Acquiring English
Often, children who are acquiring English have difficulty distinguishing between the sounds of short *e* and short *a*. Give children practice in listening to and repeating pairs of words such as *men, man; bed, bad; ten, tan;* and *bet, bat*.

In addition, speakers of Spanish, Vietnamese, or Tagalog may find it difficult to differentiate the sound of short *e* from the sound of long *a*. These children may benefit from practice with word pairs such as *red, raid; wet, wait;* and *fed, fade*. **COMPARING AND CONTRASTING**

▶ PRETEST/POSTTEST CONTEXT SENTENCES
* 1. **red** I need a **red** pen.
* 2. **hen** A **hen** is a good pet.
* 3. **help** He will **help** you.
* 4. **went** Kim **went** home.

▶ WORD FAMILY
Children might want to build a family of words that rhyme with the Spelling Word *red*. Distribute large index cards and red crayons, and have children record other words that belong to the *-ed* family, such as *bed, fed, led, sled, fled, wed,* and *shed*. Display the words on a bulletin board titled "We See Red."

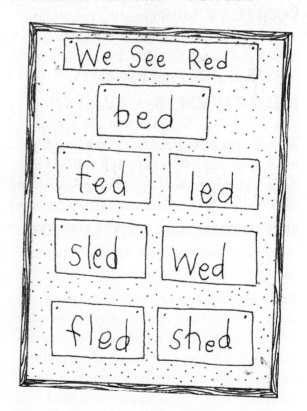

* Words appearing in "The Little Red Hen." Additional story words are *then, pecking,* and *thresh*.

NOTE: Fill in blanks on the Home Activities Master before sending it home. See the Assignment Guide on page T11.

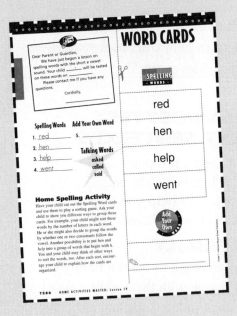

See page T286 for the Home Activities Master.

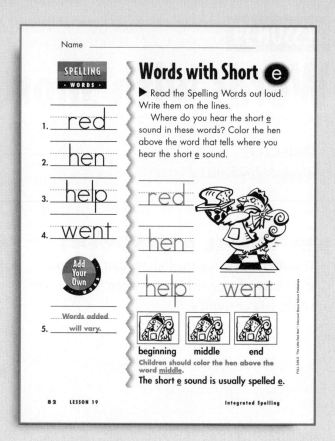

▶ Introduction

PRETEST Administer the Pretest. Say each word, and then use it in the sentence provided on page T129 before repeating the word. **ACCESSING PRIOR KNOWLEDGE**

SELF-CHECK Have children refer to their lists of Spelling Words to check their Pretests. For each word children misspell on the Pretest, remind them to follow the Study Steps to Learn a Word, found on pages 8–9 of the Pupil's Edition. **STUDENT SELF-ASSESSMENT**

INTRODUCING THE LESSON

To use the open sort, copy Home Activities Master Lesson 19, found on page T286.

Open Sort: After distributing the word cards, help children think of ways to sort the words. Possible sorts might include counting the number of letters in the words or putting the words *hen* and *help* into a group of words that begin with *h*. You may want to send home the word cards for children to use to complete the Home Activities Master.

Closed Sort: Help children read aloud the lesson title and the Spelling Words on page 82.

• Invite children to tell what they notice about the vowel sound in all the words. (All the words have the short *e* sound.)

• Ask children where they hear the short *e* vowel sound in each word. (in the middle)

Review the directions, and have children write the Spelling Words on the lines. Then have them color the hen above the word that tells where they hear the vowel sound in all four Spelling Words. **SORTING WORDS**

IN SUMMARY Have children tell what they have learned about how to spell words that have the short *e* sound in the middle. (The short *e* sound is probably spelled with the letter *e*.)
RECOGNIZING PHONIC ELEMENTS

Spelling Log Have children look through the selection for other short *e* words, and list them in their Spelling Logs and on Pupil's Edition page 82.

RECOGNIZING PATTERNS

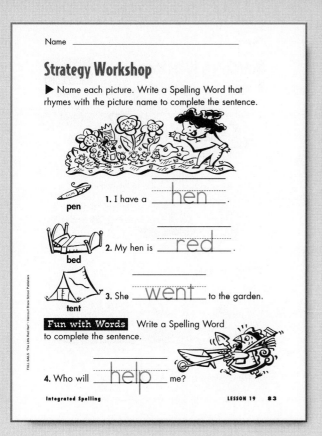

Name _____

Strategy Workshop

▶ Name each picture. Write a Spelling Word that rhymes with the picture name to complete the sentence.

pen

1. I have a ___hen___ .

bed

2. My hen is ___red___ .

tent

3. She ___went___ to the garden.

Fun with Words Write a Spelling Word to complete the sentence.

4. Who will ___help___ me?

Integrated Spelling   LESSON 19   83

▶ Strategy Workshop

RHYMING WORDS Help children read aloud the directions at the top of page 83. Point out the words *pen, bed*, and *tent* and the corresponding pictures. Then focus children's attention on the picture of the girl and the hen, and explain that the sentences they will complete tell about this picture. Explain that they can use a rhyming strategy and what they know about the sounds that letters stand for to help them write a word to complete each sentence. Invite children to share their completed sentences. APPLYING SPELLING STRATEGIES

FUN WITH WORDS Help children read the directions, and then talk about the picture with them. Explain that the question they will complete tells what the hen is saying. Have children share and discuss their answers.

MEETING INDIVIDUAL NEEDS

Children Acquiring English To reinforce the meaning of the Spelling Word *help*, direct attention to your classroom job chart and talk about ways that children help in the classroom. Then ask, "How will you help me?" and have children respond by completing this sentence: "I will help you _____."

UNDERSTANDING WORD MEANINGS

MEETING INDIVIDUAL NEEDS

Semi-Phonetic Spellers To help children remember to include the vowel in the Spelling Words, write the words on the board, omitting the medial vowel. Have children complete each word by writing the missing letter. Then have children write the whole word.

MEETING INDIVIDUAL NEEDS

Challenge If children created an *-ed* word family, as suggested on page T129, you might want to have them learn to spell one or more of these words.

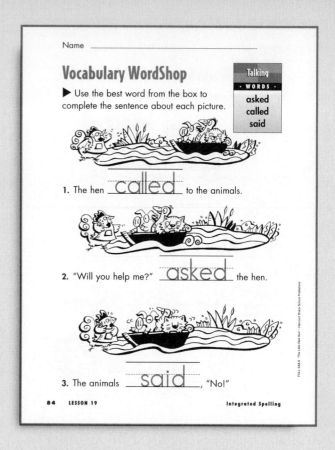

Name _____

Vocabulary WordShop

▶ Use the best word from the box to complete the sentence about each picture.

Talking
• WORDS •
asked
called
said

1. The hen **called** to the animals.

2. "Will you help me?" **asked** the hen.

3. The animals **said**, "No!"

▶ Vocabulary WordShop

WORDSHOP WORDS Ask a volunteer to read the WordShop Words on page 84 aloud. Point out that these words are used in the reading selection when characters talk to one another. Read the directions with children, and then ask them to describe what is happening in each illustration. Remind children to use picture clues to help them identify who is talking.

Phonetic Spellers Children who are spelling at this level are constructing new spelling strategies. Point out the word part *-ed* at the end of the words *asked* and *called*. Explain that the word part *-ed* is often added to a word to make it tell about something that happened in the past.

Transitional Spellers You may want to assign this level of spellers the WordShop Words as additional spelling words.

Spelling Log Invite children to look for other words used with talking, or speaker tags, in "The Little Red Hen." Suggest that they write the words they find in the Action Words section of their Spelling Logs.

EXPLORING TALKING WORDS Talk with children about the differences between saying something to someone and calling out to someone. Make the point that calling out is usually done with a raised voice because the people communicating are usually some distance apart. Explore other words used to describe ways people talk—for example, *whispered, yelled,* and *shouted.* Invite children to tell when they think each type of talking is appropriate.

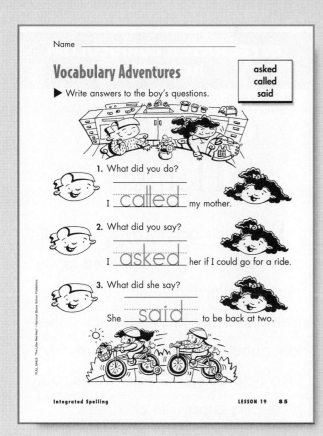

Name _____

Vocabulary Adventures

| asked |
| called |
| said |

▶ Write answers to the boy's questions.

1. What did you do?

I _called_ my mother.

2. What did you say?

I _asked_ her if I could go for a ride.

3. What did she say?

She _said_ to be back at two.

Integrated Spelling   LESSON 19   85

> "IN PARTICULAR, *categorization is intimately involved in language acquisition and the formation of verbal concepts. . . . Categorization based on feature analysis and induction enables children to recognize new words and written language structures. . . . A vehicle for this kind of systematic word study is the 'word sort.'*"
> (Jean W. Gillet and M. J. Kita)

VOCABULARY ADVENTURES

Read the directions at the top of page 85 with children. Explain that the questions and answers on this page tell what two children are saying to each other. Help children read the questions. Then have them write a word from the box to complete the answer to each question. **USING ACTION WORDS**

Working Together This activity lends itself to working in pairs. Suggest that partners take turns, with one partner reading the question, and the other partner writing the word that completes the answer. After children have finished the page, have partners read the dialogue aloud as the children in the pictures might say it.

POSTTEST
Remind children to study any Spelling Words they misspelled on the Pretest. Then use the context sentences on page T129 to administer the Posttest.

Optional Writing Idea

Shared Writing: Dialogue
Children might enjoy extending the dialogue presented on Pupil's Edition page 85. Have children suggest other questions and answers that the boy and girl might ask about their bike ride plans.

Questions	Answers
Where should we ride?	We can go to the park.
When should we go?	We can go now.

Then assign each child a partner, and have them work together to write the dialogue. Some may want to use speech balloons or draw faces beside the dialogue to show who is talking. Invite partners to read their dialogue aloud in a small group.

▶ Lesson Wrap-Up

WORDSHOP WORDS AND CONTEXT SENTENCES

1. **asked** He **asked** for help.
2. **called** She **called** the dog.
3. **said** Dad **said** I could go.

Reteach

LEARNING DIFFERENCES

Auditory processing deficits and language disorders may cause children difficulty in segmenting words and establishing sound-letter relationships. To focus attention on the sound that each letter stands for, give a child a card on which one Spelling Word is written, leaving a space for the vowel *e*. If the word is *red*, for example, have the child point to *r* as you say the initial sound. Then say the short *e* sound, and have the child write *e* in the space. Finally, pronounce the final sound as the child points to *d*. Repeat this activity for each Spelling Word in the lesson. **AUDITORY/ KINESTHETIC MODALITIES**

Community Helpers

Begin this activity by asking children to recall what happened in the reading selection when the Little Red Hen asked her friends for help. Then talk about people in the community who help others. Create a community helpers chart with children's responses. You may want to include columns that indicate who each helper is, where each helper works, and what each helper does. Invite children to add pictures to illustrate the information in the chart.

Community Helpers		
Who	**Where**	**What**
librarian	library	helps us find books
firefighter	fire house	helps put out fires
doctor	hospital	helps sick people
teacher	school	helps people learn

Words with Short *u*

OBJECTIVE

To spell words with short *u*

LESSON PLANNER

Assign words based on children's developmental levels.
See the Assignment Guide on page T11.

▶ INFORMAL ASSESSMENT

Children's writing may show that they have difficulty distinguishing between short *u* and other vowel sounds.

▼ **model**

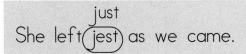

just

She left (jest) as we came.

Use this lesson to introduce the spelling of words with a medial short *u* vowel sound. Encourage children to apply what they have learned to help them spell other words with the short *u* sound. After children have completed this lesson, have them proofread their writing and correct errors they may have made.

▶ LEARNING DIFFERENCES

Use the following suggestion and the ideas on page T140 to customize learning activities.

MEETING INDIVIDUAL NEEDS

Children Acquiring English
Children may have difficulty differentiating the short *u* sound from short *a* and short *e* sounds.
Provide children with practice in listening to and pronouncing words such as *run, ran, red; must, mast; just, jest;* and *bug, bag, beg.*

In addition, children whose primary language is Vietnamese, Chinese, Spanish, Thai, or Tagalog may confuse the short *u* and short *o* sounds. Present these word pairs for them to listen to and repeat: *bug, bog; run, Ron;* and *jut, jot.* **COMPARING AND CONTRASTING**

▶ PRETEST/POSTTEST CONTEXT SENTENCES

* 1. **but** It is hard, **but** I can do it.
* 2. **must** We **must** go by ten.
* 3. **just** She came **just** in time.
* 4. **run** They **run** every day.

▶ WORD FAMILY PUZZLE

Children might want to make a word family puzzle of words that rhyme with the Spelling Words *must* and *just*. Other words in the *-ust* family include *dust, gust, rust, crust,* and *trust.* To make the puzzle, have children draw a large, irregular shape on a piece of oaktag. Then have them cut the shape into four or five pieces. On each piece, have them write a word in the *-ust* family. Children can exchange pieces with a partner and then assemble each other's puzzles.

* Words appearing in "Henny Penny." Additional story words are *Ducky Lucky, such, up,* and *until.*

NOTE: Fill in blanks on the Home Activities Master before sending it home.
See the Assignment Guide on page T11.

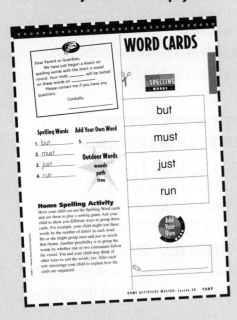

See page T287 for the Home Activities Master.

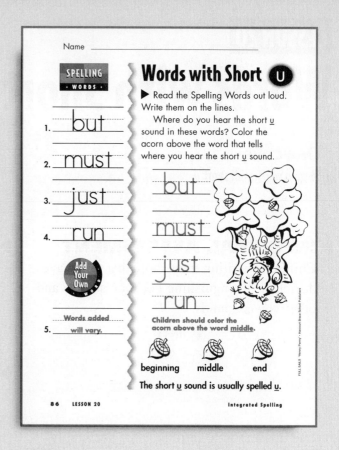

▶ Introduction

PRETEST Administer the Pretest. Say each word, and then use it in the sentence provided on page T135 before repeating the word. **ACCESSING PRIOR KNOWLEDGE**

SELF-CHECK Have children refer to their lists of Spelling Words to check their Pretests. For each word children misspell on the Pretest, remind them to follow the Study Steps to Learn a Word, found on pages 8–9 of the Pupil's Edition. **STUDENT SELF-ASSESSMENT**

INTRODUCING THE LESSON

To use the open sort, copy Home Activities Master Lesson 20, found on page T287.

Open Sort: After distributing the word cards, help children think of ways to sort the words. Children might sort the words according to the number of letters in the words. You may want to send home the word cards for children to use to complete the Home Activities Master.

Closed Sort: Help children read aloud the lesson title and the Spelling Words on page 86.

• Invite children to tell what they notice about the vowel sound in all the words. (All the words have the short *u* sound.)

• Ask children where they hear the short *u* vowel sound in each word. (in the middle)

Review the directions, and have children write the Spelling Words on the lines. Then have them color the acorn above the word that tells where they hear the vowel sound in all four Spelling Words. **SORTING WORDS**

IN SUMMARY Have children tell what they have learned about how to spell words that have the short *u* sound in the middle. (The short *u* sound is probably spelled with the letter *u*.)
RECOGNIZING PHONIC ELEMENTS

Spelling Log Encourage children to look for other short *u* words. Ask them to list the words in their Spelling Logs and on the line provided on Pupil's Edition page 86. **RECOGNIZING PATTERNS**

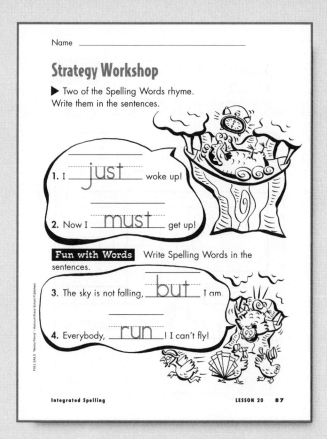

Strategy Workshop

RHYMING WORDS Help children read aloud the directions at the top of page 87. Call attention to the first two sentences and the corresponding illustration. Have children write the two Spelling Words that rhyme to complete sentences 1 and 2. After children have completed the sentences, have them share their answers. **APPLYING SPELLING STRATEGIES**

FUN WITH WORDS Read the directions with children. Have them look at and discuss the illustration. Explain that the wind is causing problems for the hen. After children have written the Spelling Words to complete the sentences, ask volunteers to read the sentences aloud as the hen might say them.

Children Acquiring English The word *but* may be confusing to children who are acquiring English. Explain that *but* is often used in place of the word *however*.

Model several examples for children:

> I want to go, <u>but</u> I can not.
> She wants to play, <u>but</u> she has to work.

Have children respond to questions such as these, using the word *but* in their responses.

> Do you want to go outside?
> Do you want to eat lunch?
> Do you want to listen to a story?

BUILDING VOCABULARY

Semi-Phonetic Spellers Children who are spelling at this level may write the wrong vowel to represent a short vowel sound. For example, they may write *jest* for *just*. Help children remember to write *u* in the Spelling Words by having them write the consonant letters in one color marker and the letter *u* in a different color marker when they practice writing their Spelling Words.

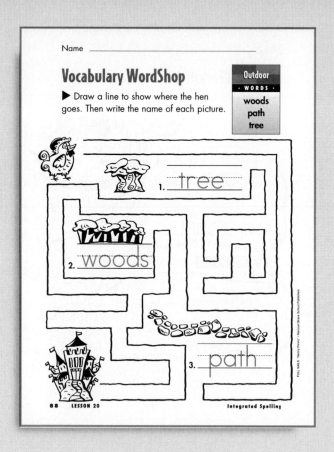

Name _____

Vocabulary WordShop

▶ Draw a line to show where the hen goes. Then write the name of each picture.

Outdoor
• WORDS •
woods
path
tree

1. tree

2. woods

3. path

88   LESSON 20   Integrated Spelling

▶ Vocabulary WordShop

Spelling Log As children write about the environment, encourage them to add other words about the outdoors to their Spelling Logs.

Transitional Spellers You may want to assign this level of spellers the WordShop Words as additional spelling words.

WORDSHOP WORDS Point out the WordShop Words on page 88, and help children read them aloud. Read the directions with children. Then suggest that they place a finger on the hen and trace a path through the maze to the king's palace. After children trace the path, have them use their pencils to complete the maze and write the words that name the pictures.

Working Together Suggest that children work with a partner to complete the maze and write the picture names.

Phonetic Spellers Have children do the activity with a partner. One child selects an Outdoor Word and makes a box for each letter on a sheet of paper. The other child guesses letters, and the first child writes correctly guessed letters where they belong in the word. When the word is complete, have both children read it.

EXPLORING OUTDOOR WORDS Help children understand the difference between the meanings of the words *woods* and *wood*. Explain that the *woods* is a place that is filled with trees, while *wood* is something that comes from a tree.

• Elicit from children other words that have almost the same meaning as *woods*. (Possible responses: *forest, grove*)

Vocabulary Adventures

Name _____

► Look at the map. Then write words to complete the directions.

| woods |
| path |
| tree |

Come to My Birthday!

1. Go down the _path_.

2. Walk into the _woods_.

3. Stop at the big oak _tree_.

A Birthday Surprise Draw four pictures of birthday gifts. Write a Spelling Word on the back of each one. Have friends choose a gift. See if they can spell the words on the pictures.

Integrated Spelling

LESSON 20   89

FULL GIRLS · "Henny Penny" · Harcourt Brace School Publishers

---

VOCABULARY ADVENTURES

Read the directions at the top of page 89 with children. Point out the illustration. Explain that it is an invitation with a map that shows how to get to the party. Before children write the words to complete the directions, suggest that they trace the route to the party with their finger. Then have children write the words to complete the directions. **USING NAMING WORDS**

 Working Together Partners can work together to complete this activity. While one child traces the route on the map and identifies the landmarks, the other child can write the words to complete the directions.

A BIRTHDAY SURPRISE
Read the directions aloud. Then have children work with a partner to complete this activity.

POSTTEST
Remind children to study any Spelling Words they misspelled on the Pretest. Then use the context sentences on page T135 to administer the Posttest.

Optional Writing Idea

Collaborative Writing: Sentences About a Picture Have children work together to create a simple classroom map on a large sheet of chart paper. Display this map, and then have children work with a partner to write sentences telling how to get from one place to another place in the classroom. Suggest they use "landmarks" that are drawn on the map. Children can exchange directions with another pair and test their accuracy by trying to follow the directions.

Directions to the Art Center
1. Walk to the board.
2. Then go to Mr. Miller's desk.
3. Stop at the art center.

▶Lesson Wrap-Up

WORDSHOP WORDS AND CONTEXT SENTENCES

1. **woods** Birds live in the **woods.**
2. **path** Stay on the **path.**
3. **tree** That is a tall **tree.**

▶Reteach

LEARNING DIFFERENCES

Children who have visual memory deficits or who are easily distracted can benefit from this strategy for copying a word. Tell children that all the Spelling Words contain the letter *u.* Write the word *must* on the board. Have children count the letters and draw four blanks on a sheet of paper. Ask children to say each letter in the word and then write it. Before they write the other Spelling Words, review the strategy to be used: count the letters, make a blank for each letter, say each letter name, and then write the letter on one of the blanks.

VISUAL/AUDITORY/KINESTHETIC MODALITIES

1. <u>M</u> <u>U</u> <u>S</u> <u>T</u>
2. <u>B</u> <u>U</u> <u>T</u>
3. <u>R</u> __ __

She'll Be Comin' Through the Woods

Have children sing and act out the following verses to the tune of "She'll Be Comin' Round the Mountain." Then work with them to make up some more verses that describe a walk through the woods.

She'll be comin' through the woods when she comes,
She'll be comin' through the woods when she comes,
She'll be comin' through the woods,
She'll be comin' through the woods,
She'll be comin' through the woods when she comes.

She'll be walking down the path when she comes, and so on.

She'll be stopping by a tree when she comes, and so on.

LESSON 21
Words with Short *i*

OBJECTIVE
To spell words with short *i*

LESSON PLANNER
Assign words based on children's developmental levels.
See the Assignment Guide on page T11.

▶ INFORMAL ASSESSMENT
Children's writing may show that they have difficulty distinguishing between short *i* and other vowel sounds.

▼ model

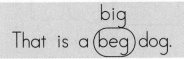

Use this lesson to introduce the spelling of words with the short *i* vowel sound. Encourage children to apply what they have learned to help them spell other words with the short *i* sound. After children have completed this lesson, have them proofread their writing and correct errors they may have made spelling words in which the letter *i* stands for the short *i* sound.

▶ LEARNING DIFFERENCES
Use the following suggestion and the ideas on page T146 to customize learning activities.

Children Acquiring English
Children who speak Spanish, Chinese, Vietnamese, or Tagalog often replace the short *i* vowel sound with the long *e* sound. Have children listen to and pronounce the following word pairs: *it, eat; bin, bean; bit, beet; hit, heat;* and *kin, keen*. Pronounce the word pairs again in random order, and have children identify the word in each pair that contains the short *i* sound. **COMPARING AND CONTRASTING**

▶ PRETEST/POSTTEST CONTEXT SENTENCES
* * 1. **in** Put the toys **in** the box.
* * 2. **it** Is **it** time to go?
* * 3. **big** I have a **big** cat.
* * 4. **him** I like to play with **him**.

▶ A BIG LADDER
Children might want to build a family of words that rhyme with the Spelling Word *big*. Draw a big ladder on a piece of chart paper. Then, on each rung, invite children to write words in the *-ig* word family. Possible words include *pig, dig, fig, jig, rig, wig, swig,* and *twig*. Have children practice going up and down the ladder by reading the words as a partner points to them.

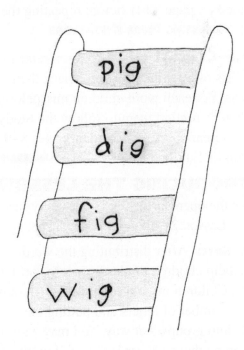

* Words appearing in "Little Lumpty." Additional story words are *still, children, his, if, did, little, king's, think,* and *mistake.*

NOTE: Fill in blanks on the Home Activities Master before sending it home. See the Assignment Guide on page T11.

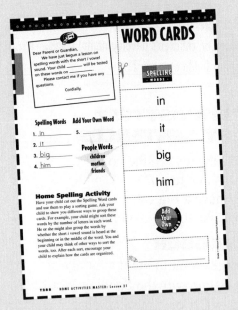

See page T288 for the Home Activities Master.

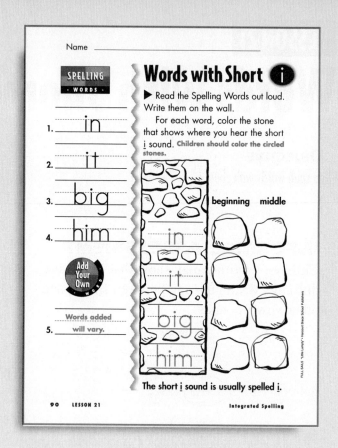

Introduction

PRETEST Administer the Pretest. Say each word, and then use it in the sentence provided on page T141 before repeating the word. **ACCESSING PRIOR KNOWLEDGE**

SELF-CHECK Have children refer to their lists of Spelling Words to check their Pretests. For each word children misspell on the Pretest, remind them to follow the Study Steps to Learn a Word, found on pages 8–9 of the Pupil's Edition. **STUDENT SELF-ASSESSMENT**

INTRODUCING THE LESSON

To use the open sort, copy Home Activities Master Lesson 21, found on page T288.

Open Sort: After distributing the word cards, help children think of ways to sort the words. Children might group words by counting the number of letters and putting the words into groups that way. You may want to send home the word cards for children to use to complete the Home Activities Master.

Closed Sort: Help children read aloud the lesson title and the Spelling Words on page 90.

• Ask children what they notice about the vowel sound in each word. (Each word has the short *i* sound.)

• Have children tell where they hear and see the vowel *i* in each word. (in the beginning—*in, it*; in the middle—*big, him*)

Review the directions, and have children write the Spelling Words on the lines. Then have them color the stone next to each Spelling Word to identify where they hear the vowel sound in the word. **SORTING WORDS**

IN SUMMARY Ask children what they have learned about how to spell words that have the short *i* sound. (The short *i* sound is probably spelled with the letter *i*.)

RECOGNIZING PHONIC ELEMENTS

Spelling Log Have children look for short *i* words in their own writing and list the words in their Spelling Logs on Pupil's Edition page 90. **RECOGNIZING PATTERNS**

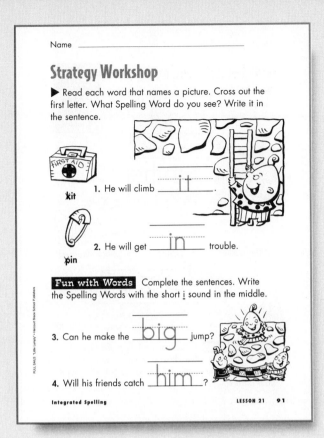

Name _____

Strategy Workshop

▶ Read each word that names a picture. Cross out the first letter. What Spelling Word do you see? Write it in the sentence.

kit

1. He will climb ___it___ .

pin

2. He will get ___in___ trouble.

Fun with Words Complete the sentences. Write the Spelling Words with the short i sound in the middle.

3. Can he make the ___big___ jump?

4. Will his friends catch ___him___ ?

▶ Strategy Workshop

RHYMING WORDS Read the directions at the top of page 91 with children. Call attention to the words *kit* and *pin* and the corresponding pictures. Have children identify the initial consonant in each of these words. After children have crossed out the initial consonants and written Spelling Words to complete sentences 1 and 2, point out that the Spelling Word *it* rhymes with the word *kit* and the Spelling Word *in* rhymes with the word *pin*.

APPLYING SPELLING STRATEGIES

Children Acquiring English Many children who are acquiring English may be unfamiliar with the idiomatic expression *to be in trouble*. Explain that this expression means "to have or experience difficulty." Have children give examples of things that might get someone *in trouble*. **UNDERSTANDING IDIOMS**

FUN WITH WORDS Help children read the directions and discuss the illustration. Invite them to share what they might say if they were watching this jump. After children write Spelling Words to complete the questions, ask them to share their responses.

Semi-Phonetic Spellers Children who are spelling at this level may omit the vowels in words. For example, they might write *hm* instead of *him*. To help children remember to include the vowel *i* in each word, focus their attention on the dot over the *i*. Suggest that children highlight this dot with a colored marker or crayon.

Challenge Suggest that children learn some of the short *i* words that appear in the reading selection "Little Lumpty," as listed on page T141.

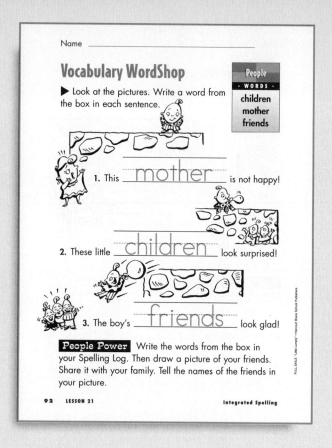

Name _____

Vocabulary WordShop

▶ Look at the pictures. Write a word from the box in each sentence.

People
· WORDS ·
children
mother
friends

1. This _mother_ is not happy!

2. These little _children_ look surprised!

3. The boy's _friends_ look glad!

People Power Write the words from the box in your Spelling Log. Then draw a picture of your friends. Share it with your family. Tell the names of the friends in your picture.

92   LESSON 21   Integrated Spelling

Vocabulary WordShop

WORDSHOP WORDS Read the WordShop Words on page 92 aloud with children, and ask how these words are alike. (They all name people.) Read the directions, and then discuss the illustrations. Explain to children that they will complete each sentence with a word from the box that names the "egg" people they see in the accompanying picture. After children have completed the sentences, call on volunteers to read them aloud.

PEOPLE POWER Provide children with drawing materials, and then help them read the directions. You may want to display children's drawings in a classroom Portrait Gallery.

Transitional Spellers You may want to assign this level of spellers the WordShop Words as additional spelling words.

Phonetic Spellers Have children write each letter of each People Word on a small card or self-stick note. Have them use the letters to spell the words.

Spelling Log As children read, encourage them to look for other words that name people. They can write the words they find in the People Words section of their Spelling Logs.

EXPLORING PEOPLE WORDS

Extend children's knowledge of words that name people by asking questions such as these:

• A mother and children can be members of a family. What other family members can you name?

• What do you call the children of your aunts and uncles? How many cousins do you have?

• What do you call your parents' parents?

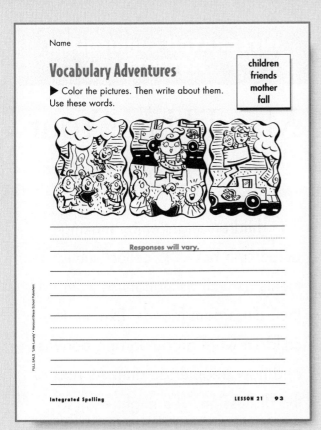

Name _____

Vocabulary Adventures

► Color the pictures. Then write about them.
Use these words.

children
friends
mother
fall

Responses will vary.

_____

FULL SAILS "Little Lumpty" • Harcourt Brace School Publishers

Integrated Spelling　　　　　　　　**LESSON 21**　**93**

> "INVENTED SPELLING REFERS *to young children's attempts to use their best judgments about spelling.*"
> *(Elaine Lutz)*

VOCABULARY ADVENTURES

Read the directions at the top of page 93 with children. Call on volunteers to read aloud the words in the box. Provide children with crayons or markers. Then invite children to tell how they plan to color the illustrations.

After children have colored the pictures, remind them to use the words in the box to write about the pictures. Suggest that children write sentences about their pictures. You may want to have children draft and revise their sentences on another sheet of paper. Have them write their final versions on the Pupil's Edition page. USING NAMING WORDS

 Working Together Some children may find it easier to work with a partner or in a small group to draft and revise their sentences.

POSTTEST
Remind children to study any Spelling Words they misspelled on the Pretest. Then use the context sentences on page T141 to administer the Posttest.

Optional Writing Idea

 Independent Writing: Journal Entry Direct children's attention to the pictures on Pupil's Edition page 93, and ask them to imagine that they are at the scene. Invite children to tell what they would do or say to help rescue the boy. Record their suggestions in a chart like the following:

What I might do.	What I might say.
Run for help.	"Hold on tight."
Look for a ladder.	"Don't look down."

Then have children write journal entries about this experience. Some may wish to illustrate their entries with a series of pictures. Encourage children to share their finished work with partners or in a small group.

Lesson Wrap-Up

WORDSHOP WORDS AND CONTEXT SENTENCES

1. **children** Ten **children** are in the play.
2. **mother** She is my **mother.**
3. **friends** Our **friends** live there.

Reteach

LEARNING DIFFERENCES

Children who have visual processing deficits may benefit from more guided learning. It may also be helpful if you limit the amount of information presented to them at one time. Try writing two of the Spelling Words across the top of a sheet of primary-ruled paper. Then fold the paper in half so that only one word is visible. At various times during the day, have children copy these models. They should start writing at the bottom of the page so that the correct model is always above their work. After children write each word, have them show it to you so that you can check to see that they are forming letters correctly and writing them in the correct order. **VISUAL MODALITY**

May I Have Your Autograph?

Children might enjoy making autograph books to collect sentiments as well as signatures from their classroom friends. Explain to children what an autograph book is and how people use one. As part of the discussion, you might want to mention that the word *autograph* refers to a person's own signature. Children can make their own autograph books by stapling blank pages between decorated construction paper covers. Then invite them to collect autograph sayings and rhymes as well as signatures from their friends.

LANGUAGE ARTS

LESSON 22
Words with *wh*

OBJECTIVE
To spell words with initial *wh*

LESSON PLANNER
Assign words based on children's developmental levels. See the Assignment Guide on page T11.

► INFORMAL ASSESSMENT
Children's writing may show that they have difficulty with initial *wh*.

▼ **model**

when

Do you know (wen) to come?

Use this lesson to introduce the spelling of words with initial *wh* such as *when*. After children complete this lesson, encourage them to proofread their writing and correct errors they may have made spelling words with the initial digraph *wh*.

► LEARNING DIFFERENCES
Use the following suggestion and the ideas on page T152 to customize learning activities.

MEETING INDIVIDUAL NEEDS

Children Acquiring English
Point out to children that the Spelling Words in this lesson are often used to ask questions. Explain that usually these words come at the beginning of a question. Model their use with these examples:

When will we go to lunch?
What are you doing?
Where do you live?
Why can't I go?

Pair children with a partner. Have them take turns asking and answering questions, using the Spelling Words at the beginning of their questions. **BUILDING VOCABULARY**

► PRETEST/POSTTEST CONTEXT SENTENCES
* 1. **when** Tell me **when** to come.
* 2. **what** Show me **what** you have.
* 3. **where** Do you know **where** she lives?
  4. **why** I know **why** he left.

► WORD WALL
Devote one section of your classroom word wall to question words. Children can begin by adding the four Spelling Words to the section. Then invite them to look through library books and other printed materials to find more examples of question words to include.

Question Words			
when	what	why	where
who	how	can	will

* Words appearing in "The Wild Woods." An additional story word is *whispered*.

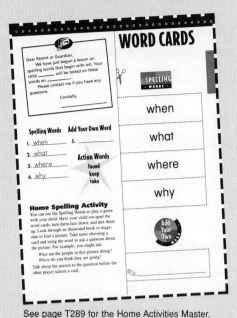

NOTE: Fill in blanks on the Home Activities Master before sending it home. See the Assignment Guide on page T11.

See page T289 for the Home Activities Master.

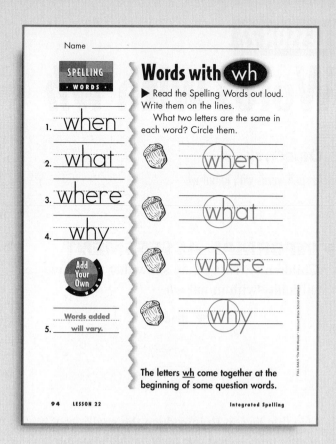

►Introduction

PRETEST Administer the Pretest. Say each word, and then use it in the sentence provided on page T147 before repeating the word. **ACCESSING PRIOR KNOWLEDGE**

SELF-CHECK Have children refer to their lists of Spelling Words to check their Pretests. For each word children misspell on the Pretest, remind them to follow the Study Steps to Learn a Word. **STUDENT SELF-ASSESSMENT**

INTRODUCING THE LESSON

Begin by helping children read the title of the lesson and the Spelling Words on page 94.

• Ask children what is the same about all the Spelling Words. (The words begin with the same sound and the same letters.)

• Explain that all the words can be used to ask questions. Model several examples of questions, and then ask volunteers to share other questions that begin with each Spelling Word.

• Read with children the directions at the top of the page. After children write the words, remind them to circle the letters *wh*.

• You may want to send home the Home Activities Master Lesson 22, found on page T289, for children to complete at home for practice. **RECOGNIZING PATTERNS**

IN SUMMARY Ask children what they have learned about how to spell question words that begin with the beginning sound they hear in *when* and *why*. (The word probably begins with the letters *wh*.) **RECOGNIZING PATTERNS**

Spelling Log Encourage children to look for words that begin with *wh* and are pronounced like *when* or *why* in classroom displays. Ask them to list the words in their Spelling Logs and on the line provided on Pupil's Edition page 94. **RECOGNIZING PATTERNS**

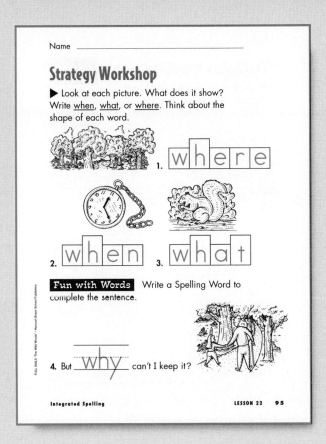

Name _____

Strategy Workshop

▶ Look at each picture. What does it show? Write <u>when</u>, <u>what</u>, or <u>where</u>. Think about the shape of each word.

1. where

2. when   3. what

Fun with Words   Write a Spelling Word to complete the sentence.

4. But _why_ can't I keep it?

Integrated Spelling

▶ Strategy Workshop

WORD SHAPES   Read the directions at the top of page 95 aloud. Then invite children to describe the shapes of the letters in the Spelling Words. Elicit that the letter *h* is tall, while the letter *y* drops below the line. Explain to children that remembering how a word looks is a strategy that can help them spell the word correctly.

Focus attention on the illustrations, and guide children to relate these pictures to the meaning of the Spelling Words. (The woods show *where*, the watch shows *when*, and the squirrel shows *what*.) Before children write the Spelling Words, encourage them to trace the word shapes with their fingers. **APPLYING SPELLING STRATEGIES**

FUN WITH WORDS   Help children read the directions, and then talk about the picture. Explain that the completed sentence will tell what the girl is saying. Ask a volunteer to read the sentence aloud, and have children write a Spelling Word to complete it.

MEETING INDIVIDUAL NEEDS

Children Acquiring English

To help children understand the meaning of the Spelling Words, explain that *when* has to do with time, *where* with a place, *what* with a person or thing, and *why* with a reason. Then use visual cues to reinforce the words as you ask children questions using the Spelling Words. For example, point to a clock when asking a *when* question. **UNDERSTANDING WORD MEANINGS**

MEETING INDIVIDUAL NEEDS

Semi-Phonetic Spellers

Some children may omit the *h* when writing the Spelling Words. Model the pronunciation of each word, emphasizing the initial sound, and have children echo you. Remind them that the letters *wh* stand for the sound they hear at the beginning of each word.

► Vocabulary WordShop

Spelling Log Invite children to look for other action words in "The Wild Woods." Suggest that they write these words in the Action Words section of their Spelling Logs.

Phonetic Spellers Say the word *keep* aloud. Then say it again so that each sound is isolated, and have children repeat it. Point out that in this word, a double *e* stands for the long vowel sound they hear. Repeat this procedure with the word *take*, pointing out that in this word, the final *e*, which is silent, is what they need to remember about the word.

WORDSHOP WORDS

Read the WordShop Words on page 96 aloud with children. Explain that these words tell about actions. Read the directions with children, and call attention to the illustrations. Explain that they will complete each sentence with the WordShop Word that describes the action in the picture. After children have completed the sentences, have them read the sentences aloud as the child in each picture might say them.

Transitional Spellers You may want to assign this level of spellers the WordShop Words as additional spelling words.

EXPLORING ACTION WORDS

Help children understand the meanings of the words *found, keep*, and *take* by playing a game of hide-and-seek in which you hide a small object. Give children clues for finding the object by saying they are hot or cold as they approach or move away from the hiding place. Have children use the WordShop Words to describe their actions when they have located the object. Example sentences might include:

I found the chalk.
I will take it to my desk.
But I will not keep it!

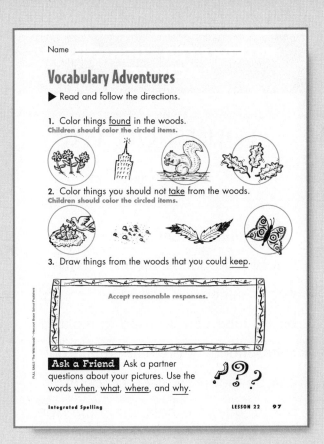

OLD ENGLISH SPELLING DID *not include the letter w. The letter u was used not only as a vowel but also to represent the consonant v. Later, the letter u was written twice to represent the sound /w/, and so the letter w (double u) was born.*

VOCABULARY ADVENTURES

After reading the direction line at the top of page 97, provide children with crayons. Then help them read the directions above each set of pictures and discuss the pictures. In the first item, children are to color things they could find in the woods; in the second item, they color things that they should *not* take from the woods. After children have shared their answers for the first two items, help them read the directions for drawing pictures, and have them complete this item. **USING ACTION WORDS**

ASK A FRIEND   Before partners ask each other questions about their pictures, encourage them to talk about the place that the items came from and the time of year they were gathered. For example, colorful leaves could be found under trees in the fall.

POSTTEST   Remind children to study any Spelling Words they misspelled on the Pretest. Then use the context sentences on page T147 to administer the Posttest.

Optional Writing Idea

Shared Writing: Journal Entry Have children look at the pictures they drew on Pupil's Edition page 97 showing things they might keep from the woods, and ask them to imagine this outing. Write *woods* in the center of a web, and add phrases suggested by children that tell *where, when,* and *what* they observed in the woods.

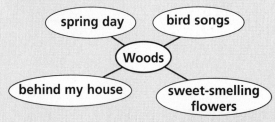

Children can dictate a group journal entry describing this outing, or you may prefer to have them work with a partner. In this case, suggest that they share their entries with the class.

▶Lesson Wrap-Up

WORDSHOP WORDS AND CONTEXT SENTENCES

1. **found** I **found** my lost coat.
2. **keep** You can **keep** this leaf.
3. **take** May I **take** this book home?

▶Reteach

LEARNING DIFFERENCES

Children with visual memory deficits do not automatically develop visual images of words. Have children use a black crayon to copy a Spelling Word on an index card. Then ask them to close their eyes and "see" a picture of the word in their minds as you spell it aloud. Tell children to keep their eyes closed, and ask them to spell the word aloud with you, while keeping a picture of the word in their minds. Tell children to open their eyes and imagine that they are seeing the word on their papers. Have them write the word by "tracing" the letters that they visualize on their papers. After they write the word, have them compare it with the model on the index card.

VISUAL MODALITY

You're on the Air

Work with children to outfit "mobile broadcast teams." Tissue paper stuffed into the top of a cardboard tube can be used to make a microphone. A pretend camcorder can be made by inserting a cardboard tube in a hole cut in the side of a shoe box. A reporter and a camera person can rove to do breaking-news stories featuring classroom activities. During their "broadcasts," children can ask questions beginning with the four Spelling Words. Suggest that children broadcast interviews, reports on school and classroom events, and local weather reports.

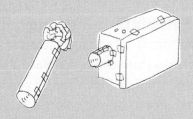

LANGUAGE ARTS

Words with Short *a*

OBJECTIVE

To spell words with short *a*

LESSON PLANNER

Assign words based on children's developmental levels. See the Assignment Guide on page T11.

▶ INFORMAL ASSESSMENT

Children's writing may show that they have difficulty distinguishing between short *a* and other vowel sounds.

▼ model

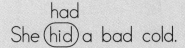

had
She (hid) a bad cold.

Use this lesson to introduce the spelling of words with initial or medial short *a*. After children complete this lesson, encourage them to proofread their writing and correct errors they may have made spelling words in which the letter *a* stands for the initial or medial short *a* sound.

▶ LEARNING DIFFERENCES

Use the following suggestion and the ideas on page T158 to customize learning activities.

MEETING INDIVIDUAL NEEDS

Children Acquiring English
Some children who are acquiring English may have difficulty distinguishing the short *a* sound from the short *e* and short *u* sounds. Provide children with practice listening to and pronouncing word pairs with these vowel sounds. As examples, use words such as the following: *had, head; and, end; cat, cut; sat, set; bag, beg, bug; ham, hem, hum;* and *bat, bet, but.* **COMPARING AND CONTRASTING**

▶ PRETEST/POSTTEST CONTEXT SENTENCES

* 1. **can** I **can** read that book.
* 2. **and** He has a dog **and** a cat.
  3. **had** We **had** fun at the park.
  4. **am** I **am** very happy.

▶ A HAND FULL OF WORDS

Children can create a bulletin board display that focuses on words that rhyme with *and*. Have children work with a partner to trace around one another's hands on a sheet of drawing paper. Then, on each finger, have them write a word that rhymes with the Spelling Word *and*. Possible words include *hand, sand, band, land, stand*, and *grand*. Display children's work on a bulletin board.

---

* Words appearing in "Wonderful Worms." Additional story words are *fat* and *damp*.

**NOTE: Fill in blanks on the Home Activities Master before sending it home.
See the Assignment Guide on page T11.**

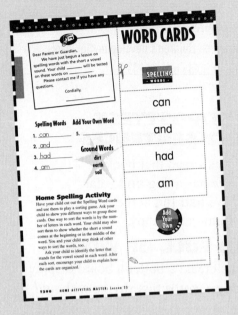

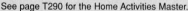

See page T290 for the Home Activities Master.

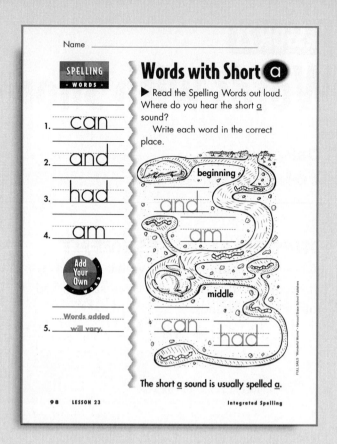

▶ Introduction

PRETEST Administer the Pretest. Say each word, and then use it in the sentence provided on page T153 before repeating the word. ACCESSING PRIOR KNOWLEDGE

SELF-CHECK Have children refer to their lists of Spelling Words to check their Pretests. For each word children misspell on the Pretest, remind them to follow the Study Steps to Learn a Word, found on pages 8–9 of the Pupil's Edition. STUDENT SELF-ASSESSMENT

INTRODUCING THE LESSON

To use the open sort, copy Home Activities Master Lesson 23, found on page T290.

Open Sort: After distributing the word cards, help children think of ways to sort the words. Children might sort by counting the number of letters and grouping words that way. They might also focus on similarities in the first or last letters to form the groups *am* and *and* or *had* and *and*.

Closed Sort: Help children read aloud the lesson title and the Spelling Words on page 98.

• Ask children what they notice about the vowel sound in each word. (Each has the short *a* sound.)

• Have children tell where they see and hear the vowel *a* in each word. (at the beginning— *and, am*; in the middle—*can, had*)

Review the directions, and have children write each Spelling Word in the space, based on where the short *a* sound is heard. SORTING WORDS

IN SUMMARY
Ask children what they have learned about how to spell words that have the short *a* sound. (The short *a* sound is probably spelled with the letter *a*.)
RECOGNIZING PHONIC ELEMENTS

Spelling Log Suggest that children look at their recent writing to locate words with the short *a* sound. Ask them to list the words in their Spelling Logs and write one on the line provided on Pupil's Edition page 98. RECOGNIZING PATTERNS

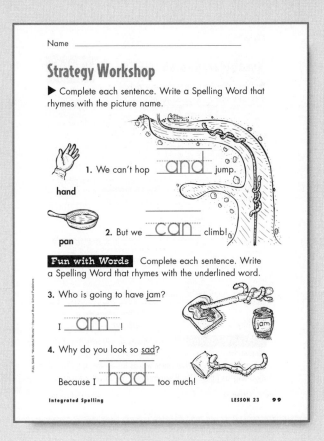

Name _____

Strategy Workshop

▶ Complete each sentence. Write a Spelling Word that rhymes with the picture name.

hand

1. We can't hop ‾and‾ jump.

pan

2. But we ‾can‾ climb!

Fun with Words Complete each sentence. Write a Spelling Word that rhymes with the underlined word.

3. Who is going to have <u>jam</u>?

I ‾am‾ !

4. Why do you look so <u>sad</u>?

Because I ‾had‾ too much!

▶Strategy Workshop

RHYMING WORDS Read the directions at the top of page 99 aloud. Call attention to the words *hand* and *pan* and the corresponding pictures. Then point out the picture of the earthworms in the tunnel, and explain that the sentences they will complete tell about this picture. Explain to children that they can use a rhyming strategy to help them write the correct Spelling Word to complete each sentence. **APPLYING SPELLING STRATEGIES**

FUN WITH WORDS Read the directions aloud. Then call on volunteers to read each sentence. Point out the underlined words, and explain to children that they will write Spelling Words that rhyme with *jam* and *sad*.

Children Acquiring English
Auxiliary verbs such as *can* may be difficult for children who speak languages that do not contain similar constructions. To practice this form, use pictures of animals, and talk

about actions the animals can perform, for example:

A worm can crawl.

Then use the picture of the worm as you model this question and answer:

What can crawl? A worm can.

Tell children the sentence *A worm can* is a shorter way of saying *A worm can crawl*.

BUILDING VOCABULARY

Semi-Phonetic Spellers
Help children remember to write the letter *a* in each word by focusing their attention on the shape of the letter *a* as they write each Spelling Word. Remind them to check that each word has the letter *a* at the beginning or in the middle.

Vocabulary WordShop

> Read the questions. Use the words from the box to answer them.

Ground · WORDS ·
dirt
earth
soil

Worm Quiz

you're wonderful

1. Where do live?

_____
_____ Possible responses: _____
They live in _____ soil, dirt, earth _____ .

2. What do eat?

_____
_____ Possible responses: _____
They eat _____ soil, dirt, earth _____ .

3. What do mix and turn?

_____
_____ Possible responses: _____
They mix and turn _____ soil, dirt, earth _____ .

Share a Meaning Synonyms are words that have almost the same meaning. The words <u>dirt</u>, <u>earth</u>, and <u>soil</u> are synonyms. What other words have almost the same meaning as <u>little</u>? Use them to tell a friend about worms.

100   LESSON 23   **Integrated Spelling**

FULL SAILS. 'Wonderful Worms' • Harcourt Brace School Publishers

---

▶ Vocabulary WordShop

Ground ★ WORDS ★

Spelling Log Help children brainstorm other words about the ground or the animals that live there. Suggest that they write these words in their Spelling Logs.

MEETING INDIVIDUAL NEEDS

Transitional Spellers You may want to assign this level of spellers the WordShop Words as additional spelling words.

WORDSHOP WORDS   Ask a volunteer to read the WordShop Words on page 100 aloud. Then read the directions with children, and explain that this quiz about worms is fun. Help children read the questions. Explain that they are to write each WordShop Word only once in this activity. As children share their responses, guide them to understand that any of the words works as an answer to each question.

SHARE A MEANING   Call on volunteers to use their own words to give examples of *synonyms*. Possible responses: *small, tiny, miniature*.

MEETING INDIVIDUAL NEEDS

Phonetic Spellers Use the words *soil* and *earth* to point out to children that sometimes two vowels come together. In the word *soil*, the two vowels together stand for a different sound than either the vowel *o* or the vowel *i*. In the word *earth*, the vowel *a* cannot be heard.

EXPLORING GROUND WORDS   Write *earth* and *Earth* on the board. Point out that one word begins with a lowercase letter and the other word begins with a capital letter.

• Display a globe, and explain that when writing about the planet Earth, we often capitalize the word *Earth*.

• Display a handful of soil, and explain that when the word *earth* is used to mean soil or dirt, it is written with a lowercase letter.

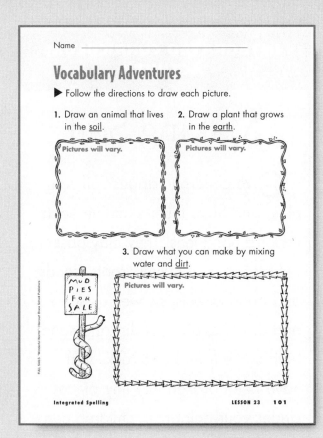

Name _____

Vocabulary Adventures

▶ Follow the directions to draw each picture.

1. Draw an animal that lives in the soil.

Pictures will vary.

2. Draw a plant that grows in the earth.

Pictures will vary.

3. Draw what you can make by mixing water and dirt.

Pictures will vary.

Integrated Spelling   LESSON 23   **101**

> "THE WORD *and* IS ONE *of the five most frequently used words in the English language. The other four are* I, the, to, *and* of."

VOCABULARY ADVENTURES

After reading the direction line at the top of page 101 to children, provide them with crayons. Then help them read the directions above each box. Point out that many pictures can be drawn for each item. You may want to have children complete each drawing before moving on to the next item. After children complete the page, invite them to describe what they drew and explain why. **USING NAMING WORDS**

Working Together You might want to have children work in pairs or small groups to do this activity. Encourage partners to agree on the picture they will draw to complete each item.

POSTTEST   Remind children to study any Spelling Words they misspelled on the Pretest. Then use the context sentences on page T153 to administer the posttest.

Optional Writing Idea

Collaborative Writing: Sentences for Pictures

Assign each child a partner. Then have the pair look at the pictures they drew as responses on Pupil's Edition page 101. Have them work with their responses to the same item to write a picture caption that uses the word *and*. You may want to explain that if one child drew a worm and the other child drew an ant as a response to the first item, they might write the following:

Worms and ants live in the soil.

Invite pairs of children to share both their pictures and the captions in a small group or with the class.

▶Lesson Wrap-Up

WORDSHOP WORDS AND CONTEXT SENTENCES

1. **dirt** Put more **dirt** in the flower pot.
2. **earth** We dug a hole in the **earth.**
3. **soil** Dad has a bag of **soil.**

▶Reteach

LEARNING DIFFERENCES

Children with auditory or visual processing problems may benefit from a multisensory review of their Spelling Words. Record an audiotape on which you pronounce each Spelling Word, spell it slowly, and then repeat the word. Have children turn off the tape player after each word is presented and attempt to write the word. Place a folder with a list of the Spelling Words beside the tape player so children can self-check each word after they write it. **AUDITORY/VISUAL MODALITIES**

Making Soil

Give children various soil samples, and have them examine each under a hand lens. They may observe pebbles, bits of leaves, roots, seeds, and dead insects, as well as sand and dirt. Explain that dirt and sand both come from large rocks that have been broken into tiny pieces. Under your guidance, children can create their own soil samples. Provide them with safety glasses and small hammers. Show children how to use a hammer to pulverize chunks of sandstone or brick that have been sealed in a grocery bag. After the rock is pulverized, children can mix in tiny pieces of organic matter. Have them compare the soil they created with the other soil samples. Ask children to describe how the soil samples are alike and different.

SCIENCE

LESSON 24
Words with Short *o*

OBJECTIVE
To spell words with short *o*

LESSON PLANNER
Assign words based on children's developmental levels. See the Assignment Guide on page T11.

▶ INFORMAL ASSESSMENT
Children's writing may show that they have difficulty distinguishing between short *o* and other vowel sounds.

▼ model

> not
> This is (nat) my hat.

Use this lesson to introduce the spelling of words with the short *o* vowel sound. Encourage children to apply what they have learned to help them spell other words with the short *o* sound. After children complete this lesson, have them proofread their writing and correct errors they may have made spelling words in which the letter *o* stands for the initial or medial short *o* sound.

▶ LEARNING DIFFERENCES
Use the following suggestion and the ideas on page T164 to customize learning activities.

Children Acquiring English
Children who speak Spanish, Chinese, Vietnamese, Thai, or Tagalog often confuse the short *o* and short *u* sounds. Have children listen to and pronounce the following word pairs: *not, nut; got, gut; hot, hut; rot, rut; pop, pup;* and *dog, dug.* Pronounce the word pairs again in random order, and have children identify the word in each pair that has the short *o* sound. **COMPARING AND CONTRASTING**

▶ PRETEST/POSTTEST CONTEXT SENTENCES
* 1. **on** Put this lid **on** the pan.
* 2. **not** The cat has **not** been fed.
* 3. **stop** Please **stop** talking.
  4. **got** We **got** wet.

▶ A POT OF WORDS
Ask children to identify *not* and *got* as the two Spelling Words that rhyme. Then involve them in creating a bulletin board display that focuses on other words in the *-ot* family. Cut a large pot from construction paper, and staple it to the board. Ask children to draw and label pictures of words that belong in this word family, such as *lot, hot, dot, cot, spot, tot, slot,* and *knot.* Have them display their labeled pictures around the pot. Then suggest that pairs of children work together to "sample" words from the pot. One child can point to a word at random and say the word aloud for the other child to spell.

* Words appearing in "Frog and Toad Together." An additional story word is *frog.*

NOTE: Fill in blanks on the Home Activities Master before sending it home. See the Assignment Guide on page T11.

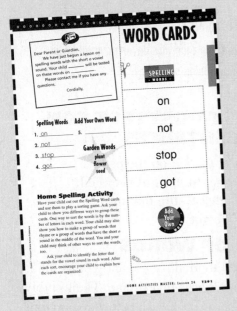

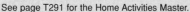

See page T291 for the Home Activities Master.

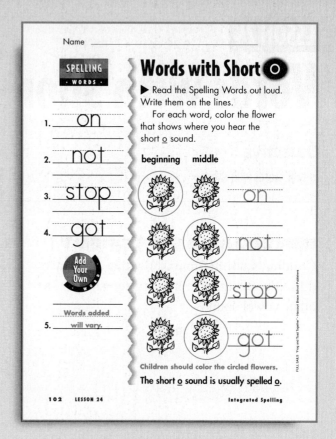

▶ Introduction

PRETEST Administer the Pretest. Say each word, and then use it in the sentence provided on page T159 before repeating the word. **ACCESSING PRIOR KNOWLEDGE**

SELF-CHECK Have children refer to their lists of Spelling Words to check their Pretests. For each word children misspell on the Pretest, remind them to follow the Study Steps to Learn a Word, found on pages 8–9 of the Pupil's Edition. **STUDENT SELF-ASSESSMENT**

INTRODUCING THE LESSON

To use the open sort, copy Home Activities Master Lesson 24, found on page T291.

Open Sort: After distributing the word cards, help children think of ways to sort the words. Children might group words by counting the number of letters or into groups of words that rhyme.

Closed Sort: Help children read aloud the lesson title and the Spelling Words on page 102.

- Ask children what they notice about the vowel sound in each word. (Each has the short *o* sound.)

- Have children tell where they see and hear the vowel *o* in each word. (at the beginning—*on*; in the middle—*not, stop, got*)

Review the directions, and have children write the Spelling Words on the lines. Then have them color the flower beside each word that shows where they hear the short *o* sound. **SORTING WORDS**

IN SUMMARY Ask children what they have learned about how to spell words that have the short *o* sound. (The short *o* sound is probably spelled with the letter *o*.) **RECOGNIZING PHONIC ELEMENTS**

 Spelling Log Invite children to find other words that have the short *o* sound. Suggest that they list these words in their Spelling Logs and write one on the line provided on Pupil's Edition page 102. **RECOGNIZING PATTERNS**

Strategy Workshop

Name _____

Strategy Workshop

▶ Two of the Spelling Words rhyme.
Write them in the sentences.

1. He did __not__ know how to plant a garden!

2. So he __got__ into trouble.

▶ Complete the sentence. Write the Spelling
Word that rhymes with the picture name.

3. The plants did not __stop__ growing.

mop

Fun with Words Complete the sentence.
Write the Spelling Word with the short o sound
at the beginning.

4. I will put water __on__ my plant!

Integrated Spelling   LESSON 24   103

▶Strategy Workshop

RHYMING WORDS Read the directions at the top of page 103 to children, and call their attention to sentences 1 and 2 and the corresponding illustration. Have children determine which two Spelling Words rhyme and then write the correct word to complete each sentence. Read the directions above sentence 3 to children, and have them identify the picture of the mop. Explain that the completed sentence will tell about the plants in the picture. Remind children to use a rhyming word strategy to help them choose the correct Spelling Word to complete sentence 3.

APPLYING SPELLING STRATEGIES

FUN WITH WORDS Read the directions to children, and discuss the illustration with them. Remind children to write the Spelling Word with the short *o* sound in the initial position to complete the sentence.

MEETING INDIVIDUAL NEEDS

Challenge You may want to challenge children to list other words containing the short *o* sound that can be spelled with the letters *s, t, o, p*. (Possible responses: *pots, tops, spot*) Suggest that children select one or more of these words and learn to spell it.

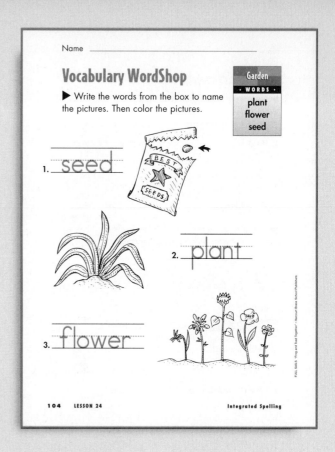

Name _____

Vocabulary WordShop
▶ Write the words from the box to name the pictures. Then color the pictures.

Garden
• WORDS •
plant
flower
seed

1. seed

2. plant

3. flower

104   LESSON 24   Integrated Spelling

▶ Vocabulary WordShop

Spelling Log As children read and write, encourage them to look for other words that are associated with growing things. Have them write the words in their Spelling Logs.

Transitional Spellers You may want to assign this level of spellers the WordShop Words as additional spelling words.

WORDSHOP WORDS Ask a volunteer to read the WordShop Words on page 104 aloud. Then talk with children about how these words are alike. (They all have to do with growing things in a garden.) Read the directions at the top of the page to children, and then distribute crayons to each child. Have children write a WordShop Word to label each illustration; then have them color the pictures.

Phonetic Spellers To practice writing the Garden Words, draw letter boxes on the board in the shape of each word. Have children write each word in the correct word shape box.

EXPLORING GARDEN WORDS
Explore with children how the same word can be used as both a naming word and an action word. Write these two sentences on the board:

This is a big *plant*.
They *plant* a garden each year.

Explain that some words, such as *plant*, can be used both as naming and action words. Help children understand that *plant* is used as a naming word in the first sentence and as an action word in the second sentence.

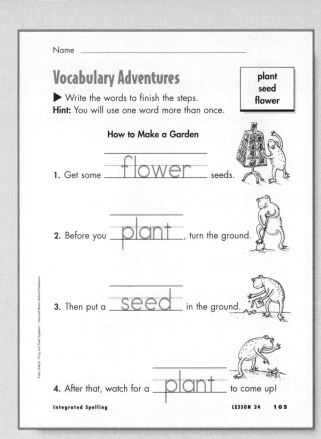

Name _____

Vocabulary Adventures

▶ Write the words to finish the steps.
Hint: You will use one word more than once.

| plant |
| seed |
| flower |

How to Make a Garden

1. Get some _flower_ seeds.

2. Before you _plant_, turn the ground.

3. Then put a _seed_ in the ground.

4. After that, watch for a _plant_ to come up!

Integrated Spelling   LESSON 24   105

VOCABULARY ADVENTURES

Help children read the directions at the top of page 105. Explain to children that they will write words from the box to complete the steps that tell how to make a garden. Have children look at the pictures and read each step, pausing for the blank, before they begin to work. If children need help in understanding the hint, remind them of the previous discussion (see Exploring Garden Words, page T162) in which they learned how a word can be used as both a naming word and an action word. **USING NAMING AND ACTION WORDS**

Challenge Have children review the completed sentences to determine whether each Garden Word is used as a naming word or an action word.

POSTTEST
Remind children to study any Spelling Words they misspelled on the Pretest. Then use the context sentences on page T159 to administer the Posttest.

Optional Writing Idea

Shared Writing: Song
Children can write a song to the tune of "The Farmer in the Dell" that describes how to plant and care for a garden. Ask children to suggest words associated with gardens, and record their responses in a web.

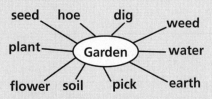

Have children use the framework of the song to develop verses that describe the process of making a garden. If you want, share the following model verse with children:

First we dig the soil.
First we dig the soil.
Heigh-ho, the derry-o,
First we dig the soil.

▶ Lesson Wrap-Up

WORDSHOP WORDS AND CONTEXT SENTENCES

1. **plant**   I gave my mom a **plant**.
2. **flower**   Did you pick that **flower**?
3. **seed**   A nut is a kind of **seed**.

▶ Reteach

LEARNING DIFFERENCES

Children who have attention deficits may find that a multisensory approach is useful in helping them master their Spelling Words. Invite the child to work at the board, which allows for greater motor activity. Write one of the Spelling Words in large letters on the board, and have the child read the word aloud. Ask the child to repeat the word again, listening for the short *o* sound. Point out the letter *o* that stands for this sound. Then have the child use a different color chalk to trace over the word as you direct the child's attention to the sensation of forming each of the letters. After the child traces the word, have the child erase the word and write it again from memory. If the word is correct, have the child say it aloud. If the word is incorrect, have the child repeat the procedure. **VISUAL/AUDITORY/ KINESTHETIC MODALITIES**

Grow, Seed, Grow!

Provide children with plastic cups, potting soil, and fast-growing seeds, such as bean or marigold seeds. Have children follow the directions on Pupil's Edition page 105 that describe how to plant a garden. After children water the seeds, have them place the cups in a sunny windowsill and regularly observe the seeds. Suggest children keep journals in which they record their observations, sketches, and measurements of their plants' growth. Show children how to record their data on vertical bar graphs showing changes in the height of their plants.

SCIENCE

Words to Remember

OBJECTIVE
To spell words that are used frequently

LESSON PLANNER
Assign words based on children's developmental levels. See the Assignment Guide on page T11.

▶ INFORMAL ASSESSMENT
Children's writing may show that they have difficulty spelling some frequently used words.

▼ model

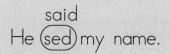

said
He (sed) my name.

Use this lesson to introduce the spelling of some words that children use frequently in their writing. After children complete this lesson, encourage them to proofread their writing and correct errors they may have made in spelling these words.

▶ LEARNING DIFFERENCES
Use the following suggestion and the ideas on page T170 to customize learning activities.

Children Acquiring English
Short vowel sounds, such as the short *i* in *with* and the short *e* in *said*, may present difficulties for children who are acquiring English. For specific suggestions regarding the short *i* sound, see Lesson 21 (page T141). For specific suggestions regarding the short *e* sound, see Lesson 19 (page T129). **COMPARING AND CONTRASTING**

▶ PRETEST/POSTTEST CONTEXT SENTENCES
* 1. **look**   Those bikes **look** old.
* 2. **said**   She **said** she would come.
* 3. **put**   Please **put** the box here.
* 4. **with**   Will you come **with** me?

▶ THE BOOK NOOK
Devote one section of your classroom word wall to words that rhyme with the Spelling Word *look*. Distribute construction paper cutouts of an open book, and have children write other words in the *-ook* word family on the shapes. In addition to the words *book* and *look*, children might include the words *cook*, *hook*, *took*, *brook*, *shook*, and *crook*.

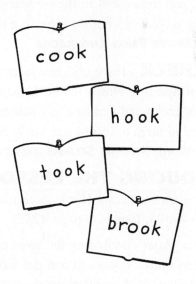

cook
hook
took
brook

* Words appearing in "Lionel in the Winter."

NOTE: Fill in blanks on the Home Activities Master before sending it home. See the Assignment Guide on page T11.

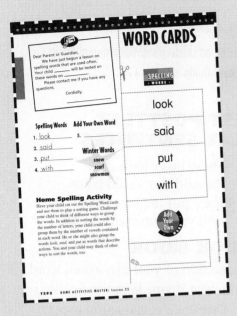

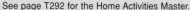

See page T292 for the Home Activities Master.

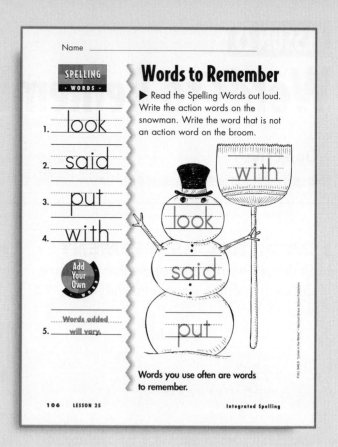

▶ Introduction

PRETEST Administer the Pretest. Say each word, and then use it in the sentence provided on page T165 before repeating the word. **ACCESSING PRIOR KNOWLEDGE**

SELF-CHECK Have children refer to their lists of Spelling Words to check their Pretests. For each word children misspell on the Pretest, remind them to follow the Study Steps to Learn a Word. **STUDENT SELF-ASSESSMENT**

INTRODUCING THE LESSON

To use the open sort, copy Home Activities Master Lesson 25, found on page T292.

Open Sort: After distributing the word cards, help children think of ways to sort the words. Children might make a group of words that have the letter *t*. They might sort *look, said,* and *with* into a group of words with four letters.

Closed Sort: Help children read aloud the lesson title and the Spelling Words on page 106. Point out that these words do not all con-

tain the same vowel sound or begin with the same consonant. Instead, they are words that are used often in writing.

• Ask children what they notice about the way the first three words could be used in a sentence. (They all name actions.)

• Tell children to write the three action words on the snowman and the word that is not an action word on the broom. **SORTING WORDS**

IN SUMMARY

Ask children what they have learned about how to spell words they use often. (You can study them to remember how to spell them.) **DEVELOPING SPELLING LISTS**

Spelling Log Suggest that children look through their writing to find other action words that they want to remember how to spell. Have them add these words to their Spelling Logs and write one on the line provided on Pupil's Edition page 106. **DEVELOPING SPELLING LISTS**

Name _____

Strategy Workshop

▶ Write a Spelling Word to complete each sentence.
Think about the shape of the word.

1. Let's `put` a hat on this one.

2. Let's make this one `with` hands.

3. They `look` like us!

Fun with Words Write a Spelling
Word to complete the sentence.

4. He `said`, "Look out!"

Integrated Spelling   LESSON 25   **107**

Strategy Workshop

WORD SHAPES Read the directions
at the top of page 107 aloud. Then invite children to describe the shapes of the letters in the
Spelling Words. Elicit that the letter *l* is tall,
while the letter *p* drops below the line. Explain
to children that remembering how a word
looks is a strategy that can help them spell the
word correctly.

Focus attention on the illustration, and have
children describe what the boys in the picture
are doing. Before children write the Spelling
Words, encourage them to trace the word
shapes with their fingers. After children have
completed the sentences, ask volunteers to
read them aloud. **APPLYING SPELLING
STRATEGIES**

FUN WITH WORDS Help children
read the directions, and then talk about the
picture. Explain that the completed sentence
will tell what the boy is saying to his friend.
Ask a volunteer to read the incomplete sentence aloud. Then have children write a
Spelling Word to complete it.

 Children Acquiring English
The word *put* has many
idiomatic meanings that may
confuse children who are
acquiring English. To help clarify some of
these meanings, present the following sentences, and talk about the meaning of *put* in
each one.

    Put your books away. (place)
    The children will *put* on a play. (present)
    Don't *put* off cleaning your room.
    (postpone)
    Always *put* out a campfire. (extinguish)

UNDERSTANDING IDIOMS

 Semi-Phonetic Spellers
Some children may omit the
double *o* when writing the
word *look*. Remind them that
every word must contain at least one vowel.
You might also point out that the two *o*'s look
like two eyes that can help them *look*.

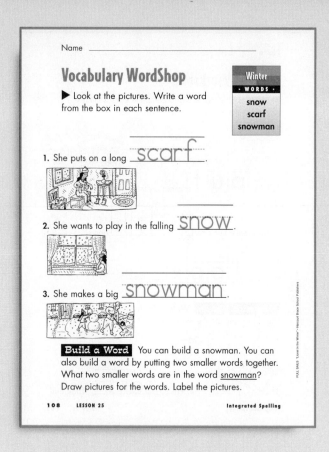

▶ Vocabulary WordShop

Spelling Log Invite children to hunt for other words associated with winter in "Lionel in the Winter." Suggest that they write these words in their Spelling Logs.

Transitional Spellers You may want to assign this level of spellers the WordShop Words as additional spelling words.

WORDSHOP WORDS Read the WordShop Words on page 108 aloud with children. Discuss how all these words are alike. (They all tell about winter.) Read the directions with children, and call attention to the illustrations. Explain that the pictures show what one girl does on a winter day. Tell children that they will complete each sentence with a WordShop Word. After children have completed the sentences, call on volunteers to read them aloud.

BUILD A WORD Read the directions aloud. Help children understand the concept of compound words by writing *snowman* on a sentence strip, and then cutting the strip into two pieces. Show children how the words *snow* and *man* can be joined to create a longer word.

EXPLORING WINTER WORDS Use this opportunity to explore additional compound words that contain the word *snow*. Write the following compound words on sentence strips: *snowflake, snowball, snowstorm, snowsuit*, and *snowdrift*. Help children read the words aloud and define them. Then cut the strips to make puzzles that consist of the two smaller words, and display them in the chalk ledge. Have children rejoin the pieces to form the compounds and then use the words in oral sentences.

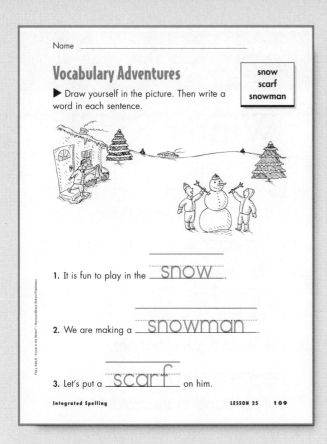

Name _____

Vocabulary Adventures

snow
scarf
snowman

▶ Draw yourself in the picture. Then write a word in each sentence.

1. It is fun to play in the ___snow___ .

2. We are making a ___snowman___ .

3. Let's put a ___scarf___ on him.

Integrated Spelling

LESSON 25   109

VOCABULARY ADVENTURES

Read the directions at the top of page 109 with children. Then have them read aloud the words in the box. Ask them to look at the illustration and describe what is happening. After children have drawn pictures of themselves in the winter scene and completed the sentences, have them share and discuss their work. **USING NAMING WORDS**

MEETING INDIVIDUAL NEEDS

Phonetic Spellers Have children write sentences, using the three Winter Words; however, instead of writing these words, have them draw blanks for the letters. Then have children exchange papers with a partner and write the words to complete the sentences.

POSTTEST   Remind children to study any Spelling Words they misspelled on the Pretest. Then use the context sentences on page T165 to administer the Posttest.

Lesson 25   **T169**

▶ Lesson Wrap-Up
WORDSHOP WORDS AND CONTEXT SENTENCES

1. **snow** It is fun to play in the **snow**.
2. **scarf** I lost my red **scarf**.
3. **snowman** We made a big **snowman**.

▶ Reteach
LEARNING DIFFERENCES

Children with visual or auditory processing deficits sometimes feel great stress when asked to perform the tasks required for spelling. To help alleviate some of this pressure, make an audiotape on which you pronounce each Spelling Word, spell it slowly, and then pronounce it again. Invite children to listen to the tape. Suggest that they turn off the tape player after each word is presented and write the word. Place a list of the Spelling Words beside the tape player so children can check their work. If they make an error, have them listen to you pronounce, spell, and pronounce the word once more before writing it again.

AUDITORY MODALITY

Winter Riddle

Display this traditional riddle on chart paper, and read it aloud. Then invite children to write their answers on snowflake cutouts.

I saw a man in white.
He looked quite a sight.
He was not old,
But he stood in the cold.
And when he felt the sun,
He started to run.
Who could he be?
Do answer me.
(snowman)

You might want to talk with children about the two meanings of *run* in this riddle and explore how the poet is having fun with words.

LANGUAGE ARTS

Words to Remember with *o*

OBJECTIVE

To spell words with different sounds for *o*

LESSON PLANNER

Assign words based on children's developmental levels. See the Assignment Guide on page T11.

▶ INFORMAL ASSESSMENT

Children's writing may show that they have difficulty distinguishing between words with *o* and words with other vowels.

▼ model

come
We will (cum) at ten.

Use this lesson to introduce words spelled with *o* that children use frequently in their writing. After children complete this lesson, encourage them to proofread their writing and correct errors they may have made in spelling these words.

▶ LEARNING DIFFERENCES

Use the following suggestion and the ideas on page T176 to customize learning activities.

Children Acquiring English
In several Spelling Words in this lesson the letter *o* stands for the short *u* sound. Because there are many languages in which the short *u* sound does not exist, it is often one of the most difficult sounds for children who are acquiring English to learn. Give children practice in listening to and pronouncing words such as *come, came; of, if;* and *one, win.* **COMPARING AND CONTRASTING**

▶ PRETEST/POSTTEST CONTEXT SENTENCES

* 1. **now** Let's clean up **now.**
* 2. **of** He is a friend **of** mine.
* 3. **come** The cats **come** when I call.
* 4. **one** I will read **one** more story.

▶ HOW NOW

Children might want to build a family of words that rhyme with the Spelling Word *now.* To help children think of words in the family, recite the following rhyme, and have them identify the rhyming words.

How now, brown cow.

Have children name other words that rhyme with *now* that end with the letters *ow,* and add them to the classroom word wall. In addition to *how, now,* and *cow,* such words might include *bow, sow, plow,* and *wow.*

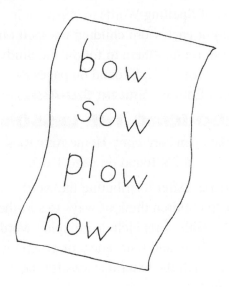

bow
sow
plow
now

---

* Words appearing in "Jenny's Journey." Additional story words are *got, out, on, some,* and *how.*

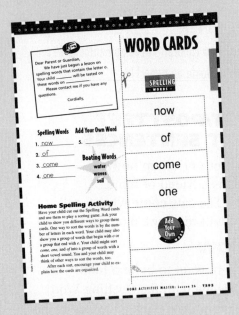

NOTE: Fill in blanks on the Home Activities Master before sending it home. See the Assignment Guide on page T11.

See page T293 for the Home Activities Master.

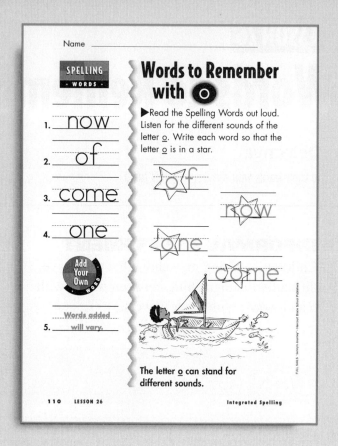

▶Introduction

PRETEST Administer the Pretest. Say each word, and then use it in the sentence provided on page T171 before repeating the word. **ACCESSING PRIOR KNOWLEDGE**

SELF-CHECK Have children refer to their lists of Spelling Words to check their Pretests. For each word children misspell on the Pretest, remind them to follow the Study Steps to Learn a Word, found on pages 8–9 of the Pupil's Edition. **STUDENT SELF-ASSESSMENT**

INTRODUCING THE LESSON

To use the open sort, copy Home Activities Master Lesson 26, found on page T293.

Open Sort: After distributing the word cards, help children think of ways to sort the words. Possible sorts include grouping words with two, three, and four letters or grouping words in which the letter *o* stands for the short *u* sound.

Closed Sort: Help children read aloud the lesson title and the Spelling Words on page 110.

• Ask children what they notice about each word. (All words contain the letter *o*.)

• Have children tell where the letter is in each word. (at the beginning—*of, one*; in the middle—*now, come*)

• Explain that children are to write each Spelling Word so that the letter *o* appears in a star. **SORTING WORDS**

IN SUMMARY Ask children what they have learned about how to spell the Spelling Words in this lesson. (Each word is spelled with the letter *o*.) **RECOGNIZING PHONIC ELEMENTS**

Spelling Log Suggest that children work in pairs to find other words in which the vowel sound is spelled with the letter *o*. Ask children to list the words in their Spelling Logs and write one on the line provided on Pupil's Edition page 110. **RECOGNIZING PATTERNS**

Name _____

Strategy Workshop

▶ Write a Spelling Word to complete each sentence. Think about the shape of the word.

1. This is a wish [of] mine.

2. I want to [come] to see you.

Fun with Words Look at the picture. What are the girls saying? Write a Spelling Word in each sentence.

3. Here comes ___one___ of my best friends!

4. I feel so happy ___now___!

Integrated Spelling   LESSON 26   111

Strategy Workshop

WORD SHAPES Read the directions at the top of page 111 aloud. Then invite children to describe the shapes of the letters in the Spelling Words. Elicit that the letter *f* is tall. Point out that none of the letters in these words drops below the line. Explain to children that remembering how a word looks is a strategy that can help them spell the word correctly.

Focus attention on the illustration, and ask children to tell what the girls are doing. Before children write the Spelling Words to complete the sentences, encourage them to trace the word shapes with their fingers. **APPLYING SPELLING STRATEGIES**

FUN WITH WORDS Help children read the directions, and then talk about the picture. Explain that the completed sentences will tell what the girls are saying to each other. Ask volunteers to read the sentences aloud, and have children write a Spelling Word to complete each sentence.

Children Acquiring English
Help children understand the difference between the numeral *one* (1) and the pronoun *one*. Begin by displaying one object, such as a pencil, and ask children how many pencils you are holding. Write the numeral 1 and the number name on the board. Then display several pencils, only one of which is red. After explaining that one of these pencils is red, ask a child to select the red one. Guide children to understand that in this case, the word *one* is used to stand for the word *pencil*.

UNDERSTANDING WORD MEANINGS

Semi-Phonetic Spellers
Help children remember to include the letter *o* when writing their Spelling Words. Have them write their words. Then provide literal "reinforcement" by having them stick a notebook-paper reinforcement over the letter *o* in each word.

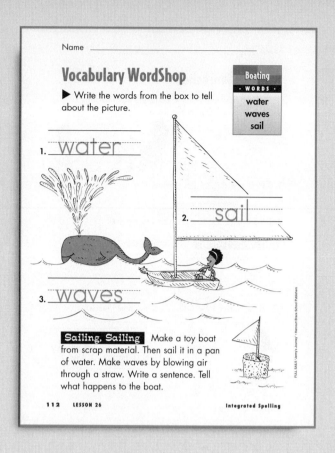

Name _____

Vocabulary WordShop

▶ Write the words from the box to tell about the picture.

Boating
• W O R D S •
water
waves
sail

1. water

2. sail

3. waves

Sailing, Sailing Make a toy boat from scrap material. Then sail it in a pan of water. Make waves by blowing air through a straw. Write a sentence. Tell what happens to the boat.

112   LESSON 26   Integrated Spelling

▶ Vocabulary WordShop

Spelling Log Invite children to look for other words that have to do with boating in "Jenny's Journey." Suggest that they write these words in their Spelling Logs.

Transitional Spellers You may want to assign this level of spellers the WordShop Words as additional spelling words.

WORDSHOP WORDS Read the WordShop Words on page 112 aloud. Then ask children to explain what each of these words has to do with boating. Read the directions with children, and call attention to the illustration. Explain that children will label each numbered object in the picture with one of the Boating Words. When children have finished, have them share their responses.

SAILING, SAILING After reading the directions with children, distribute corks, toothpicks, paste, paper, and scissors. Have children use these materials to make sailboats. Then provide the group with a shallow pan of water, and invite children to sail their boats. Give children straws, and demonstrate how to blow air through a straw to make waves in the water. Allow children to experiment on their own. Conclude the activity by having children write sentences about what they observed.

EXPLORING BOATING WORDS Talk about the multiple meanings of the word *waves*.

• Point out that wind blowing across a lake creates waves.

• Have a child wave as if saying good-bye. Have children define this meaning of *wave* as "a gesture with the hand."

• Point out a child in your class who has wavy hair. Explore that *waves* in this case refers to gentle curls.

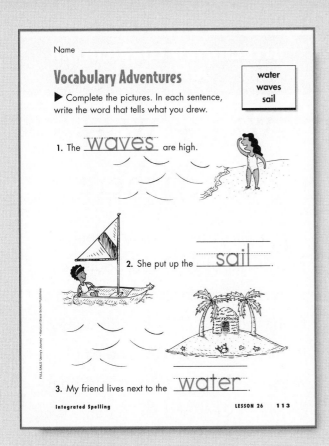

Name

Vocabulary Adventures

▶ Complete the pictures. In each sentence, write the word that tells what you drew.

| water |
| waves |
| sail |

1. The waves are high.

2. She put up the sail.

3. My friend lives next to the water.

Integrated Spelling   LESSON 26   113

VOCABULARY ADVENTURES

After reading the direction line at the top of page 113, provide children with crayons. Have them complete the pictures by drawing water, waves, and a sail. Then have them complete each sentence by writing the word that describes what they drew in each picture. After children have completed the page, invite them to share their drawings and sentences.

USING NAMING WORDS

Phonetic Spellers Children who are spelling at this level match letters to the sounds they hear in a word. Say *waves* aloud. Then say it again so that each sound is isolated, and have children repeat it. Mention that children need to remember the silent *e* in the word.

POSTTEST
Remind children to study any Spelling Words they misspelled on the Pretest. Then use the context sentences on page T171 to administer the Posttest.

Optional Writing Idea

Collaborative Writing: Riddles Invite children to work with partners to write riddles about animals that live in the water. Ask children to name a water animal and describe its characteristics. You may want to record this information in a chart.

Water Animals	
Name	Characteristics
octopus	has eight arms, has tentacles, squirts ink, can change color

Then have children work in pairs to write a riddle about one water animal. When the riddles are completed, hold a class riddle-fest in which children pose their riddles for others to solve.

▶ Lesson Wrap-Up

WORDSHOP WORDS AND CONTEXT SENTENCES

1. **water**   The **water** is very cold.
2. **waves**   The **waves** tipped over the boat.
3. **sail**   Wind filled the boat's **sail.**

▶ Reteach

LEARNING DIFFERENCES

Some children may benefit from a hands-on reinforcement of their Spelling Words. Divide the class into small groups, and give each group a Spelling Word written on a card. Have children work together to use their bodies to form the letters that spell the words. When all children are in position, have them spell the word aloud by having the children forming each letter say the letter name. After children spell the word, have the group exchange cards with another group. Repeat this procedure until each group has correctly spelled all the Spelling Words. **KINESTHETIC/ AUDITORY MODALITIES**

Water, Water Everywhere

For this activity you will need to provide maps that show bodies of water. If possible, make photocopies of the maps so children can write on them. Point out several bodies of water to children, such as a stream, a river, a lake, and the ocean. Using crayons, children can trace how the water from streams flows into rivers, and then how the rivers flow into lakes or oceans.

Talk with children about how water is useful to people. It is used not only for recreational purposes such as boating, but also as a home for water creatures, for transportation, for drinking, for irrigation, and for natural beauty. Suggest that children make posters or a collage showing one or more of the ways water is important in our lives.

Review of Lessons 19–26

OBJECTIVES

To review the spelling patterns and strategies in Lessons 19–26; to give children opportunities to recognize and use these spelling patterns and Spelling Words in their writing

▶ REVIEW OF SPELLING STRATEGIES

Guide children in reviewing the spelling strategies presented in Lessons 19–26.

Using Word Shapes Draw the following word shape boxes on the board:

Then write these words beside the word shape: *now, had, put.* Call on volunteers to read and spell each word aloud. Then trace the outline of the word shape with your finger, and ask children to identify which one of the three words has letters that fit this shape. (*had*) As children observe, write the word in the shape. Discuss how the strategy of studying and remembering word shapes can help them spell words.

Using Rhyming Words Explain to children that using what they know about rhyming words and letter sounds is another strategy to help them spell words.

• Write *hot* on the board, and ask children how they can use a rhyming strategy to spell the word *not*.

• Ask them what letter they would use to stand for the beginning sound of *not*. (*n*)

• Then have them identify the letters that stand for the middle and the ending sounds in both *hot* and *not*. (*ot*)

▶ LESSON WORDS

The following words from Lessons 19–26 are reviewed in this lesson.

Lesson 19 Words with Short *e*: help

Lesson 20 Words with Short *u*: must, run

Lesson 21 Words with Short *i*: big, in

Lesson 22 Words with *wh*: what

Lesson 23 Words with Short *a*: and

Lesson 24 Words with Short *o*: got

Lesson 25 Words to Remember: put

Lesson 26 Words to Remember with *o*: of

▶ Practice Test

OPTIONS FOR ADMINISTERING THE PRACTICE TEST

The Practice Test provides an opportunity to review Spelling Words and spelling generalizations in a standardized test format.

Option 1: Read the directions to children, and review the samples at the top of pages 114 and 115, making sure children understand that both pages use the same test format. Then have children take both pages of this Practice Test.

Option 2: After reading the directions and reviewing the sample at the top of page 114 with children, administer it as a pretest. If children need help, review the spelling generalizations on Pupil's Edition pages 82, 86, 90, 94, 98, 102, 106, and 110. Then review with children the sample at the top of page 115, and use the items on this page as a posttest.

OPTIONS FOR EVALUATION

• You may want to have children check their own Practice Tests by looking up the words in the Picture Dictionary of the Pupil's Edition or in the lessons in which they were taught. The list on page T177 contains lesson information for each Spelling Word contained in the Practice Test.

• An alternative is to assign each child a partner and have pairs check one another's Practice Tests. If you use this option, make sure that each child is using a list on which the Spelling Words are spelled correctly.

For each word misspelled on the Practice Test, remind children to follow the Study Steps to Learn a Word, found on pages 8–9 of the Pupil's Edition. **STUDENT SELF-ASSESSMENT**

Name _____

Read each sentence. Look at how the two words are spelled.
Fill in the circle next to the correct word.

SAMPLE: A bee _____ a birthday.   ● had ○ hod

1. He asked a duck _____ a cow.   ○ und ● and

2. He _____ a cake on the table.   ● put ○ pute

3. He _____ birthday hats.   ● got ○ gat

4. And _____ did his friends get him? ○ wat ● what

5. He got a bag _____ blocks.   ● of   ○ uf

Integrated Spelling   LESSON 27 • REVIEW   115

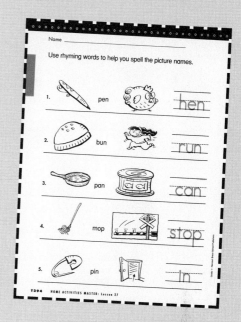

Name _____

Use rhyming words to help you spell the picture names.

1. pen — hen
2. bun — run
3. pan — can
4. mop — stop
5. pin — in

T294 HOME ACTIVITIES MASTER: Lesson 27

See page T294 for the Home Activities Master.

REVIEW OF SPELLING STRATEGIES
Review the spelling strategies discussed on pages 181–182 of the Pupil's Edition. Then distribute Home Activities Master Lesson 27, found on page T294.

The Reteach section of each Lesson Wrap-Up provides suggestions for helping children who are still having difficulty with the concepts taught in the lesson.

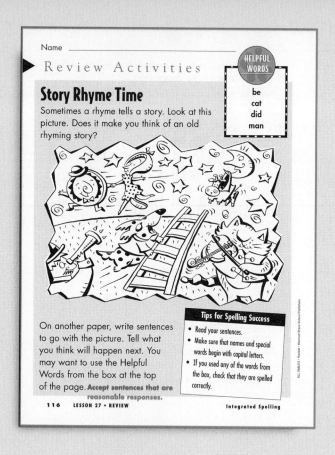

Name _____

Review Activities

HELPFUL WORDS

be
cat
did
man

Story Rhyme Time
Sometimes a rhyme tells a story. Look at this picture. Does it make you think of an old rhyming story?

On another paper, write sentences to go with the picture. Tell what you think will happen next. You may want to use the Helpful Words from the box at the top of the page. **Accept sentences that are reasonable responses.**

Tips for Spelling Success
- Read your sentences.
- Make sure that names and special words begin with capital letters.
- If you used any of the words from the box, check that they are spelled correctly.

116   LESSON 27 • REVIEW

Integrated Spelling

▶Review Activities

The activities on pages 116–117 of the Pupil's Edition emphasize writing (Story Rhyme Time) and word play (Word Magic). The Tips for Spelling Success point out the importance of knowing standard spellings and give children hints for proofreading and for applying spelling strategies.

STORY RHYME TIME Help children read the directions at the top of page 116. Then direct their attention to the illustration, which should remind them of the nursery rhyme "Hey Diddle Diddle." To refresh children's memory, lead them in reciting this rhyme.

Then read the directions under the illustration aloud. Point out and read aloud the list of Helpful Words that children may decide to use in their sentences. Then distribute primary-ruled paper, and have children write their sentences.

Point out the Tips for Spelling Success, and help children read this feature aloud.

As children proofread their work, you may want to provide them with the following checklist, or refer them to the proofreading checklist on page 180 of the Pupil's Edition.

WRITING SENTENCES/PROOFREADING

☐ Did I form the letters correctly?
☐ Did I spell the words correctly?
☐ Did I begin people's names and special words with capital letters?
☐ Did I end each sentence with the correct end mark?

If children need help in writing sentences, refer them to page 3 of the *Language Handbook*.

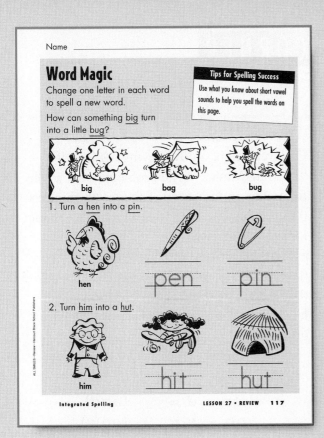

Word Magic

Change one letter in each word to spell a new word.

How can something big turn into a little bug?

Tips for Spelling Success

Use what you know about short vowel sounds to help you spell the words on this page.

big   bag   bug

1. Turn a hen into a pin.

hen   pen   pin

2. Turn him into a hut.

him   hit   hut

Integrated Spelling   LESSON 27 • REVIEW   117

"CHILDREN'S UNDERSTANDING *of spelling is based on a set of tacit hypotheses about phonetic relationships and sound-spelling correspondences, and children are able to modify these hypotheses readily as they encounter new information about standard spelling.*"

(Charles Read)

WORD MAGIC Read the directions at the top of page 117 with children. Direct their attention to the example, and help them figure out what spelling changes occurred when the word *big* was changed to *bag* and finally to *bug*. Make sure that children understand that only one letter is changed at a time to form each new word.

Focus attention on the first item, and help children identify the three pictures as a hen, a pen, and a pin. Explain that they will change one letter in the word *hen* to spell the name of the next picture. Then they will change one letter in that word to spell the word *pin*. You may want to guide children through both items in this section on the page, or you may want to have them work individually or cooperatively to complete the items.

Before children start to write, read aloud the Tips for Spelling Success. To help children use what they know about short vowel sounds, suggest that they say each picture name aloud and listen for the vowel sound to help them spell the word. Reinforce the sound-letter relationship by having children read aloud each word they write and identify the letter that they changed to create each new word. **USING SOUNDS AND LETTERS**

SPELLING SNAKES

To provide kinesthetic reinforcement of the Spelling Words in Lessons 19–26, give each child a ball of clay, and show children how to roll clay snakes. Have them use the snakes to form letters to make their Spelling Words.

STOP

SPELLING MYSTERY WORDS

Assign each child a partner, and have pairs play a mystery word game. Have each child select one of the review words listed on page T177 and write four or five clues about this mystery word. These clues might include the number of letters in the word, the vowel sound, a rhyming word clue, or a definition, synonym, or antonym for the word. Have children take turns posing their mystery words for their partners to guess, giving one clue at a time. When a word is correctly guessed, have the partners discuss the clues that were used.

SPELLING MATH

Children might enjoy playing a game of "Spelling Math." Write problems such as the following on the board. Then guide children through the first one, which involves subtracting a letter to form a Spelling Word. To extend the activity, challenge children to use the Spelling Words in Lessons 19–26 to write their own "Spelling Math" equations, and have them share them in pairs or in small groups.

$$putt - t = \underline{} \quad (put)$$
$$off - f = \underline{} \quad (of)$$
$$an + d = \underline{} \quad (and)$$
$$no + w = \underline{} \quad (now)$$
$$w + hat = \underline{} \quad (what)$$

SNOWMAN

Have children work in pairs to play a game of "Snowman." Children can take turns dictating the review words listed on page T177 for their partners to spell. Each time a child spells a word correctly, he or she may draw another part of a snowman. Continue the game until all words have been reviewed. Then have children compare their snowmen.

Words with Long *a*

OBJECTIVE

To spell words with long *a*

LESSON PLANNER

Assign words based on the children's developmental levels. See the Assignment Guide on page T11.

▶ INFORMAL ASSESSMENT

Children's writing may show that they have difficulty distinguishing between long *a* and other vowel sounds.

▼ **model**

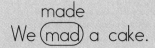

made

We (mad) a cake.

Use this lesson to introduce children to words in which the letters *a-e, ay*, or *ai* stand for the long *a* sound. Encourage children to apply what they have learned to help them spell other words with the long *a* sound. After children complete this lesson, remind them to proofread their writing and correct errors they may have made spelling the words in which the letters *a-e, ay*, or *ai* stand for the long *a* sound.

▶ LEARNING DIFFERENCES

Use the following suggestion and the ideas on page T188 to customize learning activities.

MEETING INDIVIDUAL NEEDS

Children Acquiring English

Children who are acquiring English may have difficulty distinguishing the long *a* sound from the short *e* sound. This is particularly true of children who speak Vietnamese, Spanish, or Tagalog. Provide children with practice listening to and pronouncing word pairs with these vowel sounds. As examples, use words such as the following: *wait, wet; sale, sell; wail, well; tale, tell; mate, met; gate, get; late, let;* and *main, men.*

COMPARING AND CONTRASTING

▶ PRETEST/POSTTEST CONTEXT SENTENCES

* 1. **came**   He **came** to the door.
* 2. **made**   She **made** a clay cat.
* 3. **wait**   We will **wait** for the bus.
  4. **play**   Let's **play** a game.

▶ PLAY DAY

Head a bulletin board with the words "Play Day," and ask children to say the words aloud. Elicit that the words rhyme and both end with the long *a* sound spelled *ay*. Invite children to think of things they like to do on a play day like Saturday. Challenge them to think of activities whose names contain the long *a* sound, such as skating, playing with clay, baking, sailing, or playing games. Have children draw and caption pictures of these activities to display on the "Play Day" bulletin board.

Play Day

skating | playing with clay

baking | sailing

* Words appearing in "Dreams."
Additional story words are *today, chased, sailed,* and *away.*

NOTE: Fill in blanks on the Home Activities Master before sending it home. See the Assignment Guide on page T11.

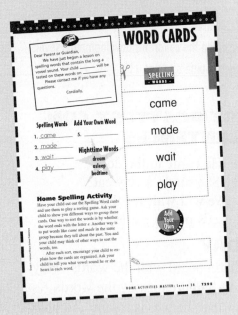

See page T295 for the Home Activities Master.

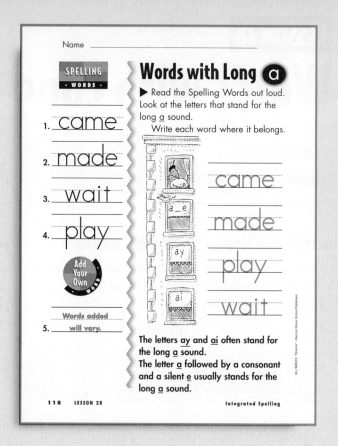

▶ Introduction

PRETEST   Administer the Pretest. Say each word, and then use it in the sentence provided on page T183 before repeating the word. **ACCESSING PRIOR KNOWLEDGE**

SELF-CHECK   Have children refer to their lists of Spelling Words to check their Pretests. For each word children misspell on the Pretest, remind them to follow the Study Steps to Learn a Word. **STUDENT SELF-ASSESSMENT**

INTRODUCING THE LESSON

To use the open sort, copy Home Activities Master Lesson 28, found on page T295.

Open Sort: After distributing the word cards, help children think of ways to sort the words. For example, they might make a group of words that end with *e*, or a group of words in which *a* is the second letter.

Closed Sort: Help children read aloud the lesson title and the Spelling Words on page 118.

• Ask children what they notice about the vowel sound in each word. (Each has the long *a* sound.)

• Have children tell what letters stand for the long *a* sound in each word. (*a-e, ay, ai*)

Review the directions, and have children write each Spelling Word in the correct space, based on which letters stand for the long *a* sound: *a-e, ay,* or *ai*. **SORTING WORDS**

IN SUMMARY   Ask children what they have learned about how to spell words that have the long *a* sound. (The long *a* sound may be spelled *a-e, ay,* or *ai*.) **RECOGNIZING PHONIC ELEMENTS**

Spelling Log   Suggest that children look at signs posted in school hallways to find other words with the long *a* sound. Ask children to list the words in their Spelling Logs and write one on the line provided on Pupil's Edition page 118. **RECOGNIZING PATTERNS**

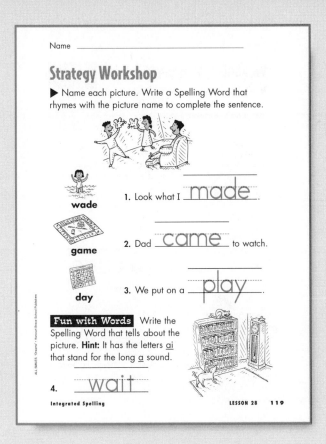

Name _____

Strategy Workshop

▶ Name each picture. Write a Spelling Word that rhymes with the picture name to complete the sentence.

wade

1. Look what I _made_.

game

2. Dad _came_ to watch.

day

3. We put on a _play_.

Fun with Words Write the Spelling Word that tells about the picture. **Hint:** It has the letters _ai_ that stand for the long _a_ sound.

4. _wait_

Integrated Spelling

LESSON 28   119

Strategy Workshop

RHYMING WORDS Read the directions at the top of page 119 aloud. Talk about the picture at the top of the page, and ask volunteers to describe what the people are doing. Then tell children to look at the pictures next to the sentences and read the label for each one aloud. Explain to children that they can use a rhyming word strategy to write the correct Spelling Word to complete each sentence.

APPLYING SPELLING STRATEGIES

FUN WITH WORDS Read the directions with children and discuss the illustration. Ask children which Spelling Word describes what the animals in the picture are doing. Have them confirm their guesses by reading the hint. After children write their responses, have them share their answers.

Children Acquiring English Some meanings of the word _play_ may be unfamiliar to children who are acquiring

English. You may want to present these example sentences and discuss the meaning of _play_ in each one:

Let's go to the park and _play_. (have fun)
We put on a puppet _play_. (a show)
I can _play_ the violin. (perform on an instrument)

UNDERSTANDING WORD MEANINGS

Phonetic Spellers Children using a phonetic system of spelling may omit the final, silent _e_ on the words _made_ and _came_. Have them segment the three sounds in each of these words and write the letters that stand for the sounds. Then have them add the silent _e_ to transform the short _a_ vowel sound into the long _a_ sound.

Name _____

Vocabulary WordShop

▶ Look at the pictures. Write a word from the box in each question. Then circle yes or no to answer.

Nighttime
· WORDS ·
dream
asleep
bedtime

1. Is it **bedtime**?
   (yes)   no

2. Will the boy fall **asleep**?
   yes   (no)

3. Will his **dream** make him happy?
   (yes)   no

120   LESSON 28   Integrated Spelling

▶ Vocabulary WordShop

Nighttime
· WORDS ·

Spelling Log Darken the room and ask children to pretend it is nighttime. Have children brainstorm words they associate with night and then write them in their Spelling Logs.

MEETING INDIVIDUAL NEEDS

Transitional Spellers You may want to assign this level of spellers the WordShop Words as additional spelling words.

WORDSHOP WORDS Help children read the WordShop Words on page 120 aloud. Ask children to tell why each word belongs in a group of Nighttime Words. Then read the directions with children. Discuss the illustrations, and have children tell what the boy is doing in each. Explain that they will complete each asking sentence by writing a Nighttime Word. Then they should circle the word below each question that tells what they think will happen. Emphasize that, as they respond, they should think of reasons to

explain their answers. After children complete the page, have them share and explain their responses.

MEETING INDIVIDUAL NEEDS

Semi-Phonetic Spellers Suggest that children count the letters in a word before they write it. After they write the word, have children check to make sure they have written the correct number of consonants and vowels.

EXPLORING NIGHTTIME WORDS Write *nighttime* and *bedtime* on the board. Guide children to conclude that both are compound words and both contain the smaller word *time*.

• Help children develop a list of other compounds containing the word *time* by asking the following:

What time is it when you play? (*playtime*)

What time is it when you eat dinner? (*dinnertime*)

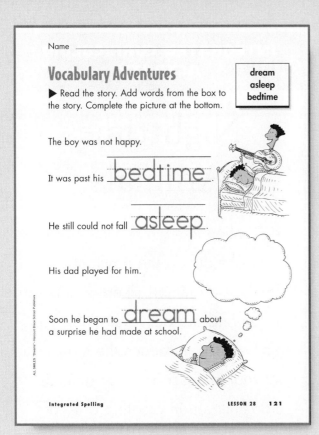

Name _____

Vocabulary Adventures

▶ Read the story. Add words from the box to the story. Complete the picture at the bottom.

| dream |
| asleep |
| bedtime |

The boy was not happy.

It was past his **bedtime**

He still could not fall **asleep**.

His dad played for him.

Soon he began to **dream** about a surprise he had made at school.

Integrated Spelling   LESSON 28   121

"CHILDREN DEVELOP *in their ability to manipulate words just as they develop in other areas. As children learn to spell, they use their increased knowledge about words and letters while they spell.*"
(James Wheelock Beers, Carol Strickland Beers, Karen Grant)

VOCABULARY ADVENTURES

Read the directions at the top of page 121, and point out the Nighttime Words in the box. Explain that children can figure out what to draw in the bubble at the bottom of the page after they write the Nighttime Words to complete the story. Before children begin to work, suggest they look at the pictures and read the story, pausing for each blank. **USING NAMING AND ACTION WORDS**

 Working Together Children can work in pairs to complete the drawing part of this activity. Encourage partners to talk about their ideas, and suggest that they might want to sketch them on scrap paper first. Have children share their final drawings in a small group.

POSTTEST Remind children to study any Spelling Words they misspelled on the Pretest. Then use the context sentences on page T183 to administer the Posttest.

Optional Writing Idea

 Collaborative Writing: Story Children can work with a partner to write a story about the boy's dream they illustrated on Pupil's Edition page 121. To help children plan their story, ask the following questions:

1. Whom is the story about?

2. Where does the story take place?

3. What happens in the story?

4. How does the story end?

Suggest children read the revised version of their story aloud.

Lesson 28   **T187**

▶Lesson Wrap-Up

WORDSHOP WORDS AND CONTEXT SENTENCES

1. **dream**   Last night, I had a bad **dream.**
2. **asleep**   The baby is **asleep** in her crib.
3. **bedtime**   Her **bedtime** is eight o'clock.

▶Reteach

LEARNING DIFFERENCES

Some children with learning and language disabilities may benefit by focusing on the letters that stand for the long *a* vowel sound. Make word cards for each Spelling Word, omitting the letters *a-e, ai,* or *ay*. Give children the cards, and have them use a red marker to write the missing letters to complete each word. Then have them read and spell the words aloud, emphasizing the letters that stand for the vowel sound. Finally, using the cards as models, have them practice writing the words on primary-ruled paper.

VISUAL/AUDITORY/KINESTHETIC MODALITIES

Nighttime Animals

Mention that while most animals are awake during the daylight hours, some animals sleep during the day and are active at night. You might want to introduce the term *nocturnal* to describe these animals. Guide children in creating a list of nocturnal animals. (Possible responses: cats, gerbils, hamsters, mice, rats, coyotes, raccoons, owls, skunks)

Suggest that children work with a partner or in a small group to create a comic-strip-style story about one of the animals on the list. In their strip, they might want to show a nighttime adventure that the animal has. Provide a place where children can display their comic strips for others to enjoy.

SCIENCE

Words with *th*

OBJECTIVE

To spell words with initial *th*

LESSON PLANNER

Assign words based on children's developmental levels. See the Assignment Guide on page T11.

▶ INFORMAL ASSESSMENT

Children's writing may show that they have difficulty with the initial *th* digraph.

▼ model

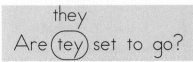

they
Are (tey) set to go?

Use this lesson to introduce the spelling of words with initial *th*, found in words such as *the* and *then*. After children complete this lesson, encourage them to proofread their writing and correct errors they may have made in spelling words with initial *th*.

▶ LEARNING DIFFERENCES

Use the following suggestion and the ideas on page T194 to customize learning activities.

MEETING INDIVIDUAL NEEDS

Children Acquiring English
Children who are acquiring English may have difficulty understanding the meanings of the Spelling Words in this lesson. Point out that the word *then* is used to describe the time that something happens, as "We will eat, and *then* we will go outside." The article *the* and the adjective *that* can be demonstrated by pointing out objects as you name them, for example, "*the* door" or "*that* book." Explain that when something is at a distance, we use the word *that*. Mention that the word *they* is used to stand for more than one person or thing, for example, "My friends missed the movie because *they* were late." **BUILDING VOCABULARY**

▶ PRETEST/POSTTEST CONTEXT SENTENCES

* 1. **the** Is **the** red hat yours?
* 2. **then** Let's eat and **then** play.
* 3. **that** Please hand me **that** ball.
  4. **they** Are **they** in your class?

▶ THIS AND THAT

Explain to children that they will frequently use words such as *the, then, that*, and *they* in their writing. Challenge them to look and listen for other words that start with the same letters and sound as the Spelling Words. Encourage children to add these and similar words to the classroom word wall in a section devoted to words that begin with the digraph *th*. Possible words might include *this, them, there, these*, and *their*.

---

* Words appearing in "Henry and Mudge in the Green Time." An additional story word is *this*.

NOTE: Fill in blanks on the Home Activities Master before sending it home. See the Assignment Guide on page T11.

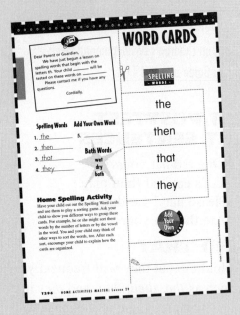

See page T296 for the Home Activities Master.

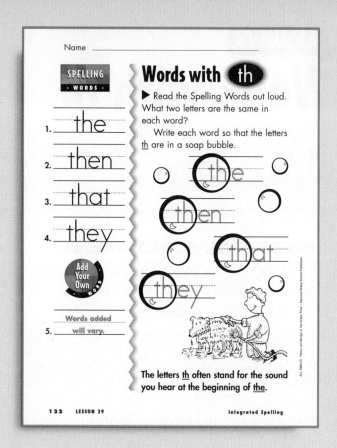

The letters th often stand for the sound you hear at the beginning of the.

▶ Introduction

PRETEST Administer the Pretest. Say each word, and then use it in the sentence provided on page T189 before repeating the word. **ACCESSING PRIOR KNOWLEDGE**

SELF-CHECK Have children refer to their lists of Spelling Words to check their Pretests. For each word children misspell on the Pretest, remind them to follow the Study Steps to Learn a Word, found on pages 8–9 of the Pupil's Edition. **STUDENT SELF-ASSESSMENT**

INTRODUCING THE LESSON

Begin by helping children read the title of the lesson and the Spelling Words on page 122.

- Direct children's attention to the Spelling Words. Then ask them what is the same about all the words. Guide them to discover that all four words begin with the same two letters.

- Have children pronounce the words and listen for the beginning sound. Elicit that the letters *th* combine to make a single sound.

- Read the directions at the top of the page. As children write the words, remind them to write the letters *th* inside the soap bubbles.

- You may want to send home the Home Activities Master Lesson 29, found on page T296. **RECOGNIZING PATTERNS**

IN SUMMARY Ask children what they have learned about how to spell words that begin with the sound they hear in *the*. (The word probably begins with the letters *th*.) **RECOGNIZING PATTERNS**

Spelling Log Have children look at story titles to find other words that begin with *th* and are pronounced like *the*. Ask children to list the words they find in their Spelling Logs and write one on the line provided on Pupil's Edition page 122. **RECOGNIZING PATTERNS**

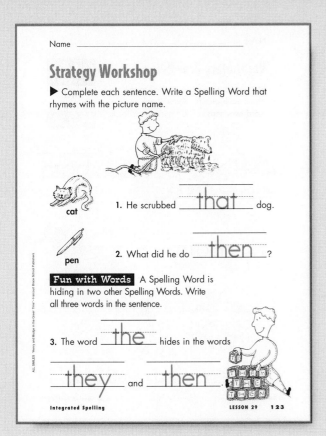

Name _____

Strategy Workshop

▶ Complete each sentence. Write a Spelling Word that rhymes with the picture name.

cat

1. He scrubbed ___that___ dog.

pen

2. What did he do ___then___ ?

Fun with Words A Spelling Word is hiding in two other Spelling Words. Write all three words in the sentence.

3. The word ___the___ hides in the words

 ___they___ and ___then___ .

Integrated Spelling   LESSON 29   123

▶ Strategy Workshop

RHYMING WORDS Help children read the directions at the top of page 123. Focus attention on the large illustration, and ask volunteers to describe what the boy is doing. Then point out the small pictures next to the sentences, and have the picture labels read aloud. Explain that children can use a rhyming strategy to help them write the correct Spelling Word to complete each sentence. After children write their responses, have them share and compare them. **APPLYING SPELLING STRATEGIES**

FUN WITH WORDS Read the directions with children. Then call attention to the illustration, and have children read aloud the three words shown on the blocks. Explain that they can find one of their Spelling Words in the other two words. Have children identify the hidden word as *the*. After children identify the two words in which they see *the* as *they* and *then*, have them complete the sentence.

Children Acquiring English Some children may mispronounce the beginning digraph sound that *th* stands for as /d/. This mispronunciation may in turn lead to incorrect spelling. To remedy this problem, model the correct pronunciation of each Spelling Word and have children repeat the word after you several times. **PRACTICING PRONUNCIATION**

Semi-Phonetic and Phonetic Spellers Remind children that two consonants together can sometimes stand for one sound. To reinforce this, have children circle the letters *th* each time they write a Spelling Word.

Challenge You may want to challenge children to learn to spell additional words that begin with the same sound they hear in the words *the* and *then*, for example, *them, there,* and *those*.

Lesson 29   **T191**

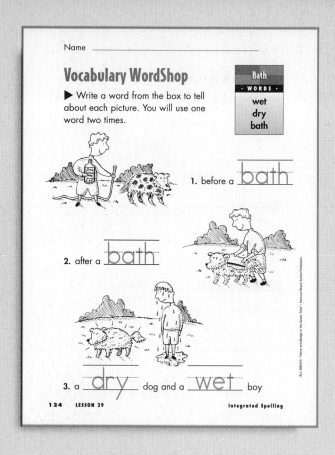

Name _____

Vocabulary WordShop

▶ Write a word from the box to tell about each picture. You will use one word two times.

Bath
• WORDS •
wet
dry
bath

1. before a bath

2. after a bath

3. a dry dog and a wet boy

124   LESSON 29   Integrated Spelling

▶ Vocabulary WordShop

Spelling Log Invite children to look for other words that have to do with bathing. Suggest that they write these words in their Spelling Logs.

Transitional Spellers You may want to assign this level of spellers the WordShop Words as additional spelling words.

WORDSHOP WORDS

Read the WordShop Words on page 124 aloud. Mention that all of these words can be used to tell about a bath. Read the directions, and ask children to describe what they see in the pictures. Explain that they will write a Bath Word to complete each phrase that tells about the pictures. Point out that children will write one of the Bath Words more than once. If necessary, give assistance with the time words *before* and *after*, making sure that children understand their meanings. After children

have completed the page, have them share and discuss their responses.

Phonetic Spellers Draw attention to the *th* digraph in the word *bath*. Remind children that even though they hear only one sound when they pronounce this digraph, they must write it as two letters, *t* and *h*.

EXPLORING BATH WORDS

Use the words on Pupil's Edition page 124 to explore both opposite and analogous relationships.

• Focus children's attention on the first and second phrases. Point out that the words *before* and *after* have opposite meanings. Have children read the third and fourth phrases and identify two other words that are opposites. (*wet* and *dry*)

• Write the following analogy on the board. Ask children to use one of the Bath Words to complete it.

Water can make you wet.

A towel can make you ____.

Name _____

Vocabulary Adventures

▶ Follow the directions.

1. Color things used to make something <u>wet</u>.
Children should color the circled items.

2. Color things used to make something <u>dry</u>.
Children should color the circled items.

3. Draw things that you use to take a <u>bath</u>.

Accept reasonable responses.

Integrated Spelling   LESSON 29   **125**

"**A**LTHOUGH THE GREEK *alphabet had separate letters (theta and delta) for the initial sounds in* then *and* thin, *the Roman alphabet did not. In English, the digraph* th *stands for each of these two differ-ent sounds.*"

VOCABULARY ADVENTURES

After reading the direction line at the top of page 125, provide children with crayons. Then help them read the directions above each set of pictures and discuss the pictures. In the first item, children are to color things used to make something *wet*; in the second item, they are to color things used to make something *dry*. After children have shared their answers for the first two items, read the directions for item 3, and have children draw their responses. **USING DESCRIBING AND NAMING WORDS**

POSTTEST
Remind children to study any Spelling Words they misspelled on the Pretest. Then use the context sentences on page T189 to administer the Posttest.

Optional Writing Idea

Shared Writing: Poem
Have children suggest words that rhyme with *wet*. You may want to record their responses in a web.

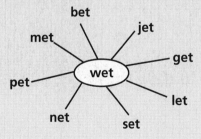

Then have the class work together to dictate a rhyming poem or a rap that describes what funny things might happen when a pet gets wet. Record suggested lines on chart paper and then revise the lines as a group. If children create a rap, suggest that they make up a clap-and-snap rhythm, and chant their rap aloud.

▶Lesson Wrap-Up

WORDSHOP WORDS AND CONTEXT SENTENCES

1. **wet**   My cat hates to get **wet**.
2. **dry**   The paint is not **dry**.
3. **bath**   We will give the dog a **bath**.

▶Reteach

LEARNING DIFFERENCES

Children with visual processing deficits may find it difficult to memorize the spelling of words. Invite children who are having difficulty with the words in this lesson to work at the board. As they observe, write a Spelling Word on the board, calling attention to each letter as you write it. While children look at the word, have them say the word, spell it orally, and then say it again. Then have children use water and paintbrushes to "paint" the word on the board. Before the water evaporates, have them check their word against the model on the board. Repeat this procedure to review all the Spelling Words. **VISUAL/ KINESTHETIC MODALITIES**

Everyday Words

Remind children that the Spelling Words for this lesson are words they use every day. Point out that the word *the* is among the five most frequently used words in the English language.

Give children four colors of crayons, and have them assign a color to one of the Spelling Words, for example:

red = *the*   green = *then*

blue = *that*   yellow = *they*

Then suggest children hunt for these words in a piece of their own writing. Each time they find one of the words, have them use the appropriate crayon to circle it. Then have them come up with a tally for each word. Conclude the activity by creating a class chart summarizing the findings.

How Many Times We Found Each Word	
the	150 times
then	30 times
that	52 times
they	47 times

More Words to Remember

OBJECTIVE
To spell words that are used frequently

LESSON PLANNER
Assign words based on children's developmental levels. See the Assignment Guide on page T11.

▶ INFORMAL ASSESSMENT
Children's writing may show that they have difficulty spelling some frequently used words.

▼ model

We will (du) our work.

Use this lesson to introduce the spelling of some words that children use frequently in their writing. After children complete this lesson, encourage them to proofread their writing and correct errors they may have made in spelling these words.

▶ LEARNING DIFFERENCES
Use the following suggestion and the ideas on page T200 to customize learning activities.

Children Acquiring English
The short vowel sounds in English often present difficulty for children who are acquiring English. Three of the words in this lesson contain the short sounds *a, i,* and *u*. For specific suggestions regarding the short sound *a,* see Lesson 23 (page T153). For the short sound *i,* see Lesson 21 (page T141). For the short *u* sound, see Lesson 20 (page T135).

COMPARING AND CONTRASTING

▶ PRETEST/POSTTEST CONTEXT SENTENCES

* 1. **have** Cats **have** sharp claws.
* 2. **live** Bats **live** in the barn.
* 3. **do** The dogs **do** need a bath.
  4. **some** The cat wants **some** water.

▶ HAVE SOME USEFUL WORDS
Devote one section of your classroom word wall to words that children use often in their writing. You might want to encourage children to add words that frequently present spelling problems for them. Possible words include the following: *love, very, could, coming, every, goes, where, thank, sure, been,* and *also.*

* Words appearing in "Pets."

**NOTE: Fill in blanks on the Home Activities
Master before sending it home.
See the Assignment Guide on page T11.**

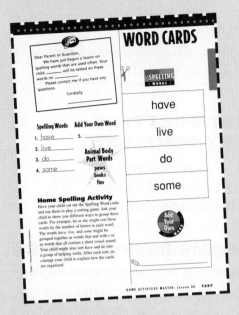

See page T297 for the Home Activities Master.

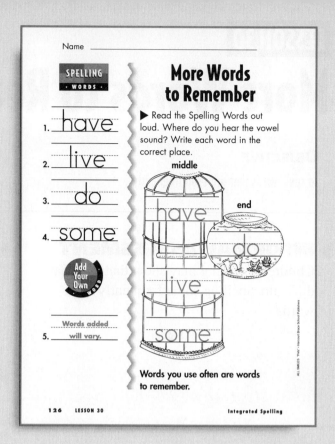

▶ Introduction

PRETEST
Administer the Pretest. Say each word, and then use it in the sentence provided on page T195 before repeating the word. **ACCESSING PRIOR KNOWLEDGE**

SELF-CHECK
Have children refer to their lists of Spelling Words to check their Pretests. For each word children misspell on the Pretest, remind them to follow the Study Steps to Learn a Word. **STUDENT SELF-ASSESSMENT**

INTRODUCING THE LESSON
To use the open sort, copy Home Activities Master Lesson 30, found on page T297.

Open Sort: After distributing the word cards, help children think of ways to sort the words. Possibilities include sorting by the number of letters, by words containing a short vowel sound, or by words ending with the letter *e*.

Closed Sort: Help children read aloud the lesson title and the Spelling Words on page 126.

- Have children say each word and listen for the vowel sound. Guide them to understand that in three of the words they hear the vowel sound in the middle, and in one word, they hear it at the end.

- Suggest that children write the words in which they hear the vowel sound in the middle under the heading *middle*. Then have them write the word in which they hear the vowel sound at the end under the heading *end*. **SORTING WORDS**

IN SUMMARY
Ask children what they have learned about spelling words they use often. (You can study the words to remember how to spell them.) **DEVELOPING SPELLING LISTS**

Spelling Log Suggest that children look through their writing to find other words that they want to remember how to spell. Have children add these words to their Spelling Logs and write one on the line provided on Pupil's Edition page 126. **DEVELOPING SPELLING LISTS**

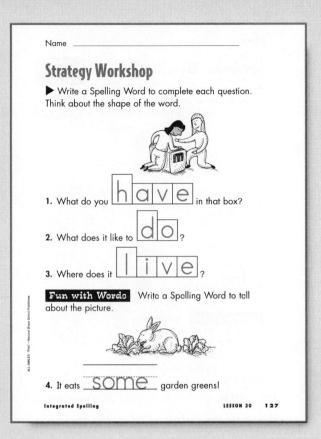

Name _____

Strategy Workshop

▶ Write a Spelling Word to complete each question.
Think about the shape of the word.

1. What do you [have] in that box?

2. What does it like to [do]?

3. Where does it [live]?

Fun with Words Write a Spelling Word to tell
about the picture.

4. It eats some garden greens!

Integrated Spelling   LESSON 30   127

Strategy Workshop

WORD SHAPES Read the directions at the top of page 127 aloud. Then call on volunteers to describe the shapes of the letters in the Spelling Words. Elicit that the letters *h, d,* and *l* are tall; however, in this group of words, none of the letters drop below the line. Help children recall that remembering how a word looks is a strategy that can help them spell the word correctly.

Focus attention on the illustration, and have children describe what the two girls are doing. Before children write the Spelling Words to complete the sentences, encourage them to trace the word shapes with their fingers. After children have completed the sentences, ask volunteers to read them aloud.

APPLYING SPELLING STRATEGIES

FUN WITH WORDS Help children read the directions, and then talk about the picture. Before children write a Spelling Word to complete the sentence, make sure they understand that *garden greens* refer to leafy vegetables such as lettuce and spinach.

MEETING INDIVIDUAL NEEDS

Semi-Phonetic and Phonetic Spellers Since children at these levels spell words the way they sound, they may omit the final, silent *e* on three of the Spelling Words. To help children remember to add the letter to the words, suggest simple mnemonics, such as the following:

Some have final *e.*
I can't *live* without final *e*!

MEETING INDIVIDUAL NEEDS

Challenge You may want to challenge children to write answers to the questions posed on Pupil's Edition page 127. Encourage children to use Spelling Words from this lesson in their responses.

►Vocabulary WordShop

Spelling Log Invite children to find other words that name animal body parts in the reading selection "Pets." Suggest that they write these words in their Spelling Logs.

Transitional Spellers You may want to assign this level of spellers the WordShop Words as additional spelling words.

WORDSHOP WORDS
Point out the WordShop Words at the top of page 128, and have them read aloud. Then talk with children about how these words are alike. (They all name animal body parts.)

Focus children's attention on the pictures, and explain that each picture shows a part of a different animal. Suggest children use picture clues to guess the animals. Then have them label each picture with the name of the animal body part that is showing. Invite children to share their responses with partners or the group.

IMAGINE THAT!
After reading the directions with children, make sure they understand that they will draw an imaginary animal. Provide children with drawing materials, and remind them to make up a name for the creature they draw.

EXPLORING ANIMAL BODY PART WORDS
Use the WordShop Words to explore characteristics of mammals, birds, and fish.

• Lead children in concluding that the WordShop Words identify three groups of animals: those with paws, those with beaks, and those with fins. Point out that the animal groups are mammals, birds, and fish.

• Discuss with children other animal body parts that are found on mammals, birds, and fish. For example, birds have feathers, fish have scales, and mammals have fur.

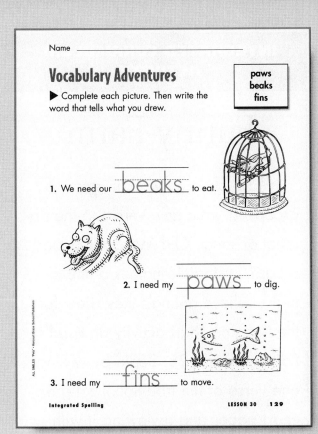

Name _____

Vocabulary Adventures

▶ Complete each picture. Then write the word that tells what you drew.

| paws |
| beaks |
| fins |

1. We need our beaks to eat.

2. I need my paws to dig.

3. I need my fins to move.

Integrated Spelling

LESSON 30   129

"**W**ALL CHARTS ARE USED *to group words around a theme: key vocabulary from a story, common words that need to be spelled correctly, content words, family words, holiday words, and so on. Lists and charts are also compiled to go along with the seasons, months, and topics of study and interest.*"
(Ethel Buchanan)

VOCABULARY ADVENTURES

Read the directions at the top of page 129 with children, and have them examine the illustrations. Explain that the words in the box name the animal body parts that are missing in the pictures. Have children read the incomplete sentences and then complete both the pictures and the sentences. **USING NAMING WORDS**

 Working Together This activity lends itself to children working in pairs. Suggest that they confer before drawing the missing animal body parts. Then have them take turns writing the words to complete the sentences.

POSTTEST
Remind children to study any Spelling Words they misspelled on the Pretest. Then use the context sentences on page T195 to administer the Posttest.

Optional Writing Idea

 Independent Writing: Friendly Letter Ask children to imagine that the animal they drew for the Imagine That! activity on Pupil's Edition page 128 comes to life. What special care does this pet need? Have children make notes and then write a letter to a friend telling how they care for this pet. Before children begin to write, display this friendly letter and review its five parts.

Date	November 30, 1999
Greeting	Dear Luis,
Body	I have a new pet. It has paws, fins, and a beak. Its name is Wally! I feed it birdseed and cat food. It sleeps in a fishbowl. I take it for walks.
Closing	Your friend,
Signature	Marissa

▶ Lesson Wrap-Up

WORDSHOP WORDS AND CONTEXT SENTENCES

1. **paws**   A dog has four **paws**.
2. **beaks**   Owls have sharp **beaks**.
3. **fins**   Sharks have big **fins**.

▶ Reteach

LEARNING DIFFERENCES

Children with attention deficits can sometimes benefit from large muscle movement when engaged in spelling activities. Try several of these techniques with children to help them master their Spelling Words.

• Have children march up and down a flight of stairs as they spell a word aloud. After they pronounce each letter, have them move to the next step.

• Have children alternately stand up and sit down as they say each letter in a word. For example: *l* (stand), *i* (sit), *v* (stand), *e* (sit).

• Have children sit on the floor when saying a vowel as they spell a word aloud.

After leading children in a variety of body movement exercises while spelling words aloud, invite volunteers to make up their own sequence of body movements to share with the class. **KINESTHETIC/AUDITORY MODALITIES**

INTEGRATED CURRICULUM ACTIVITY

Funny Farm

Have children work in small groups to write new verses to the traditional song "Old MacDonald Had a Farm" using the names of the make-believe animals they drew for the Imagine That! activity on Pupil's Edition page 128. Begin by writing one verse of the traditional song on chart paper and reviewing it with children. Then have children fill in their new animal names and funny-noise words that stand for the sounds these animals make.

Old MacDonald had a farm,
E-I-E-I-O!
And on this farm he had some ____,
E-I-E-I-O!
With a ____, ____ here,
and a ____, ____ there;
Here a ____, there a ____,
everywhere a ____, ____.
Old MacDonald had a farm,
E-I-E-I-O!

Words with Long *e*

OBJECTIVE
To spell words with long *e*

LESSON PLANNER
Assign words based on children's developmental levels. See the Assignment Guide on page T11.

▶ INFORMAL ASSESSMENT
Children's writing may show that they have difficulty distinguishing between long *e* and other vowel sounds.

▼ model

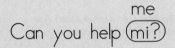

Can you help (mi?)

Use this lesson to introduce the spelling of words in which the letter *e* stands for the long *e* sound. Encourage children to apply what they have learned to help them spell other words with the long *e* sound. After children complete this lesson, have them proofread their writing and correct errors they may have made in spelling words in which the letter *e* stands for the long *e* sound.

▶ LEARNING DIFFERENCES
Use the following suggestion and the ideas on page T206 to customize learning activities.

Children Acquiring English
To help children understand the meanings of these Spelling Words, present them in context sentences. You might describe the actions of various boys and girls in the classroom, emphasizing the words *he* and *she* in sentences. For example: *He* is reading a book. *She* is playing with blocks. Have children in the group describe their own actions, using the word *we*. Then call on individual children to ask for something, using the word *me*. For example: Please give *me* that pencil.

UNDERSTANDING WORD MEANINGS

▶ PRETEST/POSTTEST CONTEXT SENTENCES
* 1. **we**   May **we** go with you?
* 2. **she**   Mom said **she** will be late.
* 3. **he**   Dad says **he** will take us to the zoo.
* 4. **me**   Will you lend **me** a pen?

▶ ME, HE, SHE DOLLS
Give each child a half sheet of drawing paper, crayons, and primary scissors. Then show children how to accordion-fold the paper into thirds. On the top fold, have them draw a doll with arms extended to the folds, as shown.

Have children cut out the figure, making sure not to cut the parts on the fold. Then have them color the dolls to show themselves, a girl, and a boy. Have them write the words *me, she*, and *he* to label the dolls. Then display the paper dolls on a bulletin board.

* Words appearing in "The Adventures of Snail at School." An additional story word is *be.*

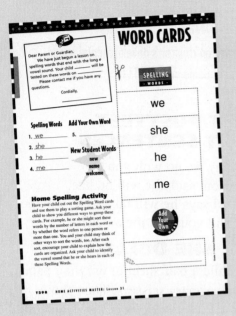

**NOTE: Fill in blanks on the Home Activities Master before sending it home.
See the Assignment Guide on page T11.**

See page T298 for the Home Activities Master.

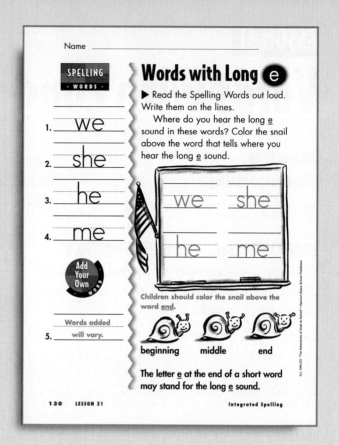

▶ Introduction

PRETEST Administer the Pretest. Say each word, and then use it in the sentence provided on page T201 before repeating the word. **ACCESSING PRIOR KNOWLEDGE**

SELF-CHECK Have children refer to their lists of Spelling Words to check their Pretests. For each word children misspell on the Pretest, remind them to follow the Study Steps to Learn a Word. **STUDENT SELF-ASSESSMENT**

INTRODUCING THE LESSON

To use the open sort, copy Home Activities Master Lesson 31, found on page T298.

Open Sort: After distributing the word cards, help children think of ways to sort the words. Possible sorts might include counting the number of letters or grouping the words by whether they refer to one person or more than one person.

Closed Sort: Help children read aloud the lesson title and the Spelling Words on page 130.

• Invite children to tell what they notice about the vowel sound in all the words. (All words have the long *e* sound.)

• Ask children where they hear the long *e* vowel sound in each word. (at the end)

Review the directions, and have children write the Spelling Words. Provide children with crayons and have them color the snail above the word that tells where they hear the vowel sound in all four Spelling Words. **SORTING WORDS**

IN SUMMARY Ask children what they have learned about how to spell words that have the long *e* sound at the end. (The long *e* sound may be spelled with the letter *e*.) **RECOGNIZING PHONIC ELEMENTS**

Spelling Log Suggest that children look through the reading selection to find other long *e* words. Have them add these words to their Spelling Logs and write one on the line provided on Pupil's Edition page 130. **RECOGNIZING PATTERNS**

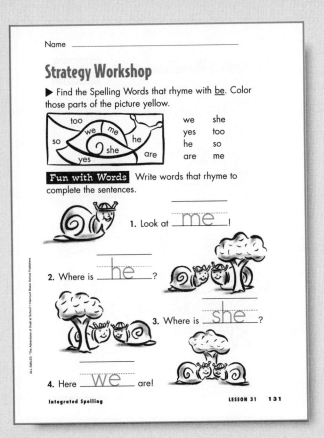

Name _____

Strategy Workshop

▶ Find the Spelling Words that rhyme with <u>be</u>. Color those parts of the picture yellow.

we	she
yes	too
he	so
are	me

Fun with Words Write words that rhyme to complete the sentences.

1. Look at __me__ !

2. Where is __he__ ?

3. Where is __she__ ?

4. Here __we__ are!

Integrated Spelling

LESSON 31   131

▶ Strategy Workshop

RHYMING WORDS Read the directions at the top of page 131 aloud. Have children read the words on the puzzle pieces aloud. Then have them use a yellow crayon to color each puzzle piece that has a word written on it that rhymes with *be*. Encourage children to share and compare their completed pictures. Conclude the activity by having children identify the animal they found in the puzzle. (snail) **APPLYING SPELLING STRATEGIES**

FUN WITH WORDS Help children read the directions and discuss the illustrations. Ask children which Spelling Word tells about each picture, giving help if necessary by identifying the gender of each character. After children have written a word to complete each sentence, call on volunteers to read the sentences aloud.

MEETING INDIVIDUAL NEEDS

Semi-Phonetic and Phonetic Spellers You can use the Spelling Words in this lesson to emphasize the importance of vowel letters. Begin by writing the initial consonant or digraph of each Spelling Word on the board, and have children pronounce the sound. Elicit from children that these sounds by themselves are not words. Explain that to spell a word, they need to write a vowel to stand for the long *e* sound that they hear in *we, she, he*, and *me*. Have volunteers use colored chalk to write the letter *e* after each consonant or digraph to form a Spelling Word. Have children pronounce each word aloud, emphasizing the long *e* sound.

MEETING INDIVIDUAL NEEDS

Challenge Explain that the long *e* sound at the end of a word can also be spelled with two *e*'s, as in the words *see, tree, free*, and *bee*. Children might want to learn to spell one or more of these words.

Lesson 31   T203

▶ Vocabulary WordShop

Spelling Log Invite children to look at materials posted on classroom bulletin boards for other words that relate to students and school. Suggest that they write these words in their Spelling Logs.

Transitional Spellers You may want to assign this level of spellers the WordShop Words as additional spelling words.

WORDSHOP WORDS

Ask a volunteer to read the WordShop Words on page 132 aloud. Point out that all these words could be used when talking about a new student. Read the directions with children, and then discuss the illustrations. Help children read the greetings in the speech balloons in the picture. If children are unfamiliar with the languages, identify the greetings as English, Spanish, and French words of welcome. After children write the WordShop Words, have them share and explain their answers.

Children Acquiring English Invite children who speak other languages to teach the class welcoming phrases in their native language. **REINFORCING SELF-ESTEEM**

EXPLORING NEW STUDENT WORDS

Talk with children about what it is like to be a new student in a school or class. To focus the discussion, you might ask the following:

• What does it feel like when you join a class where you don't know anyone?

• What are some things you might do to make a new student in our class feel welcome?

• If you were a new student, what things might you do to make friends?

Conclude the discussion by developing a list of some welcoming traditions. Playing some name games, assigning a class mentor, or giving new students a school tour are possibilities.

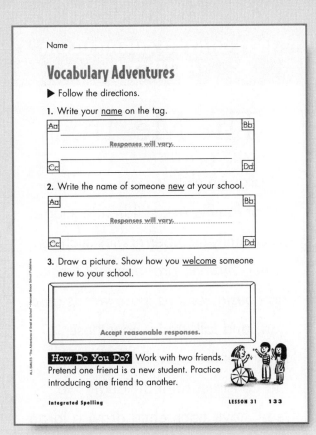

Vocabulary Adventures

▶ Follow the directions.

1. Write your <u>name</u> on the tag.

Aa		Bb
	Responses will vary.	
Cc		Dd

2. Write the name of someone <u>new</u> at your school.

Aa		Bb
	Responses will vary.	
Cc		Dd

3. Draw a picture. Show how you <u>welcome</u> someone new to your school.

Accept reasonable responses.

How Do You Do? Work with two friends. Pretend one friend is a new student. Practice introducing one friend to another.

Integrated Spelling   LESSON 31   133

> **"S**PELLING KNOWLEDGE *develops according to identifiable stages, and it is learned through reading, writing, and systematic study. It is a powerful engine that drives much of conventional reading and writing.***"**
> *(Shane Templeton)*

VOCABULARY ADVENTURES

Read the directions at the top of page 133 aloud. Then help children read the directions for item 1. You may want to have children complete the task before they work on item 2, or you may prefer to discuss all the items before children begin to work.

Have children share and discuss the names they wrote as well as their drawings. Point out that children might have drawn different pictures for item 3. Ask children to explain what they drew for that item and to tell why. **UNDERSTANDING WORD MEANINGS**

HOW DO YOU DO?
Have children follow along as you read the directions aloud. Then assign children to work in groups of three to practice their introductions. You may want to suggest that children try and use at least one of the Spelling Words in their introductions.

POSTTEST
Remind children to study any Spelling Words they misspelled on the Pretest. Then use the context sentences on page T201 to administer the Posttest.

Optional Writing Idea

Collaborative Writing: Dialogue Talk with children about what two children who had just met might say to each other. As children suggest conversation topics, you might want to record their ideas on a chart.

Child 1	Child 2
Where did you use to live?	I used to live in Florida.
What games do you like to play?	I like to play soccer.

Have children work with a partner to choose the sentences they want to include in their written dialogue. Encourage them to revise the dialogue by changing, omitting, or adding words and sentences. Have children act out their dialogues for a small group or the class.

▶Lesson Wrap-Up

WORDSHOP WORDS AND CONTEXT SENTENCES

1. **new** We have two **new** girls in our class.
2. **name** What is your **name**?
3. **welcome** We try to make new children feel **welcome**.

▶Reteach

LEARNING DIFFERENCES

Play the game "Echo Me" to help children remember the spelling of words in this lesson. Write a Spelling Word on the board, say it aloud, and have children repeat it after you. Then spell the word as you point to each letter, and have children echo you. Say the word again, and have children repeat it. Repeat this procedure with the other three Spelling Words. **AUDITORY MODALITY**

The Me Tree

Talk with children about the concept of family. Ask children to suggest some family-member names such as *mother, brother, grandmother, uncle,* and *cousin.* Record these words on a chart, and talk about how these family members are related.

To construct an individual "Me Tree," have each child draw a large tree. Then give children apple cutouts, crayons, and paste. Have children write the names of their own family members on the apples and paste them on the tree. Remind children to include themselves.

Words with Long *i*

OBJECTIVE
To spell words with long *i*

LESSON PLANNER
Assign words based on children's developmental levels. See the Assignment Guide on page T11.

▶ INFORMAL ASSESSMENT
Children's writing may show that they have difficulty distinguishing between long *i* and other vowel sounds.

▼ model

ride
I'm going to (rid) my bike.

Use this lesson to introduce the spelling of words in which the letters *i-e* stand for the long *i* sound. Encourage children to apply what they have learned to help them spell other words with the long *i* sound. After children complete this lesson, have them proofread their writing and correct errors they may have made in spelling words in which the letters *i-e* stand for the long *i* sound.

▶ LEARNING DIFFERENCES
Use the following suggestion and the ideas on page T212 to customize learning activities.

Children Acquiring English
Some children may find it difficult to differentiate the long *i* sound from the short *a* sound. You may wish to provide opportunities for children to hear and identify the difference between the vowel sounds in words such as *like, lack; nine, Nan; pine, pan; bite, bat; hide, had;* and *mine, man.* COMPARING AND CONTRASTING

▶ PRETEST/POSTTEST CONTEXT SENTENCES
* 1. **like** That dog looks just **like** mine.
* 2. **ice** My hands are as cold as **ice**!
  3. **ride** Let's go for a bike **ride**.
* 4. **nine** My cat had **nine** kittens.

▶ A LINE OF NINE PINES
Children can work together to suggest words rhyming with *nine* that belong in the *-ine* word family. Possible words include: *dine, fine, line, mine, pine, vine, shine,* and *twine.* Have children write these words as well as the word *nine* on pine tree cutouts. Then suggest they attach the cutouts in a line in one section of the classroom word wall.

The -ine Family

* Words appearing in "Planets."

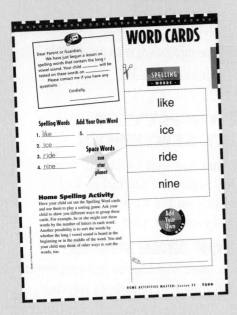

HOME ACTIVITIES MASTER: Lesson 32

NOTE: Fill in blanks on the Home Activities Master before sending it home. See the Assignment Guide on page T11.

See page T299 for the Home Activities Master.

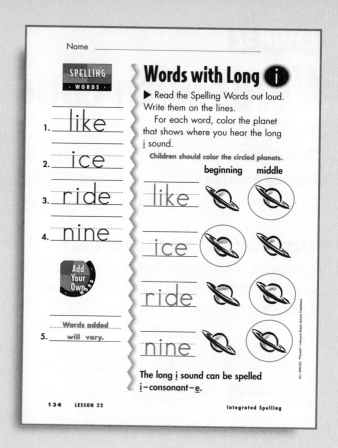

▶ Introduction

PRETEST Administer the Pretest. Say each word, and then use it in the sentence provided on page T207 before repeating the word. **ACCESSING PRIOR KNOWLEDGE**

SELF-CHECK Have children refer to their lists of Spelling Words to check their Pretests. For each word children misspell on the Pretest, remind them to follow the Study Steps to Learn a Word, found on pages 8–9 of the Pupil's Edition. **STUDENT SELF-ASSESSMENT**

INTRODUCING THE LESSON

To use the open sort, copy Home Activities Master Lesson 32, found on page T299.

Open Sort: After distributing the word cards, help children think of ways to sort the words. Possible sorts include counting the number of letters or grouping the action words together.

Closed Sort: Help children read aloud the lesson title and the Spelling Words on page 134.

- Invite children to tell what they notice about the vowel sound in all the words. (All have the long *i* sound.)

- Ask children what letter combination stands for the long *i* sound they hear in each word. (Children should identify the *i-e* combination.)

Review the directions, and have children write the Spelling Words on the lines. Provide children with crayons, and have them color the planet to show where they hear the long *i* sound in each word. **SORTING WORDS**

IN SUMMARY Ask children what they have learned about how to spell words that have the long *i* sound. (The long *i* sound may be spelled with the letters *i-e*.)

RECOGNIZING PHONIC ELEMENTS

Spelling Log Suggest that children look on schedules in the classroom to find other long *i* words. Ask children to list the words in their Spelling Logs and to write one on the line provided on Pupil's Edition page 134. **RECOGNIZING PATTERNS**

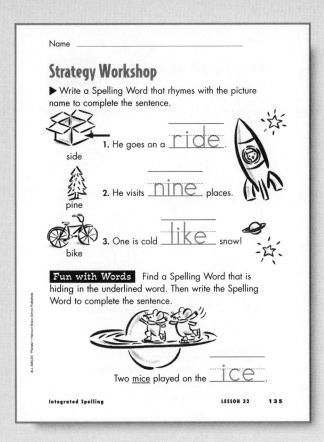

Name _____

Strategy Workshop

▶ Write a Spelling Word that rhymes with the picture name to complete the sentence.

side

1. He goes on a ride.

pine

2. He visits nine places.

bike

3. One is cold like snow!

Fun with Words Find a Spelling Word that is hiding in the underlined word. Then write the Spelling Word to complete the sentence.

Two mice played on the ice.

Integrated Spelling   LESSON 32   135

▶ Strategy Workshop

RHYMING WORDS Help children read the directions at the top of page 135. Call attention to the large illustration of the rocket, and have children describe what they see. Then direct their attention to the small pictures next to the sentences, and ask volunteers to read aloud the label for each picture. Tell children they can use a rhyming strategy to write the correct Spelling Word to complete each sentence. Encourage children to share and compare their answers. **APPLYING SPELLING STRATEGIES**

FUN WITH WORDS Read the directions with children, and invite them to talk about what the mice are doing in the illustration. Point out the underlined word in the sentence, and ask children to look for the hidden Spelling Word. Have them write this word to complete the sentence.

MEETING INDIVIDUAL NEEDS

Phonetic Spellers Children who use a phonetic system of spelling may omit the final *e* on the Spelling Words in this lesson. Teaching children this mnemonic sentence may help them remember to add this letter:

These words are **e**asy, if you remember to add final *e*.

MEETING INDIVIDUAL NEEDS

Challenge Challenge children to learn to spell the rhyming words *mice* and *nice*. Then dictate this sentence for them to write and illustrate:

Nine nice mice like the ice.

Vocabulary WordShop

► Write the words from the box to tell about the pictures.

Space
· WORDS ·
sun
star
planet

1. the hot   sun

2. a far-off   star

3. our home   planet

Sky Time Add words about space to your Spelling Log. Then draw or paint a space picture. Write the names of the things in your picture.

136   LESSON 32   Integrated Spelling

►Vocabulary WordShop

Space
· WORDS ·

Spelling Log Invite children to look through "Planets" to find other words that relate to the topic of space. They can list these words in their Spelling Logs.

MEETING
INDIVIDUAL
NEEDS

Transitional Spellers You may want to assign this level of spellers the WordShop Words as additional spelling words.

WORDSHOP WORDS Help children read the WordShop Words on page 136. Point out that these words can be used to tell about outer space. Then read the directions at the top of the page, and have children describe what they see in the illustrations. Have children read aloud the phrases that correspond to the pictures. Explain that they will write a Space Word to complete each phrase. Invite children to share and discuss their responses.

MEETING
INDIVIDUAL
NEEDS

Children Acquiring English Display a diagram of the sun and the nine planets. Help children find Earth. Then point out that Earth is the only planet that has the air and water that living things need to live.

BUILDING VOCABULARY

SKY TIME Read the directions with children, and then provide them with drawing materials. After children complete their space pictures, remind them to label the objects in their pictures.

EXPLORING SPACE WORDS
Share the following information about stars and planets with children.

• Explain that planets and stars look similar in the night sky, but it is possible to tell them apart. Stars appear to twinkle, while planets appear to shine with a steady light.

• Point out that the ancient Greeks named the planets *planetae*, which means "wanderers." This is because the planets travel in a path around the sun.

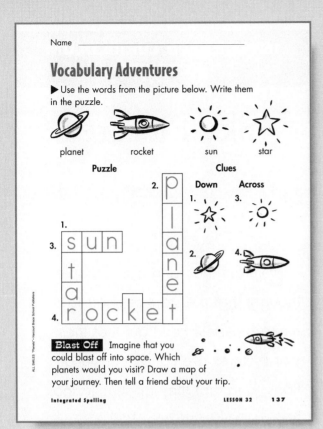

Name _____

Vocabulary Adventures

▶ Use the words from the picture below. Write them in the puzzle.

planet   rocket   sun   star

Puzzle   **Clues**

Down   Across

Blast Off Imagine that you could blast off into space. Which planets would you visit? Draw a map of your journey. Then tell a friend about your trip.

Integrated Spelling   LESSON 32   137

"**B**Y STUDYING WHAT *similarities or differences a group of words possess, children are required to categorize words to provide generalizations about how words are spelled. Open word sorts are open-ended activities that allow children to group words by self-designated categories.*" (Mary Jo Fresch and Aileen Wheaton)

VOCABULARY ADVENTURES

Read the directions at the top of page 137 with children. Direct their attention to the illustrations at the top of the page, and help them read the labels. You may want to have children work together as a group to complete the puzzle, or you may prefer to guide them through a few puzzle clues. Then have children complete the rest of the puzzle. **BUILDING VOCABULARY**

BLAST OFF
Provide children with drawing paper. Then before they draw their maps, you might want to review the planet names: Earth, Mercury, Venus, Mars, Jupiter, Pluto, Uranus, Neptune and Saturn. You may want to assign partners or have children share their work in small groups.

POSTTEST
Remind children to study any Spelling Words they misspelled on the Pretest. Then use the context sentences on page T207 to administer the Posttest.

Optional Writing Idea

Independent Writing: Journal Entry After children have completed their maps for the Blast Off activity on Pupil's Edition page 137, invite them to write a journal entry describing what happened during the trip. Before children begin to write, suggest that they write some ideas to answer these questions:

1. What happened?
2. What did I see, hear, or smell?
3. What did I do?
4. How did I feel?

After children draft and revise their entries, you might want to display them along with their maps on a bulletin board decorated with cutouts of stars and planets.

▶ Lesson Wrap-Up

WORDSHOP WORDS AND CONTEXT SENTENCES

1. **sun**   The **sun** gives us heat and light.
2. **star**   That **star** is very far away.
3. **planet**   We live on the **planet** Earth.

▶ Reteach

LEARNING DIFFERENCES

Some children with learning disabilities may benefit from large muscle movement as they practice their Spelling Words. Write the letters *l, i, k, e, c, r, d* , and *n* on large oaktag cutouts of stars. (For increased durability, laminate or cover the star shapes with clear self-stick plastic before you cut them out.) Then tape the stars down in a random pattern in a large, open area of the classroom. Say each Spelling Word, and have each child hop on the correct letters as you spell each word aloud. Then have the child say the word and spell it independently by hopping on the letters. **AUDITORY/ KINESTHETIC MODALITIES**

INTEGRATED CURRICULUM ACTIVITY

Sky Pictures

Explain that long ago, people thought that the stars seemed to make pictures. Point out that these star pictures are called constellations, and that they appear to look like animals and people.

Children can make their own star pictures. Distribute small circles of black construction paper, chalk, and sharp pencils. Have children use the chalk to create a star picture on the black paper, and then use the pencil point to poke a hole for each star. Fit each circle over the light of a flashlight, and hold it in place with a rubber band. Then turn off the classroom lights, and tell children to project their star pictures on the ceiling.

SCIENCE

More Words to Remember

OBJECTIVE
To spell words that are used frequently

LESSON PLANNER
Assign words based on children's developmental levels. See the Assignment Guide on page T11.

▶ INFORMAL ASSESSMENT
Children's writing may show that they have difficulty spelling some frequently used words.

▼ model

She (wuz) tired after the hike.

was

Use this lesson to introduce the spelling of some words that children use frequently in their writing. After children complete this lesson, encourage them to proofread their writing and correct errors they may have made in spelling these words.

▶ LEARNING DIFFERENCES
Use the following suggestion and the ideas on page T218 to customize learning activities.

MEETING INDIVIDUAL NEEDS

Children Acquiring English
Short vowel sounds, such as the short *i* in *his* and *give* and the short *u* in *was*, may present difficulties for children who are acquiring English. For specific suggestions regarding the short *i* sound, see Lesson 21 (page T141). For the short *u* sound, see Lesson 20 (page T135). Children who are acquiring English may also find the distinction between the possessive pronouns *his* and *her* confusing. Provide practice differentiating these two pronouns by displaying pictures of boys' and girls' clothing. As you display each picture, engage children in a dialogue such as the following:

Teacher: Whose shirt is that?
Children: It is *his* shirt. **COMPARING AND CONTRASTING**

▶ PRETEST/POSTTEST CONTEXT SENTENCES
* 1. **was** The cat **was** sleeping.
* 2. **his** Is that **his** mother?
* 3. **give** I want to **give** you this book.
* 4. **saw** We **saw** Jay at the lake.

▶ WORD WALL
Set aside one section of your classroom word wall for common verbs that have irregular past forms that children use often in their speaking and writing. Help children record the present and the past forms in two columns on the wall. Such words might include *is, was; give, gave; see, saw; come, came; run, ran; sit, sat; say, said;* and *go, went.*

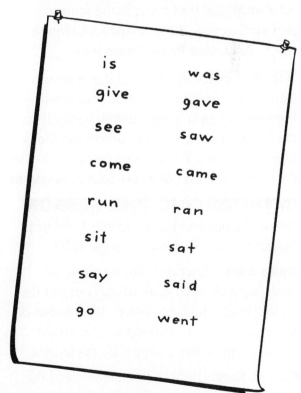

is	was
give	gave
see	saw
come	came
run	ran
sit	sat
say	said
go	went

* Words appearing in "Geraldine's Baby Brother."

**NOTE: Fill in blanks on the Home Activities Master before sending it home.
See the Assignment Guide on page T11.**

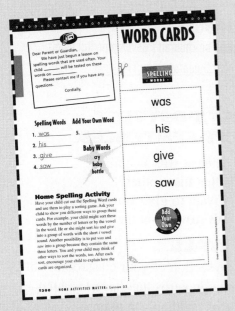

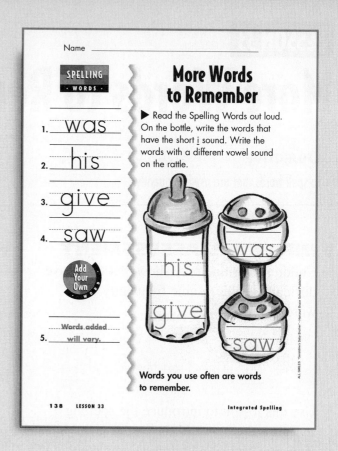

Introduction

PRETEST Administer the Pretest. Say each word, and then use it in the sentence provided on page T213 before repeating the word. **ACCESSING PRIOR KNOWLEDGE**

SELF-CHECK Have children refer to their lists of Spelling Words to check their Pretests. For each word children misspell on the Pretest, remind them to follow the Study Steps to Learn a Word, found on pages 8–9 of the Pupil's Edition. **STUDENT SELF-ASSESSMENT**

INTRODUCING THE LESSON

To use the open sort, copy Home Activities Master Lesson 33, found on page T300.

Open Sort: After distributing the word cards, help children think of ways to sort the words. Possibilities include by the number of letters, by words containing a short vowel sound, or by words ending with the letter *s*.

Closed Sort: Help children read aloud the lesson title and the Spelling Words on page

138. Point out that the Spelling Words are words that are used often in writing.

• Ask children if the vowel sound in any of the words is the same. (Two words have the short *i* vowel sound—*his, give*.)

• Suggest that children write the two words with the short *i* sound on the baby bottle and the words that do not contain the short *i* sound on the rattle. **SORTING WORDS**

IN SUMMARY Ask children what they have learned about spelling words they use often. (You can study the words in order to remember how to spell them.) **DEVELOPING SPELLING LISTS**

Spelling Log Suggest that children look through their writing to find other words that they want to remember how to spell. Have them add these words to their Spelling Logs and write one on the line provided on Pupil's Edition page 138. **DEVELOPING SPELLING LISTS**

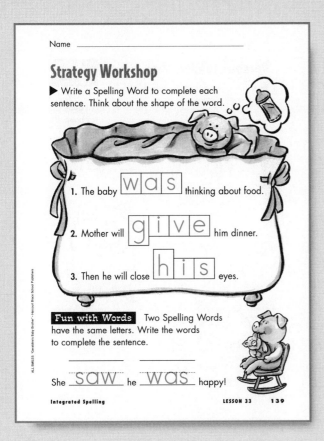

Name _____

Strategy Workshop

▶ Write a Spelling Word to complete each sentence. Think about the shape of the word.

1. The baby `was` thinking about food.

2. Mother will `give` him dinner.

3. Then he will close `his` eyes.

Fun with Words Two Spelling Words have the same letters. Write the words to complete the sentence.

She `saw` he `was` happy!

Integrated Spelling   LESSON 33   **139**

Strategy Workshop

WORD SHAPES Read aloud the directions at the top of page 139. Then invite children to describe the shapes of the letters in the Spelling Words. Elicit that the letter *h* is tall, and the letter *g* drops below the line. Remind children that remembering how a word looks is a strategy that can help them spell the word correctly.

Focus attention on the illustration, and have children describe what the baby pig is thinking about. Before children write the Spelling Words to complete the sentences, encourage them to trace the word shapes with their fingers. After children have completed the sentences, ask volunteers to read them aloud. **APPLYING SPELLING STRATEGIES**

FUN WITH WORDS Help children read the directions. Then direct attention to the illustration, and ask children how they think the baby pig is feeling. Explain that to complete the sentence, they will write two

Spelling Words that contain the same three letters but in a different order. After children have completed the sentence, ask a volunteer to read it aloud.

Children Acquiring English
Point out to children that the word *saw* can be the past form of the action word *see*. Share several example sentences to clarify this meaning. Then explain that a *saw* is also a sharp tool used for cutting wood. You may want to show a picture of this tool or sketch it on the board. **BUILDING VOCABULARY**

Semi-Phonetic Spellers
Some children may omit the final *e* on the Spelling Word *give*. To help them remember to add the letter, suggest this mnemonic cheer:

Give me a final *e!*

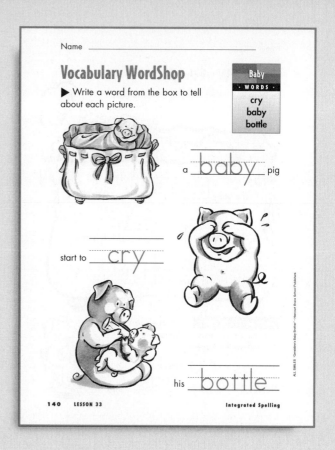

Vocabulary WordShop

▶ Write a word from the box to tell about each picture.

Baby
• WORDS •
cry
baby
bottle

a baby pig

start to cry

his bottle

140   LESSON 33   Integrated Spelling

▶Vocabulary WordShop

Baby
• WORDS •

Spelling Log Children can search for other words associated with babies in the reading selection "Geraldine's Baby Brother." Suggest that they write these words in their Spelling Logs.

MEETING
INDIVIDUAL
NEEDS

Transitional Spellers You may want to assign this level of spellers the WordShop Words as additional spelling words.

WORDSHOP WORDS
Read the WordShop Words on page 140 aloud with children, and discuss how these words relate to babies. Then read the directions at the top of the page, and focus children's attention on the three illustrations. Explain that they will complete the phrases with Baby Words to tell something about each picture. After children have completed the phrases, call on volunteers to read them aloud.

MEETING
INDIVIDUAL
NEEDS

Phonetic Spellers As a practice activity, have children write the Baby Words on large index cards. Ask a volunteer to select one of the words and act it out. Have children hold up the word that the volunteer is pantomiming. Repeat this procedure with the remaining words.

EXPLORING BABY WORDS
To expand children's awareness of other baby-related words, display a carry bag with handles, and invite children to pretend that this is a baby's diaper bag. Ask children to draw and label pictures of things that might be found in the bag. Then ask children to display and name their pictures as they deposit them in the bag. In addition to bottles and diapers, items might include safety pins, a rattle, a stuffed toy, baby powder, a bib, a pacifier, baby food, a spoon, a hat, booties, a sweater, and a blanket.

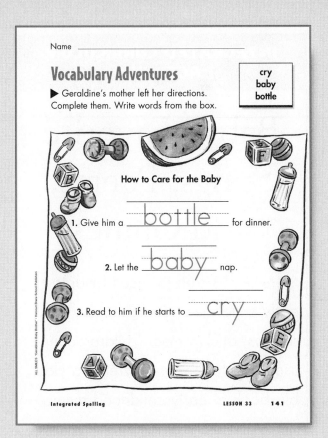

Name _____

Vocabulary Adventures

► Geraldine's mother left her directions.
Complete them. Write words from the box.

cry
baby
bottle

How to Care for the Baby

1. Give him a ___bottle___ for dinner.

2. Let the ___baby___ nap.

3. Read to him if he starts to ___cry___.

Integrated Spelling   LESSON 33   141

WORDS IN THE ENGLISH *language hardly ever end with v. Almost all words that end with the /v/ sound are spelled with a final e. One of the Spelling Words in this lesson, give, is an example. Others include* have, live, love, leave, move, glove, shove, *and* groove.

VOCABULARY ADVENTURES

Read the directions at the top of page 141 with children. Focus attention on the words in the box, and have them read aloud. Point out the list, and explain that it is a set of directions. Help children read the title of the list aloud. Then explain that they are to complete each sentence, using the best word from the box. After children have completed the sentences, have them share their answers. USING NAMING AND ACTION WORDS

Working Together You may want to have children work in pairs on this activity. Encourage partners to agree on each word before writing it in the blank.

POSTTEST Remind children to study any Spelling Words they misspelled on the Pretest. Then use the context sentences on page T213 to administer the Posttest.

Optional Writing Idea

Collaborative Writing: Poem Have children develop a list of words that rhyme with *cry*, and record their contributions on the board or on chart paper. Children might suggest the following words: *cry, dry, by, sky, fly*, and *try*.

Suggest that children work with a partner or in a small group to draft and revise a rhyming two-line poem. The poem might describe what people do when a baby starts to cry. Partners or groups can share their completed poems with the class.

▶ Lesson Wrap-Up

WORDSHOP WORDS AND CONTEXT SENTENCES

1. **cry**   He began to **cry** at six o'clock.
2. **baby**   Is that your **baby** brother?
3. **bottle**   I will fill the **bottle** with milk.

▶ Reteach

LEARNING DIFFERENCES

Learning words by visual memory may be a difficult task for some children. To help overcome visual processing deficits, try using a strategy of guided reduction of cues to reinforce the correct spelling in a way that holds children's attention.

Make a viewing device by cutting a window 1/2 inch high and two inches long in a large index card. Staple this window to another index card the same size. On a paper strip two inches wide, write a Spelling Word, omitting a letter at a time at 1/2-inch intervals, for example:

> give
> _ ive
> — ve
> ——e
> ————

Place the strip between the two index cards so that the word *give* appears in the window. Ask the child to spell the word aloud. Then pull the strip so that the next letter in the sequence shows, and ask the child to spell the word again. Continue this process, pulling the strip each time the child spells the word correctly, until the child has spelled the entire word from memory. Use this same strategy for each Spelling Word. **VISUAL MODALITY**

INTEGRATED CURRICULUM ACTIVITY

Baby's Favorite Songs, Poems, and Games

Invite children to recall favorite early childhood songs, nursery rhymes, and games. Children can use this information to create a class big book of early childhood memories. After children dictate or copy the words of songs and rhymes onto large sheets of construction paper, suggest that they add illustrations. They can also draw pictures showing the games they liked to play and write simple how-to directions.

When the book is finished, invite children to bring in a favorite loved object from their babyhood. Then have a "baby show-and-tell," in which children share these objects as well as sing songs, recite rhymes, and play games from the class big book.

More Words to Remember with *o*

OBJECTIVE
To spell words with different sounds for *o*

LESSON PLANNER
Assign words based on children's developmental levels. See the Assignment Guide on page T11.

▶ INFORMAL ASSESSMENT
Children's writing may show that they have difficulty distinguishing between words with *o* and words with other vowels.

▼ model

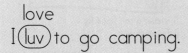

love

I (luv) to go camping.

Use this lesson to introduce words spelled with *o* that children use frequently in their writing. After children complete this lesson, encourage them to proofread their writing and correct errors they may have made in spelling these words.

▶ LEARNING DIFFERENCES
Use the following suggestion and the ideas on page T224 to customize learning activities.

MEETING INDIVIDUAL NEEDS

Children Acquiring English
Children who are acquiring English may be unfamiliar with the meaning of the conjunction *or*, which is used to signal alternatives. To help children understand the word's meaning, display pairs of objects on a table. For each pair of objects, ask children questions such as the following:

Would you like ___ or ___?
Which do you like best, ___ or ___?

When children understand the pattern, have them select their own pairs of objects and use the word *or* to ask a partner questions about the objects. **BUILDING VOCABULARY**

▶ PRETEST/POSTTEST CONTEXT SENTENCES
* 1. **love**   I **love** to sing.
* 2. **who**   Do you know **who** did this?
* 3. **no**   Getting wet in the rain is **no** fun.
* 4. **or**   You may read **or** draw.

▶ WORD FAMILIES
Children may like to construct a word family for each of the Spelling Words. Examples of word families and associated words that children might write include the following:

love—*dove, glove, shove, above*
who—*to, do, into, undo, unto*
no—*go, so, ago, hello, yo-yo*
or—*for, nor*

* Words appearing in "Julius." Additional story words are *come, old, told, so, too,* and *roll*.

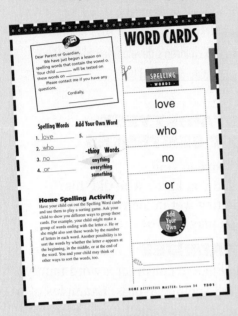

NOTE: Fill in blanks on the Home Activities Master before sending it home. See the Assignment Guide on page T11.

See page T301 for the Home Activities Master.

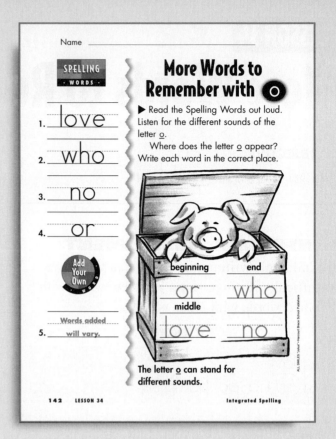

Name _____

SPELLING
· WORDS ·

1. love
2. who
3. no
4. or

Add Your Own Word

Words added will vary.

5. _____

More Words to Remember with o

▶ Read the Spelling Words out loud. Listen for the different sounds of the letter o.

Where does the letter o appear? Write each word in the correct place.

beginning	end
or	who
middle	
love	no

The letter o can stand for different sounds.

142   LESSON 34   Integrated Spelling

▶ Introduction

PRETEST Administer the Pretest. Say each word, and then use it in the sentence provided on page T219 before repeating the word. ACCESSING PRIOR KNOWLEDGE

SELF-CHECK Have children refer to their lists of Spelling Words to check their Pretests. For each word children misspell on the Pretest, remind them to follow the Study Steps to Learn a Word. STUDENT SELF-ASSESSMENT

INTRODUCING THE LESSON

To use the open sort, copy Home Activities Master Lesson 34, found on page T301.

Open Sort: After distributing the word cards, help children think of ways to sort the words. Possible sorts might include grouping words by the number of letters in each word, or grouping words that end with the letter o.

Closed Sort: Help children read aloud the lesson title and the Spelling Words on page 142.

• Ask children what they notice about the vowel in each word. (All words contain the vowel o.)

• Have children tell if the vowel is at the beginning, in the middle, or at the end of each word. (at the beginning—or; in the middle—love; at the end—who, no)

• Direct children's attention to the headings. Tell children to write each Spelling Word under the heading that tells where the letter o appears in the word. SORTING WORDS

IN SUMMARY Ask children what they have learned about how to spell the Spelling Words in this lesson. (The vowel sound in each word is spelled with the letter o.) RECOGNIZING PHONIC ELEMENTS

Spelling Log Suggest that children look through the reading selection to find other words in which the vowel sound is spelled with the letter o. Ask children to list the words in their Spelling Logs and write one on the line provided on Pupil's Edition page 142. RECOGNIZING PATTERNS

Name _____

Strategy Workshop

▶ Name each small picture. Write a Spelling Word that rhymes with the picture to complete the sentence.

glove
1. Do you love my pig?

go
2. Father says a pig is no fun!

door
3. Do not say that, or I will cry!

Fun with Words Write a Spelling Word to complete the sentence.

But who says pigs can't dance!

▶ Strategy Workshop

RHYMING WORDS Read the directions at the top of page 143 aloud. Call attention to the large illustration above the sentences, and have children tell what is happening in this picture. Then have children look at the small pictures and read the label under each one aloud. Explain to children that they can use a rhyming strategy to write the correct Spelling Word to complete each sentence. Ask volunteers to read the completed sentences aloud.

APPLYING SPELLING STRATEGIES

FUN WITH WORDS Help children read the directions, and then talk about what the pig is doing in the picture. Explain that the completed sentence will tell something about the pig. Have children write a Spelling Word to complete the sentence, and then have it read aloud.

MEETING INDIVIDUAL NEEDS

Semi-Phonetic Spellers
Distribute notebook reinforcements to children who are having difficulty remembering to include the letter *o* when writing their Spelling Words. Have children write the Spelling Words, leaving extra space around each *o*. Then have them stick a reinforcement over the letter *o* in each word.

MEETING INDIVIDUAL NEEDS

Challenge If children created word families as suggested on page T219, encourage them to select one of the word families and learn to spell several words in the family that might be useful in their writing.

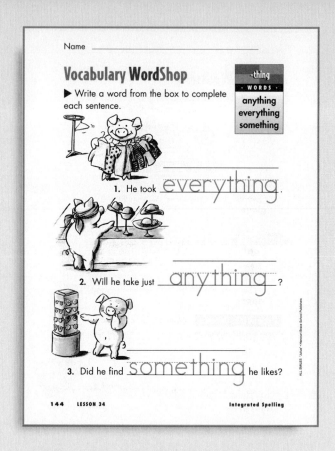

Name _____

Vocabulary WordShop

▶ Write a word from the box to complete each sentence.

-thing
· W O R D S ·
anything
everything
something

1. He took *everything*.

2. Will he take just *anything*?

3. Did he find *something* he likes?

144 LESSON 34   Integrated Spelling

▶ Vocabulary WordShop

Spelling Log Children may want to write the WordShop Words from this lesson in their Spelling Logs.

Transitional Spellers You may want to assign this level of spellers the WordShop Words as additional spelling words.

WORDSHOP WORDS Read the WordShop Words on page 144 aloud. Then ask children to look carefully at the words and tell how they are alike. (All the words are compounds; all end with *thing*.) Read the directions with children, and call attention to each illustration. Explain that they will write the best WordShop Word to complete each sentence so that it describes the picture. When children have finished, have them share and compare their responses.

Children Acquiring English Clarify the meaning of each WordShop Word for children. Point out that *everything* means "all of something"; for example, *I ate everything on my plate.* The word *something* implies a thing that is not named, for example, *I took something from the refrigerator.* The word *anything* means "any thing"; for example, *My dog will eat anything I give her.* **UNDERSTANDING WORD MEANINGS**

EXPLORING "-THING" WORDS Point out that a compound word is formed by joining two smaller words.

• Have children identify the two shorter words that make up each WordShop Word.

• Elicit other compound words that end with *thing* by giving these hints:

  Use this word to describe when everything is gone. (*nothing*)

  Use this word to describe something that is meant to be played with. (*plaything*)

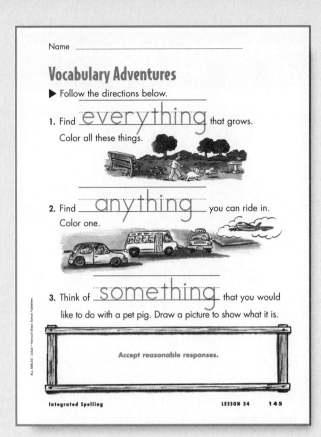

Name _____

Vocabulary Adventures

▶ Follow the directions below.

1. Find *everything* that grows.
Color all these things.

2. Find *anything* you can ride in.
Color one.

3. Think of *something* that you would
like to do with a pet pig. Draw a picture to show what it is.

Accept reasonable responses.

Integrated Spelling   LESSON 34   **145**

"**B**Y THE END OF FIRST GRADE, *children encouraged to use invented spellings typically score as well or better on standardized tests of spelling than children allowed to use only correct spellings in first drafts.*" (Constance Weaver)

VOCABULARY ADVENTURES

After reading the direction line at the top of page 145, provide children with crayons. Then help them read the directions for the first two items and discuss the pictures. In the first item, children are to color *everything* that grows. In the second item, have them name *anything* in the picture that they could ride in. Then have them color one of these objects. After reading the directions for item 3 with children, have them draw pictures to complete this item. **USING PRONOUNS**

MEETING INDIVIDUAL NEEDS **Phonetic Spellers** Help children remember to write *th* in the WordShop Words by focusing their attention on the word shape and pointing out that two tall letters come together in the middle of each word.

POSTTEST
Remind children to study any Spelling Words they misspelled on the Pretest. Then use the context sentences on page T219 to administer the Posttest.

Optional Writing Idea

Independent Writing: Friendly Letter Invite children to share the pictures they drew for item 3 on page 145 of the Pupil's Edition. Suggest children use their pictures as the basis for a letter to a classmate, telling about the things a new pet pig is able to do. To help children recall the five parts of a friendly letter, you might want to display a template, and have children refer to it as they write their letters.

```
                        Date
   Greeting
      Body of the letter
              Closing
              Signature
```

▶ Lesson Wrap-Up

WORDSHOP WORDS AND CONTEXT SENTENCES

1. **anything** The band will play **anything** you want.
2. **everything** I took one bite of **everything** on my plate.
3. **something** Choose **something** to read from this box of books.

▶ Reteach

LEARNING DIFFERENCES

Children with visual or auditory processing deficits may benefit from making their own audiotape to practice their Spelling Words. Give each child an index card with each Spelling Word. For each word, have children make a recording in which they say each word, spell it slowly while looking at the word on the card, and then say it again. Next, tell each child to replay the audiotape and listen to himself or herself say, spell, and say the word. Then have children turn off the tape player and write the word. Tell children to check the spelling by comparing each word with the word card. **AUDITORY MODALITY**

On the Ball

For each small group, you will need eight table tennis balls, a marker, and a paper bag. Write the following letters on the balls: *l, o, v, e, w, h, n,* and *r.* Then place the balls in a paper bag and shake them up. Children can take turns passing the bag around and selecting six balls for the group. After children choose the balls, have them use the letters to make as many Spelling Words as they can. To give additional practice in writing the words, suggest that children list the words they have made.

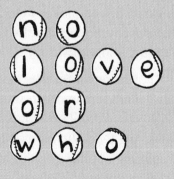

LANGUAGE ARTS

LESSON 35

Words with Long *o*

OBJECTIVE

To spell words with long *o*

LESSON PLANNER

Assign words based on children's developmental levels. See the Assignment Guide on page T11.

▶ INFORMAL ASSESSMENT

Children's writing may show that they have difficulty distinguishing between long *o* and other vowel sounds.

▼ model

old
Where is my (old) coat?

Use this lesson to introduce the spelling of words in which the letters *o* or *o-e* stand for the long *o* sound. Encourage children to apply what they have learned to help them spell other words with the long *o* sound. After children complete this lesson, have them proofread their writing and correct errors they may have made spelling words in which the letters *o* or *o-e* stand for the long *o* sound.

▶ LEARNING DIFFERENCES

Use the following suggestion and the ideas on page T230 to customize learning activities.

MEETING INDIVIDUAL NEEDS

Children Acquiring English
To help children understand the meanings of the Spelling Words, you may want to display pictures of a rose and several types of homes. For the words *go* and *old*, emphasize the words by using them in a classroom context. For example, ask a child to *go* to the pencil sharpener or to *go* to the board. Then display both a new and a well-worn crayon, and ask the child to select the one that is *old*.
UNDERSTANDING WORD MEANINGS

▶ PRETEST/POSTTEST CONTEXT SENTENCES

* 1. **old**   That **old** hat is mine.
* 2. **rose**   I gave a red **rose** to Mom.
* 3. **home**   He stayed **home** from school.
  4. **go**   Let's **go** for a bike ride.

▶ OLD GOLD

Children might enjoy building a family of words that rhyme with the Spelling Word *old*. To make a glittering display, follow this procedure. After children cover their work surfaces with old newspapers, distribute large index cards, white school glue, and small containers filled with gold glitter. Have children use the glue to write on the index cards words that rhyme with *old*. Words in the *-old* family include *bold, cold, fold, gold, hold, mold, sold,* and *told*. Before the glue dries, have children sprinkle the letters with the glitter and gently tap the cards to shake off any excess. Then display these glittering words on a bulletin board.

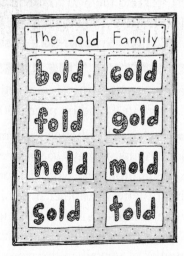

* Words appearing in "New Shoes for Silvia." Additional story words are *whole, shone, so, hold,* and *no*.

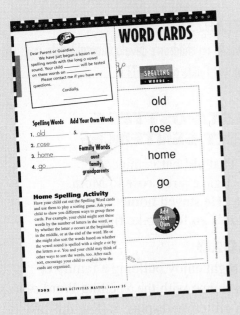

**NOTE: Fill in blanks on the Home Activities
Master before sending it home.
See the Assignment Guide on page T11.**

Dear Parent or Guardian,
We have just begun a lesson on
spelling words with the long o vowel
sound. Your child _____ will be tested
on these words on _____.
Please contact me if you have any
questions.
Cordially,

WORD CARDS

Spelling Words **Add Your Own Words**
1. old   5.
2. rose
3. home   **Family Words**
4. go   aunt
                family
                grandparents

Home Spelling Activity
Have your child cut out the Spelling Word cards
and use them to play a sorting game. Ask your
child to show you different ways to group these
cards. For example, your child might sort these
words by the number of letters in the word, or
by whether the letter o occurs at the beginning,
in the middle, or at the end of the word. He or
she might also sort the words based on whether
the vowel sound is spelled with a single o or by
the letters o-e. You and your child may think of
other ways to sort the words, too. After each
sort, encourage your child to explain how the
cards are organized.

SPELLING
WORDS

old

rose

home

go

Add
Your
Own

T302   HOME ACTIVITIES MASTER: Lesson 35

See page T302 for the Home Activities Master.

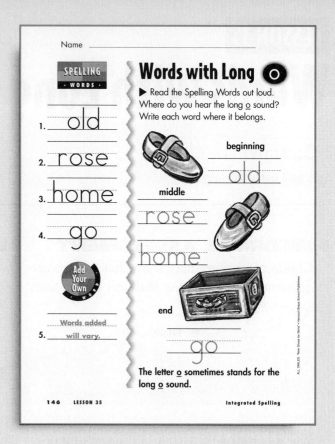

Introduction

PRETEST Administer the Pretest. Say
each word, and then use it in the sentence
provided on page T225 before repeating the
word. **ACCESSING PRIOR KNOWLEDGE**

SELF-CHECK Have children refer to
their lists of Spelling Words to check their
Pretests. For each word children misspell on
the Pretest, remind them to follow the Study
Steps to Learn a Word, found on pages 8–9 of
the Pupil's Edition. **STUDENT SELF-ASSESSMENT**

INTRODUCING THE LESSON
To use the open sort, copy Home Activities
Master Lesson 35, found on page T302.

Open Sort: After distributing the word cards,
help children think of ways to sort the words.
Children might group the words according to
the number of letters. Another possibility is to
group *rose* and *home* as words that end with
the letter *e*. They might also group the words
by the number of vowels in the word.

Closed Sort: Help children read aloud the lesson title and the Spelling Words on page 146.

• Invite children to tell what they notice about
the vowel sound in each of the words. (All
have the long *o* sound.)

• Ask children where they hear the long *o*
sound in each word. (at the beginning—*old*;
in the middle—*rose, home*; at the end—*go*)

Review the directions, and have children
write each word under the correct heading.
SORTING WORDS

IN SUMMARY Ask children what
they have learned about how to spell words
that have the long *o* sound. (The long *o* sound
may be spelled with the letters *o* or *o-e*.)
RECOGNIZING PHONIC ELEMENTS

Spelling Log Have children
find other words that contain
the long *o* sound. Ask children
to list the words they find in
their Spelling Logs and write one
on the line provided on Pupil's Edition page
146. **RECOGNIZING PATTERNS**

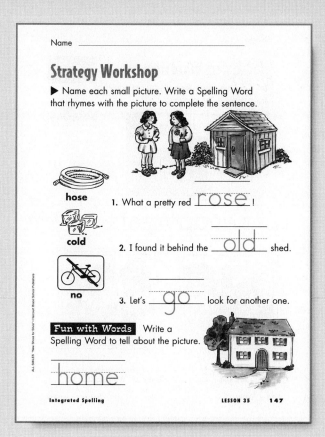

Name _____

Strategy Workshop

▶ Name each small picture. Write a Spelling Word that rhymes with the picture to complete the sentence.

hose

1. What a pretty red ⟨rose⟩ !

cold

2. I found it behind the ⟨old⟩ shed.

no

3. Let's ⟨go⟩ look for another one.

Fun with Words Write a Spelling Word to tell about the picture.

⟨home⟩

Integrated Spelling

LESSON 35   147

▶ Strategy Workshop

RHYMING WORDS Read the directions at the top of page 147 with children. Direct their attention to the large illustration, and ask children to describe what they see. Call attention to the words *hose, cold,* and *no* and the pictures that go with them. Explain that children can use a rhyming strategy and what they know about the sounds that letters stand for to help them write the correct Spelling Word to complete each sentence. After children have completed the items, have them share and discuss their answers.

APPLYING SPELLING STRATEGIES

FUN WITH WORDS Read the directions with children and discuss the picture. After children write the Spelling Word to describe the picture, invite them to compare their own homes with the one shown in the illustration. Ask children to tell how their homes are the same and how they are different.

Phonetic Spellers Children who are spelling phonetically may need to be reminded to add the final, silent *e* to the Spelling Words *home* and *rose*. To help them remember, have children write the first three letters of these words in pencil and write the final *e* with a red marker or crayon.

Challenge Suggest that children choose additional words from the *-old* family to learn to spell.

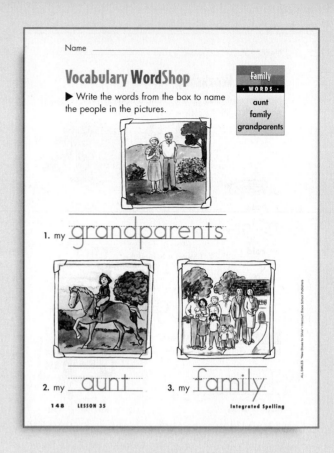

Name _____

Vocabulary WordShop

▶ Write the words from the box to name the people in the pictures.

Family
• WORDS •
aunt
family
grandparents

1. my grandparents

2. my aunt

3. my family

148   LESSON 35   Integrated Spelling

ALL SMILES "New Shoes for Silvia" • Harcourt Brace School Publishers

---

▶ Vocabulary WordShop

Spelling Log Children can look for words that are associated with the family in "Geraldine's Baby Brother" and "New Shoes for Silvia." Have them add these words to their Spelling Logs.

Transitional Spellers You may want to assign this level of spellers the WordShop Words as additional spelling words.

WORDSHOP WORDS   Help children read the WordShop Words on page 148, and ask how these words are alike. (They tell about a family and family members.) Read the directions at the top of the page with children, and then discuss the illustrations. Point out that the pictures look like those found in a family photo album. Explain to children that they can look at the people in each picture to help them figure out which Family Word to write.

Children Acquiring English Invite children who speak languages other than English to share words in their native language for *grandparents* and *aunt*.

REINFORCING SELF-ESTEEM

EXPLORING FAMILY WORDS

Use a diagram of a family tree to help children understand family relationships.

• Point out that grandparents are the parents of one's parents. A grandmother is the mother of one's father or mother, while a grandfather is the father of one's father or mother.

• Explain that an aunt is the sister of one's mother or father, and an uncle is the brother of one's mother or father. Cousins are the children of aunts and uncles.

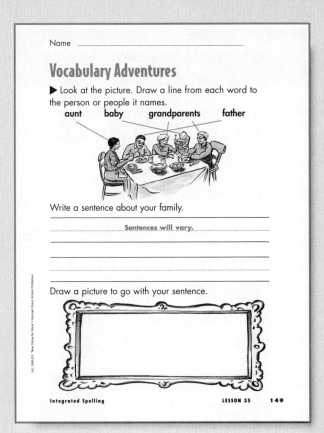

Name _____

Vocabulary Adventures

▶ Look at the picture. Draw a line from each word to the person or people it names.

aunt   baby   grandparents   father

Write a sentence about your family.

.... Sentences will vary. ....

Draw a picture to go with your sentence.

Integrated Spelling

LESSON 35   149

"SPELLING *is for writing.*"
(Donald Graves)

VOCABULARY ADVENTURES

Read the directions at the top of page 149 with children. Have them read the words above the illustration. Tell children to draw a line to match each word with the picture of the person or persons it names. After children have shared and discussed their answers, read the directions for writing a sentence and drawing a picture, and have children complete these items. **USING NAMING WORDS**

 Working Together Consider having children write their sentences and exchange them with a partner. After reading these sentences together, partners can illustrate one another's sentences on separate sheets of paper.

POSTTEST   Remind children to study any Spelling Words they misspelled on the Pretest. Then use the context sentences on page T225 to administer the Posttest.

Optional Writing Idea

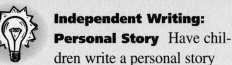 **Independent Writing: Personal Story** Have children write a personal story about something fun that they have done with their families. Possible topics include a special outing, vacation, or holiday celebration. To help children organize their pre-writing ideas, suggest that they fill in a chart such as the following:

Who was there: _____
Where we were: _____
What we did: _____
The best part was: _____

After children have drafted and revised their stories, suggest that they draw a picture to illustrate the event. Then have children proofread and publish their stories in a class book of family stories.

▶ Lesson Wrap-Up

WORDSHOP WORDS AND CONTEXT SENTENCES

1. **aunt**   My **aunt** is older than my mom.
2. **family**   There are six people in her **family**.
3. **grandparents**   Where do your **grandparents** live?

▶ Reteach

LEARNING DIFFERENCES

Children with attention deficits may benefit from a multisensory approach to practicing their Spelling Words. Invite a child to work at the board. Write one of the Spelling Words on the board, and have the child read it aloud. Point out the long *o* sound and the letter or letters that stand for that sound. Have the child trace over the word, using colored chalk. Describe the child's hand movements as each letter is formed. After the word has been traced, have the child erase the word and write it again from memory. If the word is correct, have the child say the word and spell it aloud once more. If the word is incorrect, have the child erase it, and repeat the procedure.

VISUAL/AUDITORY/KINESTHETIC MODALITIES

INTEGRATED CURRICULUM ACTIVITY

Home Sweet Home

Talk with children about the many types of homes in which people live. Briefly explore styles of housing construction and how each meets the needs of people living in a specific place. For example, people living in cold and snowy climates may have steeply sloped roofs so that the snow can slide off, while people living in very hot, dry climates may have homes with thick, flat roofs made of mud or clay.

Have children work together to create a mural that shows various types of homes, both in this country and around the world. Distribute large self-stick notes, and invite children to write captions for their mural contributions.

Review of Lessons 28–35

OBJECTIVES

To review the spelling patterns and strategies in Lessons 28–35; to give children opportunities to recognize and use these spelling patterns and the Spelling Words in their writing

▶ REVIEW OF SPELLING STRATEGIES

Guide children in reviewing the spelling strategies presented in Lessons 28–35.

Using Word Shapes On the board, draw boxes like the following, and remind children that remembering the shape of a word is a strategy they can use to help them spell words.

As children observe, write these words beside the word shape: *old, ice, who.* Point out that even though all these words have three letters, the shape of each word differs. Trace the outline of the boxes with your finger, and ask children which of the three words fits this shape. (*who*) Ask a volunteer to write the word in the shape to check the fit.

Using Rhyming Words Talk with children about how they can use what they know about rhyming words and letter sounds to help them spell words.

• Write the word *he* on the board, and have children read it. Ask them how they can use a rhyming strategy to spell the word *we.*

• Have children identify the letter that stands for the beginning sound of *we.* (*w*)

• Next, have them identify the letter that stands for the ending sound in *he* and *we.* (*e*)

• Then, have children show how they can substitute the letter *w* for the letter *h* in *he* to spell the rhyming word *we.*

▶ LESSON WORDS

The following words from Lessons 28–35 are reviewed in this lesson.

Lesson 28 Words with Long *a*: made

Lesson 29 Words with *th*: then, they

Lesson 30 More Words to Remember: some, do

Lesson 31 Words with Long *e*: we

Lesson 32 Words with Long *i*: ride

Lesson 33 More Words to Remember: give

Lesson 34 More Words to Remember with *o*: or

Lesson 35 Words with Long *o*: home

▶ Practice Test

OPTIONS FOR ADMINISTERING THE PRACTICE TEST

The Practice Test provides an opportunity to review Spelling Words and spelling generalizations in a standardized test format.

Option 1: Read the directions, and review the samples at the top of Pupil's Edition pages 150–151. Then have children complete the rest of these pages as a pretest. After they check the words, have children study any that they missed. Several days later, dictate the underlined Spelling Words in the context sentences on these pages as a posttest.

Option 2: Have children review any words they found difficult in Lessons 28–35. For extra support, you may want to review the spelling generalizations focused on in each of these lessons. Then administer the Practice Test on pages 150–151 to determine children's level of mastery.

OPTIONS FOR EVALUATION

• Have children check their own Practice Tests. They can either look up the words in each lesson, or you may choose to write on the board the words listed on page T231.

• An alternative is to have children exchange Practice Tests and correct one another's work. In this case, ask children to use their own lists of Spelling Words as they check their partners' tests.

For each word children misspell on the Practice Test, remind them to follow the Study Steps to Learn a Word, found on pages 8–9 of the Pupil's Edition. **STUDENT SELF-ASSESSMENT**

NOTE: Use as an extra activity to reinforce spelling strategies.

Name _____

Read each pair of sentences. Look at how the underlined words are spelled. Then fill in the circle next to the correct sentence.

SAMPLE: ● A pet could live here.
○ A pet could liv here.

1. ○ We maad a little home.
● We made a little home.

2. ○ We put in sume water.
● We put in some water.

3. ○ And theen we got a big rock.
● And then we got a big rock.

4. ● Do they like this home?
○ Do thay like this home?

5. ● We think they do!
○ We think they doo!

Integrated Spelling   LESSON 36 • REVIEW   151

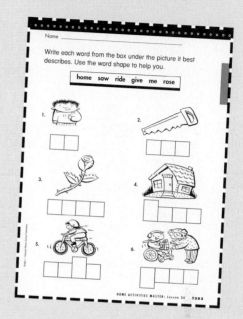

Name _____

Write each word from the box under the picture it best describes. Use the word shape to help you.

| home | saw | ride | give | me | rose |

1.

2.

3.

4.

5.

6.

HOME ACTIVITIES MASTER: Lesson 36   T303

See page T303 for the Home Activities Master.

REVIEW OF SPELLING STRATEGIES

Review the spelling strategies discussed on pages 181–182 of the Pupil's Edition. Then distribute Home Activities Master Lesson 36, found on page T303.

The Reteach section of each Lesson Wrap-Up provides suggestions for helping children who are still having difficulty with the concepts taught in the lesson.

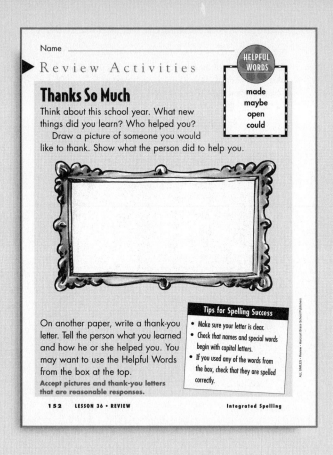

Name _____

Review Activities

HELPFUL WORDS

Thanks So Much

Think about this school year. What new things did you learn? Who helped you?

Draw a picture of someone you would like to thank. Show what the person did to help you.

made
maybe
open
could

On another paper, write a thank-you letter. Tell the person what you learned and how he or she helped you. You may want to use the Helpful Words from the box at the top.

Accept pictures and thank-you letters that are reasonable responses.

Tips for Spelling Success
• Make sure your letter is clear.
• Check that names and special words begin with capital letters.
• If you used any of the words from the box, check that they are spelled correctly.

152   LESSON 36 • REVIEW   Integrated Spelling

ALL SMILES • Review • Harcourt Brace School Publishers

▶ Review Activities

The activities on pages 152–153 of the Pupil's Edition emphasize writing (Thanks So Much) and word play (Rhyme Time). The Tips for Spelling Success point out the importance of knowing standard spellings and give children hints for proofreading and for applying spelling strategies.

THANKS SO MUCH Help children read the directions at the top of page 152. Encourage them to talk about new things they have learned this school year. Help them identify people who have helped them learn. Then distribute crayons, and have children draw their pictures.

After children have shared their drawings, help them read the directions below the picture frame. Point out the list of Helpful Words, and call on volunteers to read the words aloud. Explain to children that they may want to use these words in their thank-you letters. Before children begin, you may want to review the five parts of a friendly let-

ter. Then distribute primary-ruled paper, and have children write their letters.

Have a volunteer read the Tips for Spelling Success aloud. As children proofread their letters, they may find it helpful to refer to the proofreading checklist on page 180 of the Pupil's Edition, or you may want to provide them with the following checklist.

WRITING LETTERS/PROOFREADING

☐ Did I spell the words correctly?
☐ Did I write complete sentences?
☐ Did I begin each sentence, people's names, and special words with capital letters?
☐ Did I capitalize the word *I*?

If children need help with the friendly letter format, suggest they look at page 6 of the *Language Handbook*.

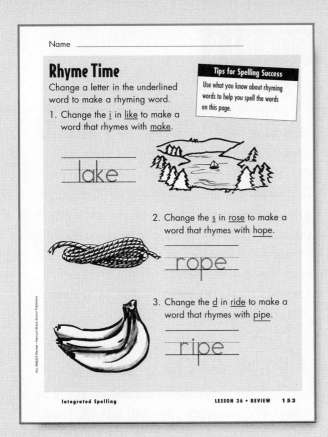

Name _____

Rhyme Time

Change a letter in the underlined word to make a rhyming word.

1. Change the i in <u>like</u> to make a word that rhymes with <u>make</u>.

lake

2. Change the s in <u>rose</u> to make a word that rhymes with <u>hope</u>.

rope

3. Change the d in <u>ride</u> to make a word that rhymes with <u>pipe</u>.

ripe

Integrated Spelling   LESSON 36 • REVIEW   153

"EVEN IN A PRINT-RICH *environment, spelling development does not just happen for many children. There must be a predictable period of time set aside each day for the specific, intentional study of words and their spellings.*"
(*J. Richard Gentry and Jean Wallace Gillet*)

RHYME TIME   Read the directions at the top of page 153 aloud. Point out the illustrations, and explain that they provide clues to the rhyming words that children are to write. You may want to work through the first item with the group and then have them complete the remaining items, working independently or in pairs. An alternative is to read and discuss each set of clues and have children work cooperatively in a large group to complete each item.

Before children begin to work, suggest that they read the Tips for Spelling Success. Encourage them to recall and use a rhyming word strategy to solve these rhyming puzzles.
USING RHYMING WORDS

BAG A WORD

To provide reinforcement of vowel sounds, divide the class into groups of three, and ask each child to be responsible for copying the Spelling Words from Lesson 31, 32, or 35 onto large index cards. Then give each group three paper bags labeled Long *e*, Long *i*, and Long *o*. Have children place the cards face down on the table and mix them up. Have children perform a word sort by taking turns selecting a card, reading the word, and depositing it in the appropriate bag. When all the cards have been sorted, have the group review the cards in each bag and identify the letters that stand for the long vowel sounds.

CELEBRATE SPELLING

Have a celebration to mark the completion of the last spelling lesson! Invite children to share their favorite words they learned to spell this year. One way to review these words is to have children write them on graham crackers, using colored frosting that comes in tubes. After the words have been shared with the group, allow time for everyone to "internalize" their hard work!

ACT OUT A WORD

Many of the Spelling Words in Lessons 28–35 can be pantomimed. Divide the class into small collaborative groups. Give each group three words to act out. As each group presents its words to the class, have the other teams work together to guess the words. Have each group write its guess on a slate or erasable marker board and display it to the performing group for confirmation.

SPIN AND SPELL

Create a spinner, using a cardboard pizza wheel, a large paper clip, and a brad. Then, with a marker, divide the circle into four parts. Using self-stick notes, write four Spelling Words you want a small group to review, and attach one word in each segment of the wheel. Ask one child in each group to spin the paper clip and then dictate the indicated word to the rest of the group. After children have written the word, have the spinner spell the word aloud so children can check their work. When these four words have been reviewed, replace the words and ask a new child to serve as the spinner.

Spelling Picture Dictionary

THE SPELLING PICTURE DICTIONARY, *which appears on pages 154–177 of the Pupil's Edition, contains all the Spelling Words and many of the Vocabulary WordShop Words from the spelling lessons.*

▶ FEATURES OF THE PICTURE DICTIONARY

The information on pages 154–155 introduces the Picture Dictionary to children. The following features of a dictionary are pointed out and explained:

• What a dictionary is

• When to use a dictionary

• How to use alphabetical order to find a word in the Picture Dictionary

In addition to these standard dictionary features, the Picture Dictionary includes a context phrase or sentence for each entry word that illustrates the word's meaning.

▶ INTRODUCING THE PICTURE DICTIONARY

Remind children that a dictionary shows the meaning and spelling of words and that the words are listed in alphabetical order. Then read pages 154–155 to them. Invite volunteers to explain in their own words or to demonstrate how to look up a word, using alphabetical order. Questions such as these may be used to guide the discussion.

• Why do you think the words in the Picture Dictionary are in alphabetical order?

• How might the picture that goes with each Spelling Word help you?

• How might the sentence or the words that go with each Spelling Word help you? (Make sure that children understand that the context of the sentence or the phrase helps them know what the word means.)

Next, ask children when they think they should use the Picture Dictionary. Make sure they understand these points:

• A dictionary can be used when you are reading to look up the meaning of unfamiliar words.

• A dictionary can be used when you are writing to check the spelling of words.

▶ USING THE TOPIC AND CONCEPT PAGES

Work with children to make a web of words about the circus. Explain that all the ideas would be about one topic—the circus. The web may include some of the following ideas.

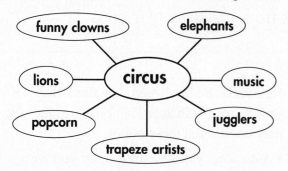

Then have children look at pages 172–177 to preview the topics and the concepts that are illustrated. Discuss with children how they can use these pages.

PAGE 154

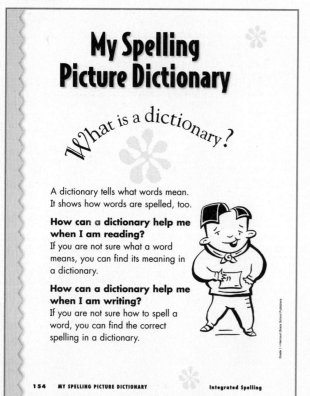

PAGE 155

PAGE 172

Action Words

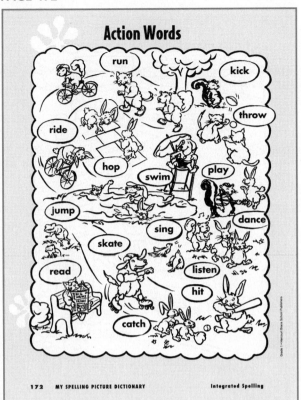

PAGE 173

Food Words

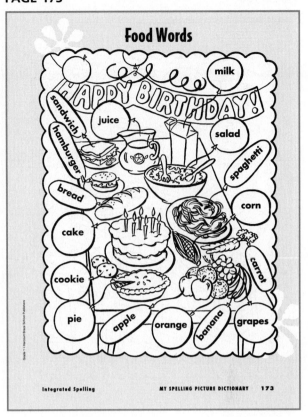

PAGE 174

Place Words

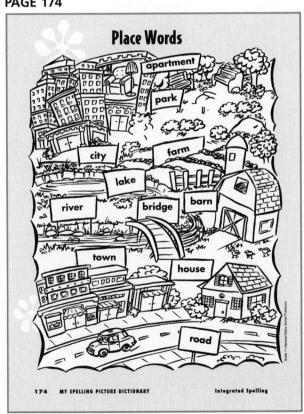

PAGE 175

Position Words

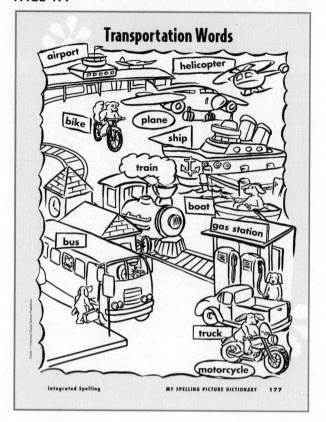

The Writing Process

USING THE WRITING PROCESS can help children not only in thinking about, creating, revising, and polishing original written works, but also in improving their spelling.

PRODUCING AN ERROR-FREE piece of writing involves a combination of creative thinking, critical evaluation, and checking for errors in spelling and mechanics. Although the writing process is a recursive one in which children may move back and forth between stages as necessary, it also allows children to focus on one task at a time.

The basic stages of the writing process are

Prewriting Children identify their task, audience, and purpose for writing. Then they select a topic and organize their information. Pictures, lists, charts, and webs are effective graphic organizers for the prewriting stage.

Drafting Children write a rough draft from their prewriting information. They focus on the message rather than on correct spelling, punctuation, usage, or mechanics at this stage.

Responding and Revising Children reread their writing and make changes. They might also work in pairs or with a group to make evaluations or suggestions.

Proofreading Children find and correct errors in spelling, grammar, usage, mechanics, and punctuation.

Publishing Children prepare their writing to share with others.

▶ SPELLING AS PART OF WRITING

Learning correct spelling in the context of their writing helps children focus on the relationships between words as well as the spelling of individual words. As children learn about written language, they apply that knowledge to words they wish to use in their own writing.

▶ PRACTICE THROUGH PROOFREADING

The proofreading stage of the writing process provides an excellent opportunity for children to learn spelling skills. Children will more readily understand the need for correct spelling when they recognize misspellings in their own writing. Teaching spelling as part of the writing process, together with the direct teaching of reading vocabulary and problem words taken from children's own writing, is both natural and effective. Such teaching works because it is based on the desire of children to communicate clearly as writers.

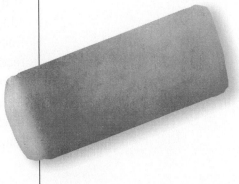

▶ INTRODUCING THE WRITING PROCESS

Ask children to name some things they like to write, such as stories or letters. Explain that they will learn about a plan that will help them become better writers. Then read Pupil's Edition pages 178–180 to the children. Next, help volunteers reread the different stages of the writing process aloud. Use questions such as these to discuss the writing process with children:

• How many steps are there in the writing process?

• What do you do in each step?

• How can the writing process help you when you write?

• Why do you think it is important to fix up your writing? How can others help you with this stage?

Help children understand that not every piece of writing they produce needs to be constructed according to the stages of the writing process. The writing process is intended for works they want to share, such as stories or friendly letters, and works they hope to develop into finished form.

▶ SUGGESTIONS FOR USING THE WRITING PROCESS

Here are suggestions for helping children become familiar with the writing process and use it to improve their spelling:

Prewriting Children can sometimes benefit from group brainstorming sessions. Write idea webs on the board to help children consider a variety of topics before they select one to write about. Children may need some guidance in identifying their purpose and audience. Use these questions to guide them:

• What will you try to do in this piece of writing? Are you going to write something that gives information or something that entertains your readers?

• Who will read your work? What can you do to make your writing interesting to your readers?

Drafting Remind children that when they use the stages of the writing process, they can go back to what they have written as many times as they like. As children write their first drafts, or as you write collaboratively with children, encourage them to write freely. Point out to them that they will have opportunities to correct their work later.

Note that children who are acquiring English may need some assistance with writing a first draft. You might encourage them to draw pictures to show story events and then work with a peer to whom they can dictate a caption for each picture.

Responding and Revising Have children work with you, a partner, or a small group to revise their writing. Point out to children that at this stage of the writing process, they can add, delete, move, or replace information. Encourage children to ask one another for feedback and to offer honest but constructive responses. Also, ask children to begin checking for spelling. However, note that it is at the proofreading stage that children will concentrate on making sure spelling is correct.

Proofreading Discuss with children the importance of proofreading as a way to prepare their writing for their readers. Point out that correct spelling is important because their writing will be shared with others, and misspelled words can make it difficult for readers to understand the writer's message.

Proofreading instruction may be carried out in small groups or as a class. Suggest these procedures to help children proofread for spelling errors:

• Children should proofread their writing twice. The first time, they should circle any words they know are misspelled. The second time, they should circle words they suspect are misspelled.

• Children can work with a partner to correct spellings by using the Picture Dictionary, by referring to their Spelling Logs, by applying spelling generalizations, and by asking others how to spell words.

• Help children understand that the correct spelling of words that are most commonly misspelled, such as *too/to/two,* can be determined by sentence context. Remind children that good spellers think about the meaning of the sentence in which a troublesome word appears.

• Have children add to their Spelling Logs the words they have misspelled. Remind them that a Spelling Log is a useful resource for recording words they have trouble spelling.

Publishing You might give children an opportunity to generate creative ideas for publishing their work and allow them to choose from among these ideas when they share their writing:

• Children can organize an "Authors Circle" in which child authors read their work aloud. Afterward, have children discuss the spelling errors they found, and how and when they corrected them.

• Children can collect their finished works and bind them, with all drafts of their writing, into individual books for the classroom library.

• Children might create posters, dioramas, or murals to display their writing.

• Children can make puppets and act out their writing.

The Writing Process

When you write, follow the five steps of the Writing Process.

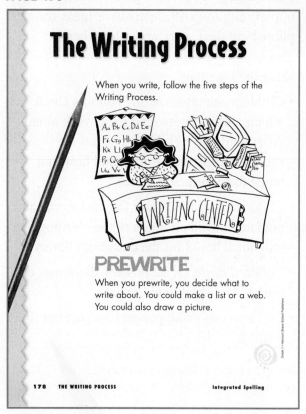

PREWRITE

When you prewrite, you decide what to write about. You could make a list or a web. You could also draw a picture.

DRAFT

When you write a draft, you put your ideas on paper. Don't worry about making mistakes. Just write what you want to say.

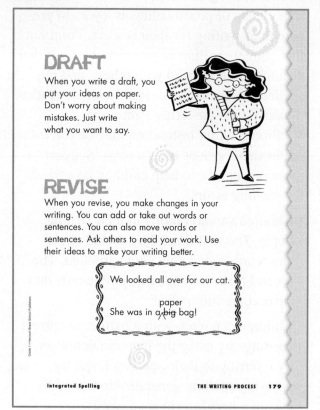

REVISE

When you revise, you make changes in your writing. You can add or take out words or sentences. You can also move words or sentences. Ask others to read your work. Use their ideas to make your writing better.

We looked all over for our cat.
paper
She was in a ~~big~~ bag!

PROOFREAD

When you proofread, you look for mistakes. Correct any mistakes you find.

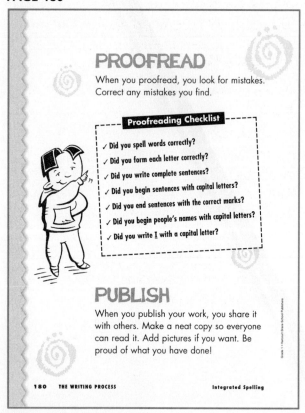

Proofreading Checklist

✓ Did you spell words correctly?

✓ Did you form each letter correctly?

✓ Did you write complete sentences?

✓ Did you begin sentences with capital letters?

✓ Did you end sentences with the correct marks?

✓ Did you begin people's names with capital letters?

✓ Did you write I with a capital letter?

PUBLISH

When you publish your work, you share it with others. Make a neat copy so everyone can read it. Add pictures if you want. Be proud of what you have done!

Spelling Strategies

THE LESSONS IN INTEGRATED SPELLING *are designed around and utilize two major strategies of instruction: (a) phonology—consistent spelling patterns based on sound-letter relationships; and (b) analogy—common characteristics of words as the basis for predicting the spelling of unfamiliar words.*

▶ SPECIFIC STRATEGIES FOR SPELLING

These specific strategies and others are presented in *Integrated Spelling*:

Study Steps to Learn a Word Children are encouraged to use the five study steps to help them learn the spelling of new words.

Picture a Word and Sound It Out Children picture a word they want to write, and think about the sounds the letters stand for.

Try Different Spellings Children think about the vowel sound in a word, consider different ways this sound can be represented by letters, and try different spellings until the word looks right.

Guess and Check Children guess the spelling of a word and then check its spelling in their Picture Dictionary.

Rhyming Words/Word Families Children often can figure out the spelling of a word by thinking about word families or rhyming words that share the same spelling pattern and sound-letter relationship.

Use a Dictionary Children can simply look up the spelling of a word in their Picture Dictionary.

▶ STRATEGIES FOR IDENTIFYING SPELLING ERRORS IN WRITING

These particular strategies are helpful to children as they proofread:

Proofread Twice By proofreading their writing twice, children identify spelling errors they know they have made, as well as possible misspellings.

Proofread with a Partner Children work with a partner to check and discuss each other's spelling.

Proofread Backward By beginning with the last word in a sentence and reading each word in isolation, children are apt to notice misspellings because the words are not in context.

▶ SPELLING PROCESS

To aid children in developing the tools to become competent independent spellers, spelling strategies are provided to maximize their learning. The strategies help children think about spelling as a skill they can develop through a variety of processes such as the following:

• Utilizing a five-step strategy can help them learn the spelling of new words.

- Using a variety of spelling strategies can help them remember the spelling of troublesome words.

- Using possible spellings, thinking about word families, and using a dictionary can help them figure out how to spell new words.

- Proofreading can help them identify spelling errors in their own writing.

▶ INTRODUCING THE STRATEGIES

Ask children to name some things they can do to help them figure out how to spell a word that is new to them and to remember the spelling of words they know. List their suggestions on the board. Explain to children that they will learn about some additional spelling strategies they can use as they write and proofread. Read pages 181–182 to children. Then invite volunteers to read the information about the strategies aloud.

Encourage children to summarize the strategies by asking questions such as these:

- Which strategies might you use when you are trying to figure out how to spell a word you don't know?

- Imagine that you want to spell the word *tree*. How can thinking about the words *see* and *bee* help you?

Discuss with children when to use spelling strategies. Point out that these strategies are also useful as they are writing. Encourage children to refer to pages 181–182 as they write.

PAGE 181

PAGE 182

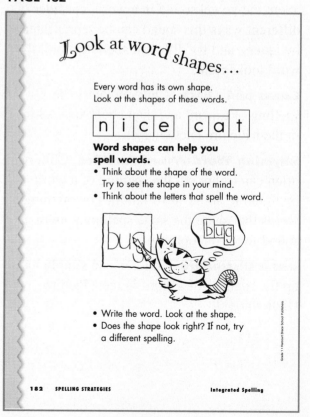

SUGGESTIONS FOR
Using the Spelling Log

THE SPELLING LOG *is on pages 183–192 of the Pupil's Edition. There are two parts to the Spelling Log: Vocabulary WordShop Words and My Own Word Collection.*

WORDSHOP WORDS

Spelling Log pages 184–189 correspond to the WordShop Words section of the spelling lessons. Children can group the WordShop Words any way they like, but they should be encouraged to place the words on the pages where they belong. These pages are organized according to the following categories:

> *Action Words*: page 184
> *Describing Words*: page 185
> *People Words*: page 186
> *Position Words*: page 187
> *Science Words*: page 188
> *Time and Place Words*: page 189

After children have completed each spelling lesson, have them write the WordShop Words on the pages where they belong. Encourage children to use the pictures on the pages to help them group words.

Some words might be placed in more than one category. Encourage children to discuss the reasons a word fits in both categories. Have children write the word in both categories.

MY OWN WORD COLLECTION

Pages 190–192 of the Spelling Log provide space for children to record words they have gathered from other sources and want to remember. Make sure children understand that they can create their own word groups on these pages. Suggestions for word groups are also provided on the pages. Children can choose from among these ideas or think of their own ways to categorize words.

From time to time, invite volunteers to share the words they have written in this part of the Spelling Log. Children can read words aloud and explain how they have chosen to group them. Encourage children who have created the same groups to compare the words they have included.

▶ REVIEWING THE SPELLING LOGS

You might want to monitor children's progress in using their Spelling Logs. Periodically or at the end of each unit, encourage children to share with you the words they have written in each part of the Spelling Log. Discuss with children their reasons for grouping different words. Encourage children to use in their writing the words they have written in their Spelling Logs.

My Spelling Log

What's a Spelling Log? It's a special place for words that are important to you. Here's what you'll find in this Spelling Log!

WordShop
· WORDS ·

VOCABULARY WORDSHOP WORDS

Every spelling lesson has Vocabulary WordShop Words. List them where you think they belong on these special pages.

Action Words • page 184

Describing Words • page 185

People Words • page 186

Position Words • page 187

Science Words • page 188

Time and Place Words • page 189

Add Your Own
· WORDS ·

MY OWN WORD COLLECTION, *pages 190–192*

Be a word collector. Keep your collection here! Group words you want to remember any way you please!

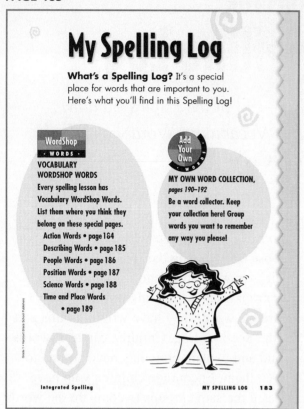

Integrated Spelling   MY SPELLING LOG   183

WordShop
· WORDS ·
Action Words

On this page, you can write Action Words.

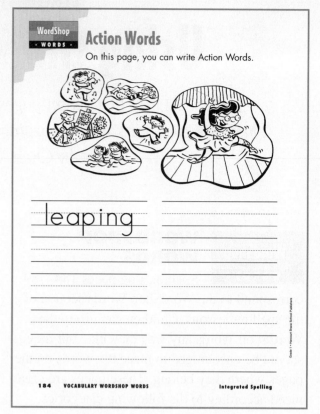

leaping

184   VOCABULARY WORDSHOP WORDS   Integrated Spelling

Describing Words

WordShop
· WORDS ·

This page is for Describing Words. These words tell how things look, feel, taste, smell, and sound. They also tell how many or what color.

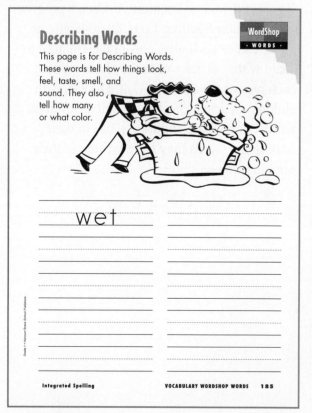

wet

Integrated Spelling   VOCABULARY WORDSHOP WORDS   185

WordShop
· WORDS ·
People Words

You can write People Words on this page.

baby

186   VOCABULARY WORDSHOP WORDS   Integrated Spelling

Position Words

WordShop
• WORDS •

This page is for writing Position Words.

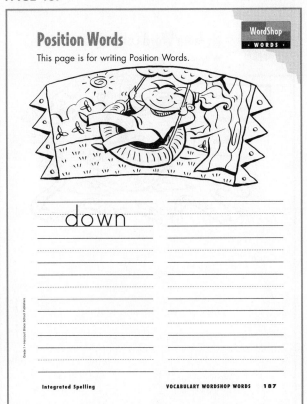

down

Grade 1 • Harcourt Brace School Publishers

WordShop
• WORDS •

Science Words

You can write Science Words on this page. Clues can help you remember a word. Your clues can be words or pictures like this one.

web

Grade 1 • Harcourt Brace School Publishers

Time and Place Words

WordShop
• WORDS •

Time and Place Words belong on this page.

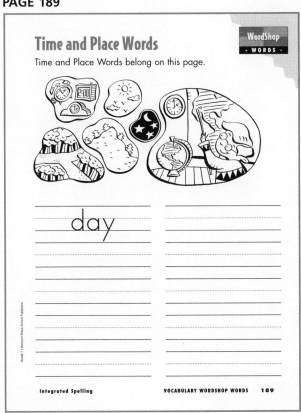

day

Grade 1 • Harcourt Brace School Publishers

Add Your Own
• WORDS •

My Own Word Collection

What's a word collection?

It's like a sticker collection. You choose words you like. Then you put them in groups with other words.

Weather Words
School Words
Sports Words
Story Words
Play Words

What kinds of groups?

Look at the pictures to get some ideas. Use your own ideas, too.

Group _____   Group _____

Grade 1 • Harcourt Brace School Publishers

My Own Word Collection

Add words that you want to know how to spell. Then you can use them in your writing.

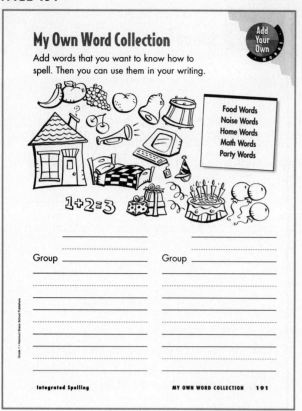

Food Words
Noise Words
Home Words
Math Words
Party Words

1+2=3

Group _____

Group _____

Integrated Spelling

MY OWN WORD COLLECTION   191

My Own Word Collection

Write more of your own words on this page.

Happy Words
Sad Words
Silly Words
Long Words
Short Words

Group _____

Group _____

192   MY OWN WORD COLLECTION

Integrated Spelling

Answer Key for Lessons

LESSON 1

Page 10
Pictured objects whose names begin with the letters *b*, *h*, *d*, and *t*:
b — boy, bananas, basket, buns
h — hot dogs
d — dog, dishes
t — table, tail
Accept reasonable responses.

Page 11
1. dog 2. hat 3. tie 4. boy
5. dog, boy

Page 12
1. hat 2. pie 3. bee
Plan a Picnic Accept pictures and words that are reasonable responses.

Page 13
1. pie 2. bee 3. hat

LESSON 2

Page 14
Pictured objects whose names end with the phonogram *-ap*:
tapping drum, snapping fingers, clapping hands, map, cap
Accept reasonable responses.

Page 15
1. tap 2. map 3. cap 4. nap
5. tap, map

Page 16
1. farm 2. duck 3. hen
Act Like an Animal Accept reasonable responses.

Page 17
Hidden words, across: farm, cat, hen
Hidden word, down: duck
1. hen 2. duck 3. cat
4. farm

LESSON 3

Page 18
Pictured objects whose names end with the phonogram *-ot*:
cot, hot, pot, dot, tot
Accept reasonable responses.

Page 19
1. dot 2. pot 3. tot 4. hot 5. dot, pot

Page 20
1. I 2. me 3. you
What I Like Accept pictures that are reasonable responses.

Page 21
1. I 2. you 3. me

LESSON 4

Page 22
Pictured objects whose names end with the phonogram *-an*:
pan, can, van, man, fan
Accept reasonable responses.

Page 23
1. fan 2. van 3. man 4. pan
5. man, van

Page 24
1. three 2. one 3. two

Page 25
1. one 2. three 3. two
Draw and Count Accept reasonable responses.

LESSON 5

Page 26
Pictured objects whose names end with the phonogram *-at*:
mat, cat, bat, hat, patting of the ducklings, flat tire
Accept reasonable responses.

Page 27
1. hat 2. bat 3. cat 4. mat 5. cat, mat

Page 28
1. red 2. yellow 3. green
Color Signs Accept signs that are reasonable responses.

Page 29
Children should color the trees green, the sign red, and the flowers yellow. They should also include a drawing of themselves in the scene.

LESSON 6

Page 30
Pictured objects whose names end with the phonogram *-op*:
mop, girl doing a hop, top, stop sign, lollipop design
Accept reasonable responses.

Page 31
1. pop 2. hop 3. mop 4. top
5. top, mop

Page 32
1. pot 2. pop 3. hot
Get It While It's Hot! Accept pictures that are reasonable responses.

Page 33
1. pot 2. hot 3. pop 4. popcorn
Accept pictures that are reasonable responses.

LESSON 7

Page 34
Pictured objects whose names end with the phonogram *-et*:
jet, net, pet and vet on book covers, wet rain on window
Accept reasonable responses.

Page 35
1. jet, 2. net 3. vet 4. wet 5. get, jet

Page 36
1. blue 2. brown 3. paint

Paint a Picture Accept pictures and words that are reasonable responses.

Page 37
Children should do the following: **1.** circle the bears that are painting **2.** color the bigger bear brown **3.** color the little bear's hat blue

LESSON 8

Page 38
Pictured objects whose names end with the phonogram -ell:
shell, wishing well, bell, skunk who has a smell, girl giving a yell
Accept reasonable responses.

Page 39
1. well **2.** yell **3.** fell **4.** bell
5. fell **6.** yell

Page 40
1. shell **2.** butterfly **3.** worm
Nature Flash Cards Accept pictures and words that are reasonable responses.

Page 41
1. butterfly; Children should complete the picture of the butterfly. **2.** shell; Children should complete the picture of the shell. **3.** worm; Children should complete the picture of the worm.

LESSON 9

Page 42
Pictured objects whose names end with the phonogram -en:
men, numeral ten, pen, hen
Accept reasonable responses.

Page 43
1. ten **2.** pen **3.** men **4.** hen
5. ten, men

Page 44
1. sunny **2.** cloudy **3.** gray
Weather Report Accept pictures and sentences that are reasonable responses.

Page 45
1–3. Accept words and pictures that are reasonable responses.
4. Sentences will vary.

LESSON 10

Page 46
Pictured objects whose names end with the phonogram -ick:
brick, fox licking his chops, chick, stick, boy picking apples
Accept reasonable responses.

Page 47
1. kick **2.** pick **3.** lick **4.** sick
5. pick, kick

Page 48
1. moving **2.** box **3.** going
Pack a Box Accept words and pictures that are reasonable responses.

Page 49
1. box **2.** going **3.** moving
4. dog

LESSON 11

Page 50
Pictured objects whose names end with the phonogram -ip:
monkey doing a flip, hippo sipping a drink, bowl of chips, gorilla dipping toes in water, toy ship
Accept reasonable responses.

Page 51
1. zip **2.** rip **3.** lip **4.** tip **5.** rip

Page 52
1. teeth **2.** feet **3.** tail
Animal Body Parts Accept pictures and words that are reasonable responses.

Page 53
1. teeth **2.** feet **3.** tail

LESSON 12

Page 54
Pictured objects whose names end with the phonogram -ad:
smiling face—glad; unpleasant face—bad; frowning face—sad;

angry face—mad; note pad
Accept reasonable responses.

Page 55
1. pad **2.** mad **3.** dad **4.** sad
5. dad, pad

Page 56
1. threw **2.** ran **3.** caught
Game Time Accept sentences that are reasonable responses.

Page 57
Hidden words, across: ran, threw
Hidden word, down: caught
1. caught **2.** ran **3.** threw

LESSON 13

Page 58
Pictured objects whose names end with the phonogram -in:
child about to win the race, twins, fish fin, bin, person with a grin
Accept reasonable responses.

Page 59
1. fin **2.** bin **3.** win **4.** pin
5. win, pin

Page 60
1. ears **2.** nose **3.** legs

Page 61
1. nose **2.** ears **3.** legs
Favorite Animals Accept pictures and words that are reasonable responses.

LESSON 14

Page 62
Pictured objects whose names end with the phonogram -ill:
act of filling the glass, pills, hill, windmill, windowsill
Accept reasonable responses.

Page 63
1. sill **2.** fill **3.** pill **4.** hill **5.** pill, sill

Page 64
1. listen **2.** peek **3.** see

Page 65
1. listen **2.** peek **3.** see
Act It Out Accept reasonable responses.

LESSON 15

Page 66
Pictured objects whose names end with the phonogram -ug:
bug, tug, rug, plug, mug
Accept reasonable responses.

Page 67
1. rug 2. tug 3. mug 4. bug
5. bug, rug

Page 68
1. swim 2. ride 3. paint
Friends Together Accept sentences that are reasonable responses.

Page 69
1–3. Accept pictures that are reasonable responses to the questions.

LESSON 16

Page 70
Pictured objects whose names end with the phonogram -ig:
pig, cow that is digging, twig, fig, wig
Accept reasonable responses.

Page 71
1. pig 2. dig 3. fig 4. wig
5. pig, wig

Page 72
1. little 2. long 3. happy

Page 73
1. happy 2. little 3. long
Describe Something Accept pictures and words that are reasonable responses.

LESSON 17

Page 74
Pictured objects whose names end with the phonogram -un:
children who run, bun, sun, children having fun
Accept reasonable responses.

Page 75
1. sun 2. run 3. fun 4. bun
5. run, sun

Page 76
1. reading 2. learn 3. math

Page 77
1. learn 2. math 3. reading
School Time Accept pictures that are reasonable responses.

LESSON 18

Page 78
Pictured objects whose names end with the phonogram
-ack:
seed pack, sack, tack, rack, jack
Accept reasonable responses.

Page 79
1. tack 2. jack 3. pack 4. back
5. pack, sack

Page 80
1. music 2. step 3. dance

Page 81
1. music 2. dance 3. step

LESSON 19

Page 82
(*left column*) **5.** (possible response: **then**) Words added by children will vary.
(*right column*) red, hen, help, went; Children should color the picture of the hen above the label *middle*.

Page 83
1. hen 2. red 3. went
Fun with Words help

Page 84
1. called 2. asked 3. said

Page 85
1. called 2. asked 3. said

LESSON 20

Page 86
(*left column*) **5.** (possible response: **such**) Words added by children will vary.
(*right column*) but, must, just, run; Children should color the picture of the acorn above the label *middle*.

Page 87
1. just 2. must
Fun with Words 3. but **4.** run

Page 88
1. tree 2. woods 3. path

Page 89
1. path 2. woods 3. tree
A Birthday Surprise Accept reasonable responses.

LESSON 21

Page 90
(*left column*) **5.** (possible response: **his**) Words added by children will vary.
(*right column*) in, it; Children should color the picture of the stone under the label *beginning* for these words.
big, him; Children should color the picture of the stone under the label *middle* for these words.

Page 91
1. Children should write an X over the letter *k* in *kit*; it
2. Children should write an X over the letter *p* in *pin*; in
Fun with Words 3. big **4.** him

Page 92
1. mother 2. children 3. friends
People Power Accept pictures that are reasonable responses.

Page 93
Accept reasonable responses.

LESSON 22

Page 94
(*left column*) **5.** (possible response: **which**) Words added by children will vary.
(*right column*) when, what, where, why; Children should circle the letters *wh* in each of these words.

Page 95
1. where 2. when 3. what
Fun with Words 4. why

Page 96
1. found 2. take 3. keep

Page 97
1. Children should color the pictures of the flowers, the squirrel, and the fallen leaves.
2. Children should color the pictures of the nest and the butterfly.
3. Accept pictures that are reasonable responses.
Ask a Friend Accept questions that are reasonable responses.

LESSON 23

Page 98
(*left column*) 5. (possible response: **fat**) Words added by children will vary.
(*right column*) and, am; Children should write these words under the label *beginning*.
can, had; Children should write these words under the label *middle*.

Page 99
1. and 2. can
Fun with Words 3. am
4. had

Page 100
1–3. (possible responses: dirt, earth, soil)
Share a Meaning Accept words that are reasonable responses.

Page 101
1–3. Accept pictures that are reasonable responses.

LESSON 24

Page 102
(*left column*) 5. (possible response: **box**) Words added by children will vary.
(*right column*) on; Children should color the picture of the flower under the label *beginning* for this word.
not, stop, got; Children should color the picture of the flower under the label *middle* for these words.

Page 103
1. not 2. got 3. stop
Fun with Words 4. on

Page 104
1. seed 2. plant 3. flower

Page 105
1. flower 2. plant 3. seed
4. plant

LESSON 25

Page 106
(*left column*) 5. (possible response: **took**) Words added by children will vary.
(*right column*) look, said, put; Children should write these words on the snowman.
with; Children should write this word on the broom.

Page 107
1. put 2. with 3. look
Fun with Words 4. said

Page 108
1. scarf 2. snow 3. snowman
Build a Word snow, man; Accept pictures that are reasonable responses.

Page 109
Accept pictures that are reasonable responses.
1. snow 2. snowman 3. scarf

LESSON 26

Page 110
(*left column*) 5. (possible response: **some**) Words added by children will vary.
(*right column*) of, now, one, come; Children should write each of these words so that the letter *o* is written in a star.

Page 111
1. of 2. come
Fun with Words 3. one 4. now

Page 112
1. water 2. sail 3. waves
Sailing, Sailing Accept reasonable responses.

Page 113
1. waves; Children should draw a picture of waves.
2. sail; Children should draw a picture of a sail.
3. water; Children should draw a picture of water.

LESSON 27

Page 114
1. must 2. big 3. run
4. in 5. help

Page 115
1. and 2. put 3. got 4. what 5. of

Page 116
Accept sentences that are reasonable responses.

Page 117
1. pen; pin 2. hit; hut

LESSON 28

Page 118
(*left column*) 5. (possible response: **stay**) Words added by children will vary.
(*right column*) came, made; Children should write these words next to the label *a–e*.
play; Children should write this word next to the label *ay*.
wait; Children should write this word next to the label *ai*.

Page 119
1. made 2. came 3. play
Fun with Words wait

Page 120
1. bedtime; Children should circle the word *yes*.
2. asleep; Children should circle the word *no*.
3. dream; Children should circle the word *yes*.

Page 121
bedtime; asleep; dream
Accept pictures that are reasonable responses.

LESSON 29

Page 122
(*left column*) 5. (possible response: **this**) Words added by children will vary.

(*right column*) the, then, that, they; Children should write each of these words so that the letters *th* are written in a soap bubble.

Page 123
1. that **2.** then
Fun with Words the; they *or* then; then *or* they

Page 124
1. bath **2.** bath **3.** dry; wet

Page 125
1. Children should color the pictures of the hose, the watering can, and the faucet.
2. Children should color the pictures of the towel, the hair dryer, and the paper towels.
3. Accept pictures that are reasonable responses.

LESSON 30

Page 126
(*left column*) **5.** (possible response: **come**) Words added by children will vary.
(*right column*) have, live, some; Children should write these words under the label *middle*.
do; Children should write this word under the label *end*.

Page 127
1. have **2.** do **3.** live
Fun with Words some

Page 128
1. paws **2.** fins **3.** beaks
Imagine That! Accept pictures and names that are reasonable responses.

Page 129
beaks; Children should draw a picture of beaks.
paws; Children should draw a picture of paws.
fins; Children should draw a picture of fins.

LESSON 31

Page 130
(*left column*) **5.** (possible response: **be**) Words added by children will vary.
(*right column*) we, she, he, me; Children should color the picture of the snail above the label *end*.

Page 131
Children should color the parts of the puzzle that show the words *we, she, he,* and *me.*
Fun with Words 1. me **2.** he **3.** she **4.** we

Page 132
1. new **2.** name **3.** welcome

Page 133
1. Children should write their own names. **2.** Children should write the name of a new student. **3.** Accept pictures that are reasonable responses.
How Do You Do? Accept reasonable responses.

LESSON 32

Page 134
(*left column*) **5.** (possible response: **five**) Words added by children will vary.
(*right column*) like, ride, nine; Children should color the picture of the planet under the label *middle*.
ice; Children should color the picture of the planet under the label *beginning*.

Page 135
1. ride **2.** nine **3.** like
Fun with Words ice

Page 136
1. sun **2.** star **3.** planet
Sky Time Accept pictures and words that are reasonable responses.

Page 137
Puzzle words, down: **1.** star **2.** planet
Puzzle words, across: **3.** sun

4. rocket
Blast Off Accept maps that are reasonable responses.

LESSON 33

Page 138
(*left column*) **5.** (possible response: **in**) Words added by children will vary.
(*right column*) his, give; Children should write these words on the baby bottle.
was, saw; Children should write these words on the baby rattle.

Page 139
1. was **2.** give **3.** his
Fun with Words saw; was

Page 140
baby; cry; bottle

Page 141
1. bottle **2.** baby **3.** cry

LESSON 34

Page 142
(*left column*) **5.** (possible response: **so**) Words added by children will vary.
(*right column*) or; Children should write this word under the label *beginning*.
love; Children should write this word under the label *middle*.
who, no; Children should write these words under the label *end*.

Page 143
1. love **2.** no **3.** or
Fun with Words who

Page 144
1. everything **2.** anything **3.** something

Page 145
1. everything; Children should color the following items: pig, girl, cat, bushes, bird, grass, flowers, and trees.
2. something; Children should color one of the following items: car, taxi, bus, or plane.
3. anything; Accept pictures

that are reasonable responses.

LESSON 35

Page 146
(*left column*) **5.** (possible
response: **nose**) Words added
by children will vary.
(*right column*) old; Children
should write this word under
the label *beginning*.
rose, home; Children should
write these words under the
label *middle*.
go; Children should write this
word under the label *end*.

Page 147
1. rose **2.** old **3.** go
Fun with Words home

Page 148
1. grandparents **2.** aunt **3.** family

Page 149
Children should draw a line
between each of the following
pictures and the word that
represents the picture: *aunt;
baby; grandparents; father*.
Accept sentences and pictures
that are reasonable responses.

LESSON 36

Page 150
1. we **2.** ride **3.** give **4.** or
5. home

Page 151
1. made **2.** some **3.** then **4.** they
5. do

Page 152
Accept pictures and thank-you
letters that are reasonable
responses.

Page 153
1. lake **2.** rope **3.** ripe

Copying Masters

USING THE COPYING MASTERS
T264
This page provides information about using the reproducible record-keeping charts and Home Activities Masters.

PERCENT CONVERSION CHART
T265
This chart converts Pretest, Posttest, and Practice Test scores to percentages.

SPELLING PROGRESS RECORD
T266
This chart may be used to track children's test scores for Lessons 19–36.

CLASS RECORD-KEEPING CHART
T267
This chart is useful for tracking class progress for Lessons 19–36 of Integrated Spelling.

HOME ACTIVITIES MASTERS
T268–T303
This section contains one copying master for each lesson in Integrated Spelling.

USING THE
Copying Masters

THIS SECTION OF THE TEACHER'S EDITION *contains the following reproducible record-keeping charts and Home Activities Masters.*

▶ PERCENT CONVERSION CHART

The Percent Conversion Chart indicates percentage scores on tests that have from 4 to 24 test items. The horizontal row of numbers across the top of the chart represents the number of items answered correctly. The vertical row of numbers that runs along the left side of the chart represents the number of items in a test. To find the percentage score that a particular child has earned, find the box where the appropriate horizontal and vertical rows meet. The percentage score appears in that box.

▶ SPELLING PROGRESS RECORD

The Spelling Progress Record may be used to track individual children's scores for the Pretests, Posttests, and Practice Tests in Lessons 19–36. Make one photocopy of the Spelling Progress Record for each child. Keep a copy of this chart in each child's portfolio, and refer to it during child-teacher conferences. You may prefer to allow children to record their own scores and keep a copy of the record to monitor their progress as a form of self-assessment.

The Practice Tests are designed to give children practice with the standardized-test format and to help them become comfortable with test-taking procedures. The number of correctly spelled words should be recorded in the appropriate column of the chart.

▶ CLASS RECORD-KEEPING CHART

Use the Class Record-Keeping Chart to keep track of the progress of your class. This master can hold all children's scores for the Pretests, Posttests, and Practice Tests. Make two copies of this page. Use one copy with Lessons 19–27 and one copy with Lessons 28–36.

▶ HOME ACTIVITIES MASTERS

One Home Activities Master is provided for each spelling lesson. The Answer Key for the copying masters appears on page T304.

For Developmental Lessons After children have completed the Strategy Workshop, copy the Home Activities Master for the corresponding lesson. Distribute the word cards to children, and guide them in an open-sort activity. In this activity, children group the word cards according to a criterion they decide on themselves. They might group words that share the same beginning or middle sound, words that are related by topic, or words that have a similar shape. You may also want to have children take home the Home Activities Master with the word cards and complete the spelling activity with a family member.

For Review Lessons Use the Home Activities Master as an extra activity to reinforce the spelling strategies taught in previous lessons. Begin by having children review the spelling strategies in the corresponding lessons in the Pupil's Edition.

PERCENT CONVERSION CHART

Use the matrix below to convert the raw score for each test to a percentage.

NUMBER OF TEST ITEMS	NUMBER CORRECT																						
	2	3	4	5	6	7	8	9	10	11	12	13	14	15	16	17	18	19	20	21	22	23	24
For 4-item tests	50	75	100																				
For 5-item tests	40	60	80	100																			
For 6-item tests		50	67	83	100																		
For 7-item tests		43	57	71	86	100																	
For 8-item tests			50	63	75	88	100																
For 9-item tests			44	56	67	78	89	100															
For 10-item tests				50	60	70	80	90	100														
For 11-item tests				45	55	64	73	82	91	100													
For 12-item tests					50	58	67	75	83	92	100												
For 13-item tests					46	54	62	69	77	85	92	100											
For 14-item tests						50	57	64	71	79	86	93	100										
For 15-item tests						47	53	60	67	73	80	87	93	100									
For 16-item tests							50	56	63	69	75	81	88	94	100								
For 17-item tests							47	53	59	65	71	76	82	88	94	100							
For 18-item tests								50	56	61	67	72	78	83	89	94	100						
For 19-item tests								47	53	58	63	68	74	79	84	89	95	100					
For 20-item tests									50	55	60	65	70	75	80	85	90	95	100				
For 21-item tests									48	52	57	62	67	71	76	81	86	90	95	100			
For 22-item tests										50	55	59	64	68	73	77	82	86	91	95	100		
For 23-item tests										48	52	57	61	65	70	74	78	83	87	91	96	100	
For 24-item tests											50	54	58	63	67	71	75	79	83	88	92	96	100

Spelling Progress Record

Lesson	NUMBER OF WORDS CORRECTLY SPELLED		PROGRESS	
	Pretest	**Posttest**	**Showed Improvement**	**Mastered Words**
Lesson 19			◯	◯
Lesson 20			◯	◯
Lesson 21			◯	◯
Lesson 22			◯	◯
Lesson 23			◯	◯
Lesson 24			◯	◯
Lesson 25			◯	◯
Lesson 26			◯	◯
Lesson 27	PRACTICE TEST		◯	◯
Lesson 28			◯	◯
Lesson 29			◯	◯
Lesson 30			◯	◯
Lesson 31			◯	◯
Lesson 32			◯	◯
Lesson 33			◯	◯
Lesson 34			◯	◯
Lesson 35			◯	◯
Lesson 36	PRACTICE TEST		◯	◯

DIRECTIONS: Write in Pretest, Posttest, and Practice Test scores. If a child shows improvement but has missed one or more items, fill in the circle under *Showed Improvement*. For a perfect score, fill in the circle under *Mastered Words*.

Class Record-Keeping Chart

NAME	LESSON Pretest	Posttest	LESSON Pretest	Posttest	LESSON Pretest	Posttest	LESSON Pretest	Posttest	LESSON Pretest	Posttest	LESSON Pretest	Posttest	LESSON Pretest	Posttest	LESSON Pretest	Posttest	REVIEW LESSON Practice	Test
1.																		
2.																		
3.																		
4.																		
5.																		
6.																		
7.																		
8.																		
9.																		
10.																		
11.																		
12.																		
13.																		
14.																		
15.																		
16.																		
17.																		
18.																		
19.																		
20.																		
21.																		
22.																		
23.																		
24.																		
25.																		
26.																		
27.																		
28.																		
29.																		
30.																		
31.																		
32.																		
33.																		
34.																		
35.																		
36.																		

DIRECTIONS: Make copies of this page, and use one copy with Lessons 19–27 and one copy with Lessons 28–36.

Dear Parent or Guardian,

We have just begun a lesson on the sounds and spellings of words that begin with the consonants *b, h, d,* and *t.* Next time you go for a walk or a drive with your child, _____, look for people and objects whose names begin with these sounds and letters. Examples include a baby, a house, a dog, and a toy.

Please contact me if you have any questions.

Cordially,

_____

Home Spelling Activities

Have your child look through discarded magazines, catalogs, or store advertisements to find pictures of items whose names begin with the sounds for the letters *b, h, d,* and *t.* He or she might find pictures of bottles, hats, dishes, and tubs. Have your child cut out the pictures and paste them to newspaper pages, using a separate page for each letter. Encourage your child to say each picture name and identify the initial consonant while sharing each collage with family members.

Talk with your child about the picture below. Then ask him or her to find and color the pictures of things whose names begin with the sounds for the letters *b, h, d,* and *t.* (bubbles, bicycle, hat, house, dog, doll, tail, table) After your child finishes coloring, have him or her tell the names of the pictures and the beginning consonants.

Dear Parent or Guardian,
We have just begun a lesson on the sounds and spelling of words ending with the letters *ap*. You can help by encouraging your child, —————, to listen for words you use in everyday conversation that end with these sounds and letters, such as *clap*, *tap*, and *nap*.
Please contact me if you have any questions.

Cordially,

—————

Home Spelling Activities

You can use words that end with the sounds the letters *ap* stand for to play a game. Have your child draw pictures on slips of paper to show these words: *cap, nap, map*. Then read the riddles below, and have your child point to the picture and say the word that answers each riddle.

- People use this to help them find a new place. (*map*)
- Babies do this when they are tired. (*nap*)
- Baseball players wear this type of hat. (*cap*)

Read the rhyme below with your child. Then ask your child to color the pictures of things whose names end with the sounds for the letters *ap*. Talk about the things your child colored. (rapping fingers, tapping nose, clapping hands, tapping toes, cap, map)

Rap on the table.

Tap your nose.

Clap your hands.

Then tap your toes.

Dear Parent or Guardian,

We have just begun a lesson on the sounds and spelling of words ending with the letters *ot*. You can help by encouraging your child, _____, to listen for words you use in everyday conversation that end with these sounds and letters, such as *hot, got, pot,* and *not.*

Please contact me if you have any questions.

Cordially,

_____

Home Spelling Activities

Play a word association game with your child. Ask him or her to name a word that matches each clue below and ends with the letters *ot*:

- not a little but a _____ (*lot*)
- not too cold and not too _____ (*hot*)
- not a pan but a _____ (*pot*)
- not a line but a _____ (*dot*)
- not an infant but a _____ (*tot*)

Talk with your child about the picture below. Then have him or her find and color four things whose names end with the sounds for the letters *ot*. (pot, dot, tot, hot) Ask your child to name the things he or she colored. This will help your child hear that the words rhyme and that they end with the sounds the letters *ot* stand for.

Grade 1 • Harcourt Brace School Publishers

Dear Parent or Guardian,

We have just begun a lesson on the sounds and spelling of words ending with the letters *an*. Next time you go for a walk or drive in the neighborhood with your child, _____, look for people and objects whose names end with these sounds and letters. For example, you might see a van, a man, a can, and a fan.

Please contact me if you have any questions.

Cordially,

_____

Home Spelling Activities

Have your child look through magazines to find pictures of items whose names end with the sounds the letters *an* stand for. Have your child cut out the pictures and then glue them in a colorful arrangement on a piece of newspaper. Encourage your child to name each picture that he or she uses in this collage.

Talk with your child about the picture below. Then have him or her color the five things that are hidden in the picture whose names end with the letters *an*. (van, man, fan, pan, can) Ask your child to say the names of the things he or she colored. This will help your child to confirm that all those words rhyme and that they end with the sounds the letters *an* stand for.

Dear Parent or Guardian,

We have just begun a lesson on the sounds and spelling of words that end with the letters *at*. As you drive or walk through your neighborhood, encourage your child, ——————, to point out objects whose names contain these sounds and letters or can be described by words containing these sounds. For example, you might see a fat cat, a welcome mat, a baseball bat, and a funny hat.

Please contact me if you have any questions.

Cordially,

——————————

Home Spelling Activities

You can use words ending with the letters *at* to play a spelling game. Write these words on slips of paper: *bat, cat, fat, hat, mat, pat, rat,* and *sat.* Before you show each word, cover the first letter with your finger. Say the word. Ask your child to repeat it and tell which letter it begins with. Then lift your finger so he or she can check the answer.

Read the rhyme below with your child, and invite him or her to act it out. Then ask your child to color the pictures of the things whose names end with the sounds the letters *at* stand for. Talk about the things your child colored. (mat, hat, bat, cat)

Use the mat.

Take off your hat.

Put away the bat.

Now pet the cat.

Grade 1 • Harcourt Brace School Publishers

Dear Parent or Guardian,

We have just begun a lesson on the sounds and spelling of words ending with the letters *op*. You can help your child, _____, recognize words that have these sounds and letters by saying words such as *top, drop, pop, stop,* and *mop* and by asking your child to do a little hop while repeating each word with you.

Please contact me if you have any questions.

Cordially,

_____

Home Spelling Activities

You can use words ending with the sounds for the letters *op* to play a spelling game. Write the words *top, hop, pop,* and *mop*. Then say each word, covering the first letter with your finger. Ask your child to repeat the word and tell which letter it begins with. Then lift your finger so your child can check the answer.

Talk with your child about the picture below. Then have him or her find and color the four hidden things whose names end with the letters *op*. (top, lollipop, stop sign, mop) Ask your child to say the names of the things he or she colored. This will help your child to confirm that those words rhyme and that they end with the sounds the letters *op* stand for.

Dear Parent or Guardian,

We have just begun a lesson on the sounds and spelling of words ending with the letters *et*. You can help by encouraging your child, _____, to listen for words you use in everyday conversation that end with these sounds and letters. Possible examples include *let, get, set, wet,* and *pet.*

Please contact me if you have any questions.

Cordially,

_____

Home Spelling Activities

Begin a rhyming word game with your child by asking the following riddle:

> *B-e-t* spells *bet.*
> Change *b* to *n.* What word do you get?
> (*net*)

Continue the game by using the format of this riddle for other words that end with the letters *et*. These might include words such as *get, wet, met, pet,* and *let.*

Talk with your child about the picture below. Then have him or her find and color the three things whose names end with the sounds the letters *et* stand for. (a wet pet, net, jet) Ask your child to name the things he or she colored. This will help your child hear that those words rhyme and that they end with the sounds the letters *et* stand for.

Dear Parent or Guardian,

We have just begun a lesson on the sounds and spelling of words ending with the letters *ell*. You can help by encouraging your child, ——————, to listen for words you use in everyday conversation that end with these sounds and letters. Possible examples include *well, tell, yell, smell, sell, fell,* and *spell.*

Please contact me if you have any questions.

Cordially,

——————————

Home Spelling Activities

Begin a rhyming word game with your child by reading the following riddle:

I'll tell what I can spell:
S-e-l-l spells *sell.*
Now change the *s* to *w,*
And tell what you can spell.
(*well*)

Continue the game by using the format of this riddle for other words that end with the sounds for the letters *ell*. These might include words such as *bell, well, fell, yell, shell,* and *smell.*

Invite your child to use a pencil to mark the correct path in the maze below from the mouse to the cheese. Tell your child to figure out which path to take by looking for pictures whose names end with the same sounds as *spell*. (bell, wishing well, shell, a skunk that smells)

Grade 1 • Harcourt Brace School Publishers

Dear Parent or Guardian,

We have just begun a lesson on the sounds and spelling of words ending with the letters *en*. Next time you go on a family outing with your child, —————, encourage him or her to look for people and objects whose names end with these sounds and letters; for example, a group of men, a pen, and the numeral for ten. If you live in a rural area, you might even spot a hen!

Please contact me if you have any questions.

Cordially,

—————————————

Home Spelling Activities

You can use words that end with the sounds the letters *en* stand for to play a riddle game. Have your child draw pictures on small pieces of paper to illustrate these words: *men, pen, ten,* and *hen*. Then share these riddles, and ask your child to point to the picture whose name answers the riddle.

- A mother chicken is called this. (hen)
- This number comes after nine. (ten)
- Boys grow up to be these. (men)
- Use this to write with. (pen)

Talk with your child about the picture below. Then have him or her find and color the four hidden things whose names end with the letters *en*. (pen, ten, men, hen) Ask your child to name the things he or she colored. This will help your child to confirm that those words rhyme and that they end with the sounds the letters *en* stand for.

Dear Parent or Guardian,

We have just begun a lesson on the sounds and spelling of words ending with the letters *ick*. You can help your child, _____, recognize words that have these sounds and letters by saying words such as *brick, chick, kick, pick, quick, sick,* and *trick* and by asking your child to make a clicking sound after repeating each word with you.

Please contact me if you have any questions.

Cordially,

_____

Home Spelling Activities

You can play a guessing game using words that end with the sounds the letters *ick* stand for. Help your child write the following words on cards: *lick, click, tick, pick, sick, quick,* and *thick.* Then turn all the cards face down on a table. With your child, take turns selecting a word and acting it out so it can be guessed. Once a guess has been made, display the card to check if the response is correct.

Read the rhyme below with your child. Then have him or her name the pictures, cut them out, and paste them where they belong to illustrate the rhyme. (chick, brick, stick)

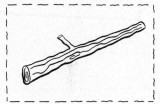

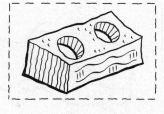

Do this magic trick.

Turn a duck into a <u>chick</u>.

Turn a rock into a <u>brick</u>.

Turn a leaf into a <u>stick</u>.

Dear Parent or Guardian,

We have just begun a lesson on the sounds and spelling of words ending with the letters *ip*. You can help by encouraging your child, _____, to use a doll or a stuffed animal to act out these rhyming action words as you say them aloud: *dip, trip, skip, flip,* and *slip.*

Please contact me if you have any questions.

Cordially,

_____

Home Spelling Activities

Play a matching game with your child, using these words: *dip, trip, sip, flip, tip, hip, nip, rip,* and *drip.* Work with your child to write each word on two separate cards. Take two cards and have your child take two cards. Then place the other cards face down in a pile. Take turns with your child selecting cards from the pile and either laying down a matching pair or discarding a card until all the cards have been matched.

Invite your child to use a pencil to mark the correct path in the maze below from the gorilla to the bananas. Tell your child to figure out which path to take by looking for pictures whose names end with the same sounds as *flip.* Ask your child to show you which pictures they are. (ship, whip, lip, faucet with a drip)

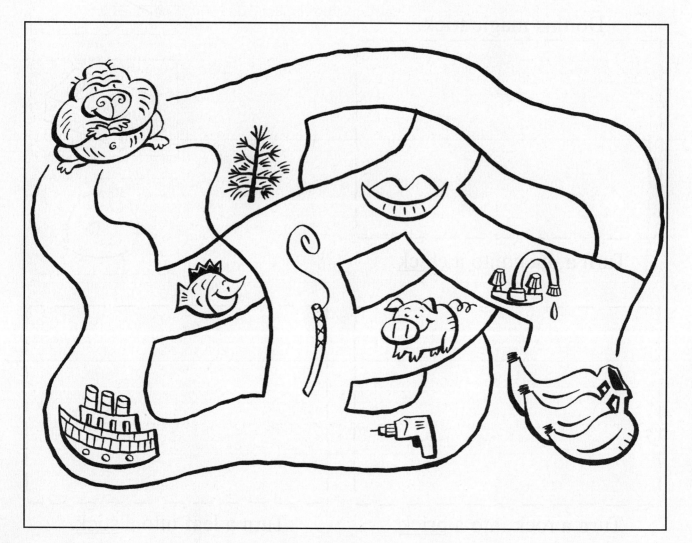

Grade 1 • Harcourt Brace School Publishers

Dear Parent or Guardian,

We have just begun a lesson on the sounds and spelling of words ending with the letters *ad*. Help your child, —————, recognize words that have these sounds and letters by saying words such as *bad*, *had*, *mad*, and *pad*. As you do so, alternate saying words that do not end with *ad*. Ask your child to look glad whenever he or she hears a word ending with the letters *ad*.

Please contact me if you have any questions.

Cordially,

—————————————

Home Spelling Activities

You can play a riddle game using words that end with the sounds for the letters *ad*. Have your child draw pictures to illustrate these words: *dad*, *lad*, *sad*, *glad*, and *pad*. Then share these riddles, and ask your child to point to the picture whose name answers the riddle.

- I'm not your mom. I'm your _____. (dad)
- I'm not a lass. I'm a _____. (lad)
- I'm not happy. I'm _____. (sad)
- I'm not unhappy. I'm _____. (glad)
- You can write on me. I'm a _____. (pad)

Read the rhymes below with your child, and invite him or her to draw pictures to go with the rhymes. Then ask your child to explain how each picture shows words whose names end with the letters *ad*. This will help your child to hear that those words rhyme and that they end with the sounds the letters *ad* stand for.

Show a lad
Who is sad.

Show a dad
Who is glad.

Dear Parent or Guardian,

We have just begun a lesson on the sounds and spelling of words ending with the letters *in*. The next time you go to a supermarket with your child, —————, encourage him or her to look for objects whose names end with these sounds and letters. Possible examples include a trash bin, a safety pin, and a fish's fin.

Please contact me if you have any questions.

Cordially,

—————————————

Home Spelling Activities

You can use words that end with the sounds the letters *in* stand for to play a riddle game. Have your child draw pictures to illustrate these words: *pin*, *bin*, *fin*, and *win*. Help your child label the pictures. Then read these riddles, and have your child point to the picture and read the word that answers each riddle.

- A fish has more than one. (fin)
- It can hold two pieces of cloth together. (pin)
- It's a big box. (bin)
- The first one to finish a race will do this. (win)

Invite your child to use a pencil to mark the path in the maze below from the little girl to the finish line. Explain that she or he can figure out which path to take by looking for pictures whose names end with the letters *in*. Then ask your child to color and name the pictures on the correct path. (fish fin, safety pin, child with a grin, trash bin)

Grade 1 • Harcourt Brace School Publishers

Home Spelling Activities

Play a word association game with your child. Ask her or him to name a word that ends with the sounds the letters *ill* stand for and that corresponds with one of these clues:

- window (*sill*)
- mountain (*hill*)
- dollar (*bill*)
- vitamin (*pill*)
- pickle (*dill*)

Talk with your child about the picture below. Then have him or her find and color four things whose names end with the letters *ill*. (bill, dill pickle, the glass the waiter fills, windowsill) Ask your child to name the things he or she colored. This will help your child to verify that those words rhyme and that they end with the sounds the letters *ill* stand for.

Dear Parent or Guardian,

We have just begun a lesson on the sounds and spelling of words ending with the letters *ug*. You can help by encouraging your child, _____, to write labels for objects in your home that end with these sounds and letters. Possible objects might include a jug, a mug, a rug, and a plug.

Please contact me if you have any questions.

Cordially,

_____

Home Spelling Activities

You can use words that end with the sounds for the letters *ug* to play a synonym game with your child. Explain that you are going to name an object. Ask your child to say a word that has almost the same meaning and that rhymes with the word *bug*.

- A pitcher is called a _____. (*jug*)
- A large cup is called a _____. (*mug*)
- A carpet is called a _____. (*rug*)

Invite your child to use a pencil to mark the three paths in the maze below that the bug could take to get to the flower. Tell your child to figure out which paths to take by looking for pictures whose names end with the same sounds as *bug*. Ask your child to show you which pictures they are. (mug, rug, jug)

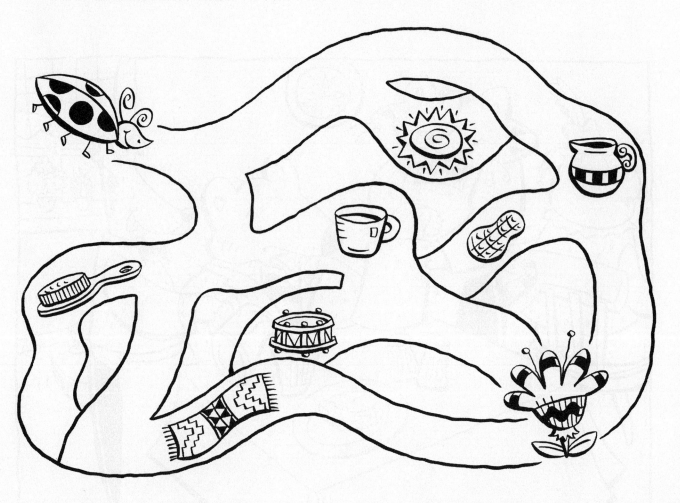

Grade 1 • Harcourt Brace School Publishers

Dear Parent or Guardian,

We have just begun a lesson on the sounds and spelling of words ending with the letters *ig*. The next time you go on an outing with your child, ——————, help him or her find objects whose names end with these sounds and letters or that can be described by words containing these sounds. On the street you might pass a big dog, for example. In a store, you might see a wig on display; on a farm, you might notice a pig.

Please contact me if you have any questions.

Cordially,

——————————————

Home Spelling Activities

Write these words on cards and mix them up: *big*, *dig*, *fig*, *jig*, *pig*, and *wig*. Then take turns with your child selecting a card and making up a riddle about the word. For example, for the word *pig*, you might make up this riddle: "This word names a pink animal that has a curly tail. What word is it?"

Talk with your child about the picture below. Then have him or her find and color three things whose names end with the letters *ig*. (twig, pig, wig) Ask your child to name the things he or she colored. This will help your child to confirm that those words rhyme and that they end with the sounds the letters *ig* stand for.

Dear Parent or Guardian,

We have just begun a lesson on the sounds and spelling of words ending with the letters *un*. You can help by encouraging your child, ——————, to identify words that you use in everyday conversation that end with these sounds and letters. Possible examples include *fun, run, sun,* and *bun.*

Please contact me if you have any questions.

Cordially,

——————

Home Spelling Activities

Play a word association game with your child by asking him or her to name a word that ends with the sounds for the letters *un* and that corresponds with one of these clues:

- hot dog or hamburger (*bun*)
- sneakers (*run*)
- heat wave (*sun*)
- circus clowns (*fun*)

Talk with your child about the picture below. Then have him or her find and color the three things whose names end with the letters *un.* (sun, children who run, bun) Ask your child to name the things he or she colored. This will help your child to confirm that those words rhyme and that they end with the sounds the letters *un* stand for.

Dear Parent or Guardian,

We have just begun a lesson on the sounds and spelling of words ending with the letters *ack*. You can help by encouraging your child, _____, to write labels for objects in your home that end with these sounds and letters. Possible objects might include a sack, a rack, a tack, and a backpack.

Please contact me if you have any questions.

Cordially,

_____

Home Spelling Activities

You can use words ending with the sounds for the letters *ack* to play a spelling game. Write the words *tack, sack, jack,* and *back* on a sheet of paper. Cover the first letter of each word, and then say the word aloud. Ask your child to tell which letter the word begins with. Then uncover the letter so that your child can check the answer.

Point out the picture below. Explain that three things whose names rhyme with *back* belong in the sack. Ask your child to name each object and then color the ones whose names end with the letters *ack*. (black crayon, tack, backpack)

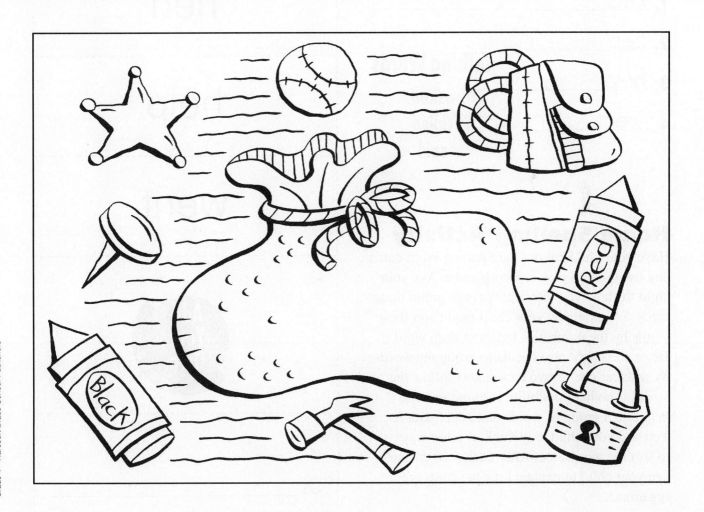

Dear Parent or Guardian,
We have just begun a lesson on spelling words with the short e vowel sound. Your child _____ will be tested on these words on _____.
Please contact me if you have any questions.

Cordially,

_____

WORD CARDS

SPELLING ★ WORDS ★

Spelling Words

1. red
2. hen
3. help
4. went

Add Your Own Word

5. _____

Talking Words
asked
called
said

Home Spelling Activity

Have your child cut out the Spelling Word cards and use them to play a sorting game. Ask your child to show you different ways to group these cards. For example, your child might sort these words by the number of letters in each word. He or she might also decide to group the words by whether one or two consonants follow the vowel. Another possibility is to put *hen* and *help* into a group of words that begin with *h*. You and your child may think of other ways to sort the words, too. After each sort, encourage your child to explain how the cards are organized.

red

hen

help

went

Add Your Own ★ WORD

_____

Grade 1 • Harcourt Brace School Publishers

WORD CARDS

Dear Parent or Guardian,
   We have just begun a lesson on spelling words with the short *u* vowel sound. Your child _____ will be tested on these words on _____.
   Please contact me if you have any questions.

   Cordially,

   _____

Spelling Words

1. but
2. must
3. just
4. run

Add Your Own Word

5. _____

Outdoor Words

woods
path
tree

Home Spelling Activity

Have your child cut out the Spelling Word cards and use them to play a sorting game. Ask your child to show you different ways to group these cards. For example, your child might sort these words by the number of letters in each word. He or she might group *must* and *just* as words that rhyme. Another possibility is to group the words by whether one or two consonants follow the vowel. You and your child may think of other ways to sort the words, too. After each sort, encourage your child to explain how the cards are organized.

but

must

just

run

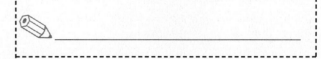

WORD CARDS

Dear Parent or Guardian,
We have just begun a lesson on spelling words with the short *i* vowel sound. Your child ———— will be tested on these words on ————.
Please contact me if you have any questions.

Cordially,

_____

Spelling Words

1. in
2. it
3. big
4. him

Add Your Own Word

5. _____

People Words

children
mother
friends

Home Spelling Activity

Have your child cut out the Spelling Word cards and use them to play a sorting game. Ask your child to show you different ways to group these cards. For example, your child might sort these words by the number of letters in each word. He or she might also group the words by whether the short *i* vowel sound is heard at the beginning or in the middle of the word. You and your child may think of other ways to sort the words, too. After each sort, encourage your child to explain how the cards are organized.

SPELLING
· WORDS ·

in

it

big

him

Grade 1 • Harcourt Brace School Publishers

WORD CARDS

Dear Parent or Guardian,
We have just begun a lesson on spelling words that begin with *wh*. Your child _____ will be tested on these words on _____.
Please contact me if you have any questions.

Cordially,

_____

when

what

where

why

Spelling Words

1. when
2. what
3. where
4. why

Add Your Own Word

5. _____

Action Words
found
keep
take

Home Spelling Activity

You can use the Spelling Words to play a game with your child. Have your child cut apart the word cards, turn them face down, and mix them up. Look through an illustrated book or magazine to find a picture. Take turns choosing a card and using the word to ask a question about the picture. For example, you might ask:

What are the people in this picture doing?
Where do you think they are going?

Talk about the answer to the question before the other player selects a card.

WORD CARDS

Dear Parent or Guardian,
   We have just begun a lesson on spelling words with the short *a* vowel sound. Your child _____ will be tested on these words on _____.
   Please contact me if you have any questions.
               Cordially,
   _____

SPELLING · WORDS ·

Spelling Words

1. <u>can</u>
2. <u>and</u>
3. <u>had</u>
4. <u>am</u>

Add Your Own Word

5. _____

Ground Words

dirt
earth
soil

Home Spelling Activity

Have your child cut out the Spelling Word cards and use them to play a sorting game. Ask your child to show you different ways to group these cards. One way to sort the words is by the number of letters in each word. Your child may also sort them to show whether the short *a* sound comes at the beginning or in the middle of the word. You and your child may think of other ways to sort the words, too.

   Ask your child to identify the letter that stands for the vowel sound in each word. After each sort, encourage your child to explain how the cards are organized.

can

and

had

am

Add Your Own · WORD ·

_____

WORD CARDS

Dear Parent or Guardian,

We have just begun a lesson on spelling words with the short *o* vowel sound. Your child ———— will be tested on these words on ————.

Please contact me if you have any questions.

Cordially,

————————

Spelling Words   ## Add Your Own Word

1. on   5. ————

2. not

3. stop   ### Garden Words
               plant
4. got   **flower**
               seed

Home Spelling Activity

Have your child cut out the Spelling Word cards and use them to play a sorting game. Ask your child to show you different ways to group these cards. One way to sort the words is by the number of letters in each word. Your child may also show you how to make a group of words that rhyme or a group of words that have the short *o* sound in the middle of the word. You and your child may think of other ways to sort the words, too.

Ask your child to identify the letter that stands for the vowel sound in each word. After each sort, encourage your child to explain how the cards are organized.

on

not

stop

got

Grade 1 • Harcourt Brace School Publishers

WORD CARDS

Spelling Words

1. look
2. said
3. put
4. with

Add Your Own Word

5. _____

Winter Words

snow
scarf
snowman

Home Spelling Activity

Have your child cut out the Spelling Word cards and use them to play a sorting game. Challenge your child to think of different ways to group the words. In addition to sorting the words by the number of letters, your child could also group them by the number of vowels contained in each word. He or she might also group the words *look, said,* and *put* as words that describe actions. You and your child may think of other ways to sort the words, too.

look

said

put

with

_____

WORD CARDS

Dear Parent or Guardian,
    We have just begun a lesson on spelling words that contain the letter o. Your child _____ will be tested on these words on _____.
    Please contact me if you have any questions.

                    Cordially,

    _____

Spelling Words

1. now
2. of
3. come
4. one

Add Your Own Word

5. _____

Boating Words

water
waves
sail

Home Spelling Activity

Have your child cut out the Spelling Word cards and use them to play a sorting game. Ask your child to show you different ways to group these cards. One way to sort the words is by the number of letters in each word. Your child may also show you a group of words that begin with *o* or a group that end with *e*. Your child might sort *come, one,* and *of* into a group of words with a short vowel sound. You and your child may think of other ways to sort the words, too.

    After each sort, encourage your child to explain how the cards are organized.

now

of

come

one

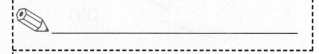

Name _____

Use rhyming words to help you spell the picture names.

1.  pen    hen

2.  bun    run

3. 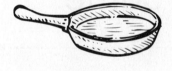 pan    can

4.  mop    stop

5.  pin    in

WORD CARDS

Dear Parent or Guardian,
    We have just begun a lesson on spelling words that contain the long *a* vowel sound. Your child ———— will be tested on these words on ————.
    Please contact me if you have any questions.

                Cordially,

                _____

Spelling Words

1. came
2. made
3. wait
4. play

Add Your Own Word

5. _____

Nighttime Words

dream
asleep
bedtime

Home Spelling Activity

Have your child cut out the Spelling Word cards and use them to play a sorting game. Ask your child to show you different ways to group these cards. One way to sort the words is by whether the word ends with the letter *e*. Another way is to put words like *came* and *made* in the same group because they tell about the past. You and your child may think of other ways to sort the words, too.

    After each sort, encourage your child to explain how the cards are organized. Ask your child to tell you what vowel sound he or she hears in each word.

came

made

wait

play

Grade 1 • Harcourt Brace School Publishers

WORD CARDS

Spelling Words

1. the
2. then
3. that
4. they

Add Your Own Word

5. _____

Bath Words

wet
dry
bath

Home Spelling Activity

Have your child cut out the Spelling Word cards and use them to play a sorting game. Ask your child to show you different ways to group these cards. For example, he or she might sort these words by the number of letters or by the vowel in the word. You and your child may think of other ways to sort the words, too. After each sort, encourage your child to explain how the cards are organized.

SPELLING ★ WORDS ★

the

then

that

they

Add Your Own WORD

_____

Grade 1 • Harcourt Brace School Publishers

Dear Parent or Guardian,
    We have just begun a lesson on spelling words that are used often. Your child _____ will be tested on these words on _____.
    Please contact me if you have any questions.

Cordially,

_____

Spelling Words

1. have
2. live
3. do
4. some

Add Your Own Word

5. _____

Animal Body Part Words

paws
beaks
fins

Home Spelling Activity

Have your child cut out the Spelling Word cards and use them to play a sorting game. Ask your child to show you different ways to group these cards. For example, he or she might sort these words by the number of letters in each word. The words *have, live,* and *some* might be grouped together as words that end with *e* or as words that all contain a short vowel sound. Your child might also sort *have* and *do* into a group of helping verbs. After each sort, encourage your child to explain how the cards are organized.

SPELLING WORDS

have

live

do

some

Add Your Own Word

_____

WORD CARDS

Dear Parent or Guardian,
    We have just begun a lesson on spelling words that end with the long e vowel sound. Your child _____ will be tested on these words on _____.
    Please contact me if you have any questions.

Cordially,

_____

Spelling Words

1. we_____
2. she_____
3. he_____
4. me_____

Add Your Own Word

5. _____

New Student Words

new
name
welcome

Home Spelling Activity

Have your child cut out the Spelling Word cards and use them to play a sorting game. Ask your child to show you different ways to group these cards. For example, he or she might sort these words by the number of letters in each word or by whether the word refers to one person or more than one. You and your child may think of other ways to sort the words, too. After each sort, encourage your child to explain how the cards are organized. Ask your child to identify the vowel sound that he or she hears in each of these Spelling Words.

SPELLING
★ WORDS ★

we

she

he

me

Add
Your
Own
WORD

_____

Grade 1 • Harcourt Brace School Publishers

WORD CARDS

Spelling Words   Add Your Own Word

1. like   5. _____

2. ice

3. ride   **Space Words**

4. nine   sun
                       star
                       planet

Home Spelling Activity

Have your child cut out the Spelling Word cards and use them to play a sorting game. Ask your child to show you different ways to group these cards. For example, he or she might sort these words by the number of letters in each word. Another possibility is to sort the words by whether the long *i* vowel sound is heard at the beginning or in the middle of the word. You and your child may think of other ways to sort the words, too.

like

ice

ride

nine

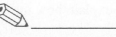

_____

WORD CARDS

Dear Parent or Guardian,
    We have just begun a lesson on spelling words that are used often. Your child _____ will be tested on these words on _____.
    Please contact me if you have any questions.

                        Cordially,

                        _____

Spelling Words

1. was
2. his
3. give
4. saw

Add Your Own Word

5. _____

Baby Words

cry
baby
bottle

Home Spelling Activity

Have your child cut out the Spelling Word cards and use them to play a sorting game. Ask your child to show you different ways to group these cards. For example, your child might sort these words by the number of letters or by the vowel in the word. He or she might sort *his* and *give* into a group of words with the short *i* vowel sound. Another possibility is to put *was* and *saw* into a group because they contain the same three letters. You and your child may think of other ways to sort the words, too. After each sort, encourage your child to explain how the cards are organized.

SPELLING
★ W O R D S ★

was

his

give

saw

Add
Your
Own
★ WORD ★

Grade 1 • Harcourt Brace School Publishers

Dear Parent or Guardian,

We have just begun a lesson on spelling words that contain the vowel o. Your child _____ will be tested on these words on _____.

Please contact me if you have any questions.

Cordially,

_____

SPELLING WORDS

Spelling Words

1. love
2. who
3. no
4. or

Add Your Own Word

5. _____

"-thing" Words

anything
everything
something

Home Spelling Activity

Have your child cut out the Spelling Word cards and use them to play a sorting game. Ask your child to show you different ways to group these cards. For example, your child might make a group of words ending with the letter *o*. He or she might also sort these words by the number of letters in each word. Another possibility is to sort the words by whether the letter *o* appears at the beginning, in the middle, or at the end of the word. You and your child may think of other ways to sort the words, too.

love

who

no

or

WORD CARDS

Dear Parent or Guardian,
   We have just begun a lesson on spelling words with the long o vowel sound. Your child _____ will be tested on these words on _____.
   Please contact me if you have any questions.

                    Cordially,

   _____

SPELLING
★ WORDS ★

Spelling Words   Add Your Own Words

1. old   5. _____

2. rose

3. home

4. go

Family Words
aunt
family
grandparents

Home Spelling Activity

Have your child cut out the Spelling Word cards and use them to play a sorting game. Ask your child to show you different ways to group these cards. For example, your child might sort these words by the number of letters in the word, or by whether the letter *o* occurs at the beginning, in the middle, or at the end of the word. He or she might also sort the words based on whether the vowel sound is spelled with a single *o* or by the letters *o–e*. You and your child may think of other ways to sort the words, too. After each sort, encourage your child to explain how the cards are organized.

old

rose

home

go

Add
Your
Own
★ WORD

Grade 1 • Harcourt Brace School Publishers

Write each word from the box under the picture it best describes. Use the word shape to help you.

home	saw	ride	give	me	rose

1.

2.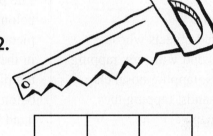

3.

4.

5.

6.

ANSWER KEY FOR
Home Activities Masters

Lesson 1
Pictured objects whose names begin with the letters *b, h, d, t*: bubbles, bicycle, hat, house, dog, doll, tail, table

Lesson 2
Pictured objects whose names end with *-ap*: rapping fingers, tapping nose, clapping hands, tapping toes, cap, map

Lesson 3
Pictured objects whose names end with *-ot*: pot, dot, tot, hot

Lesson 4
Hidden objects whose names end with *-an*: van, man, fan, pan, can

Lesson 5
Pictured objects whose names end with *-at*: mat, hat, bat, cat

Lesson 6
Hidden objects whose names end with *-op*: top, lollipop, stop sign, mop

Lesson 7
Pictured objects whose names end with *-et*: a wet pet, net, jet

Lesson 8
Pictured objects in the maze whose names end with *-ell*: bell, wishing well, shell, skunk that smells

Lesson 9
Hidden objects whose names end with *-en*: pen, numeral ten, men, hen

Lesson 10
The picture of the chick belongs in the top box; the picture of the brick belongs in the bottom left-hand box; the picture of the stick belongs in the bottom right-hand box.

Lesson 11
Pictured objects in the maze whose names end with *-ip*: ship, whip, lip, a drip from the faucet

Lesson 12
In the first box, children should draw a picture of a lad who is sad. In the second box, children should draw a picture of a dad who is glad.

Lesson 13
Pictured objects in the maze whose names end with *-in*: fish fin, safety pin, child with a grin, trash bin

Lesson 14
Pictured objects whose names end with *-ill*: bill, dill pickle, the glass the waiter fills, windowsill

Lesson 15
Pictured objects in the maze whose names end with *-ug*: mug, rug, jug

Lesson 16
Pictured objects whose names end with *-ig*: twig, pig, wig

Lesson 17
Pictured objects whose names end with *-un*: sun, children who run, bun

Lesson 18
Pictured objects whose names end with *-ack*: tack, black crayon, backpack

Lessons 19–26
Children's word sorts will vary.

Lesson 27
1. hen **2.** run **3.** can **4.** stop **5.** in

Lessons 28–35
Children's word sorts will vary.

Lesson 36
1. me **2.** saw **3.** rose **4.** home **5.** ride **6.** give

Assessment

FORMAL ASSESSMENT OPTIONS
T308

This section provides options that may be used with children to determine instructional level and evaluate work.

INFORMAL ASSESSMENT OPTIONS
T308

This section provides options for evaluation of spelling, using children's writing.

OPTIONS FOR
Assessment

► FORMAL ASSESSMENT OPTIONS

Spelling Placement Inventory See pages T14–T17 for administering and interpreting the Spelling Placement Inventory. The inventory will help you devise an instructional plan for each child by assessing his or her developmental level.

Pretest/Posttest/Practice Test The Pretests/Posttests for Lessons 19–36 provide sets of numbered context sentences for the Spelling Words. Children are asked to write each Spelling Word after hearing the word and context sentence read aloud.

The Pretest should be given at the beginning of each lesson, encouraging children to draw on their prior knowledge. It determines which spelling patterns or generalizations have been mastered and which areas need improvement. The Self-Check activities encourage children to play an active role in evaluating their work. Assign partners or have children choose partners for assessing their own words.

The Posttest given at the end of each lesson is an effective diagnostic tool for determining whether extra practice is needed. In addition, the Practice Test at the end of each unit may be used to assess children's progress.

► INFORMAL ASSESSMENT OPTIONS

Research has shown that spelling instruction is most effective when it is linked to authentic writing tasks. For children to develop the skills and habits of proficient spellers, they need to view correct spelling within the broader context of reading, writing, and the communication of ideas. Therefore, the natural starting point for the assessment of spelling awareness is the written work that children complete in all subject areas as part of their daily assignments.

Error Analysis Chart for Writing Activities *Integrated Spelling* supports you in the ongoing informal assessment of each child's developing spelling skills. The chart on page T310 of this Teacher's Edition enables you to record and analyze the words children misspell as they complete their writing activities. It is designed to help you analyze the nature of children's spelling errors and thereby customize instruction to meet individual needs. These findings will help you determine which lessons in *Integrated Spelling* will be of greatest benefit.

Writing Activity Error Analysis In Lessons 19–36, each lesson in the *Integrated Spelling* Teacher's Edition includes a writing model that contains common grade-level error patterns. Children's daily writing can be compared to these models to determine which lessons will be of greatest benefit.

▼ model

> rode   light
> I (road) my bike to the (lite.)

You can then compare these models to the error patterns you find and record on children's Error Analysis Charts for Writing Activities. As children work through each lesson, mastering spelling and acquiring skills, update the charts. This process will enable you to identify areas of achievement and to informally assess areas that need improvement.

Portfolio Conferences To develop independent spelling awareness, *Integrated Spelling* teaches spelling as part of the writing process. Writing samples, including unfinished work and proofread drafts, should be included in an evaluation portfolio and reviewed periodically. The proofreading phase provides important clues to a child's progress. For informal assessment during this stage, children can work independently, in pairs, or in small groups.

Periodic conferences give children, teachers, and family members a chance to reflect on each child's writing and developing knowledge of spelling. An evaluation portfolio should be created for each child. See the Guidelines for Portfolio Conferences on pages T311–T313 for suggestions of items to include in each evaluation portfolio.

You may want to monitor children's performance, observing how effectively they edit their work and how successfully they select resources to confirm spellings. Children's personalized Spelling Logs are another useful measure of their growth as independent, competent spellers.

PERFORMANCE-BASED ASSESSMENT

The lessons in *Integrated Spelling* are designed to engage children actively in integrated listening, speaking, reading, and writing activities and to help them develop a "spelling consciousness." All the writing activities provide excellent opportunities for ongoing performance-based assessment. Clues to children's developing word knowledge and attitudes toward spelling may also be revealed in oral summarizing activities. Throughout the lessons, children are encouraged to assess their progress and to help their classmates evaluate their work.

▶ A COMPREHENSIVE ASSESSMENT PROGRAM

Integrated Spelling offers a comprehensive, holistic assessment program. The components of informal assessment, combined with the formal assessment of the Spelling Placement Inventory and the Pretests/Posttests, ensure that every child receives individualized instruction and is recognized for her or his achievements.

Name _____

Error Analysis Chart for Writing Activities

Misspelling	Correct Spelling	Where the Error Appears in the Word			Substitutions, Omissions, Insertions, Reversals				Other		
		Beginning	Middle	End	Vowel	Consonant	"Silent" Letters	Double Letters	Compounds, Homophones, Contractions	Irregular Words	Inflectional Endings and Suffixes

DIRECTIONS: Make as many copies of this chart as necessary.

GUIDELINES FOR
Portfolio Conferences

SINCE SPELLING OCCURS NATURALLY within the context of writing, a portfolio provides an effective means of illustrating children's development as spellers. The following pages provide suggestions for including indicators of spelling progress in children's portfolios. They also offer guidelines for discussing spelling progress in conferences with children and with family members.

▶ INCORPORATING SPELLING SAMPLES INTO THE PORTFOLIO

Help each child organize the contents of the portfolio according to a system he or she feels comfortable with. Several methods of organization are suggested in the *Portfolio Assessment Teacher's Guide* that accompanies *Signatures*.

After children have decided on an organizational system, suggest that they think about ways they can include examples of their spelling work. Help them decide how their spelling work best fits in with other categories in the portfolio.

If a child has organized a portfolio by topics, she or he may want to place topic-related Spelling Words in the appropriate sections of the portfolio. If a child's portfolio is organized chronologically, spelling-related work might be placed in the portfolio according to when the work was done. Some children may prefer to create a separate section just for spelling work.

▶ ITEMS TO INCLUDE IN A PORTFOLIO

In addition to selecting several examples of completed spelling assignments, children might choose to include the following items in their portfolios:

Writing Samples Encourage children to add writing samples that show spelling corrections they have made. Drafts that show errors that children have discovered and corrected while proofreading are good indicators of their spelling progress.

Pretests and Posttests You may want to have children include Pretests and Posttests in their portfolios to show the progress they have made with particular groups of words. Such items should not be included as part of a formal assessment or as a means of judging children's weaknesses. Rather, they should be used as a method of demonstrating progress and as a way for children to assess their own achievements.

Spelling Logs If children are keeping individual Spelling Logs of unusual and interesting words, encourage them to photocopy some of these pages and add them to the portfolio. These pages provide insight into a child's interests.

Language Discovery Sheets From time to time, children learn language facts or patterns that prove especially useful. For instance, learning about the -og word family may help a child understand and spell a variety of rhyming words that end with this phonogram, such as *dog* and *frog*. Encourage children to record their facts or patterns on a "Language Discovery Sheet" and add the sheet to their portfolios.

Optional Writing Idea Children may want to include in their portfolios the activity they did for the Optional Writing Idea that is suggested at the end of each spelling lesson.

▶ CONFERENCES BETWEEN A FAMILY MEMBER AND A TEACHER

Discuss with the family member how the child has chosen to incorporate indicators of his or her spelling progress into the portfolio. Then share examples of the child's work that reveal spelling development, such as process-writing activities, Spelling Log pages, and Pretest and Posttest pages. The following checklist may be used to help you emphasize the progress individual children have made and point out areas that need improvement:

✓ Awareness of spelling patterns

✓ Ability to apply knowledge of known words to unfamiliar words that share a similar pattern or origin

✓ Developmental level of the child

▶ CONFERENCES BETWEEN A TEACHER AND A CHILD

Try to conduct the conference so that the child does most of the talking. Prompts such as these will help generate discussion:

• Tell me how you organized your spelling work in your portfolio.

• Let's look at a piece of writing that shows some corrections you made in spelling. How did you find the mistakes? How did you figure out how to spell the words correctly?

• What spelling strategies are most helpful to you when you are trying to spell new words?

• How often do you use your Picture Dictionary? How is the dictionary helpful?

• What kind of progress do you think you have made in spelling?

The child's responses to questions such as these will provide valuable insight into her or his attitudes, habits, and strengths. Help the child plan ways to increase his or her proficiency in spelling. These might include using the Picture Dictionary or another dictionary more often during proofreading, consulting with peers when troublesome words are encountered, or referring to spelling strategies more often.

▶ CONFERENCES BETWEEN A TEACHER AND A SMALL GROUP

Peer portfolio conferences offer valuable opportunities for children to discuss their progress, to share the things they find most challenging, and to compare problem-solving strategies with each other. The following questions may be helpful in focusing a peer portfolio conference.

- How did you arrange the work in your portfolio?

- Where did you put your spelling work? What kinds of work did you include?

- What do you like about spelling? What is hard for you about spelling?

- What do you do when you want to write a word but don't know how to spell it?

- What are some difficult words you can spell? How did you learn to spell them?

Encourage children to share the strategies they have discovered that are the most useful for spelling new words and remembering the spelling of troublesome words. Ask children to try to be as specific as they can. You may want to take notes as children discuss their ideas.

Also, encourage children to become resources for one another in sharing their solutions and strategies. Encourage them to actively listen during their peer conferences and to try out some of the suggestions and strategies identified by their classmates.

Teacher Resources

SPELLING ACTIVITIES AND GAMES
T316

This section provides activities that may be used with children to enhance spelling strategies learned within the lessons.

INTEGRATING SPELLING AND LITERATURE
T322

The chart in this section links each spelling lesson to a selection in the Grade 1 Signatures Student Anthology.

SPELLING WORD LIST DEVELOPMENT
T324

The lists of words to be taught at each level in Integrated Spelling reflect the words children use most often as they write and read. Information on the research base and the compilation process for the program's word lists is presented in this section.

CUMULATIVE WORD LIST FOR GRADES 1–6
T325

This section presents a comprehensive list of all the words taught in Integrated Spelling. For each word, the grade level and the number of the lesson in which it is taught are included.

BIBLIOGRAPHY
T335

This bibliography includes informative professional articles and books about how children develop spelling proficiency as well as how they acquire related literacy skills. It also suggests a number of books for children to enjoy and learn from.

SCOPE AND SEQUENCE
T338

The chart in this section identifies the grade levels at which specific spelling strategies and skills are developed.

INDEX
T340

Spelling Activities and Games

THE FOLLOWING ACTIVITIES *may be used with children of all ability levels. They provide children with opportunities to develop higher-order spelling strategies that will enable them to predict the spelling of English words. The activities do more than have children write spelling words; they also have children apply spelling knowledge to write other words—words they need to use in their writing across the curriculum.*

ACTIVITIES are for whole-class participation, for use with small groups, or for individual children. The activities may be adapted to reinforce a variety of spelling generalizations. You may select those activities that best suit the needs and interests of your children.

RHYME TIME

Players	Materials
WHOLE CLASS	NONE

Directions To play "Rhyme Time," invite children to form a circle in an open area of the classroom. As they march, lead them in chanting the following rhyme:

> Come join in,
> Play a rhyming game.
> Invite your friends
> To do the same.
> All join hands,
> Let's circle around.
> Clap if these words
> Have rhyming sounds.

Then ask children to listen to pairs of words. Some should be rhyming pairs, ending with the phonograms you wish to reinforce or review. After each pair, children should clap if the words rhyme.

LEAVE A TRACE

Players	Materials
PAIRS	PLASTIC TRAYS FILLED WITH SAND, CORNMEAL, SALT, OR OATMEAL

Directions To help reinforce Spelling Words, provide partners with clean plastic trays filled with sand, cornmeal, salt, or oatmeal. Children can take turns dictating and finger-tracing their Spelling Words in the tray. A quick swipe with the side of the hand "erases" the word and creates a smooth writing surface.

YUMMY WORDS

Players	Materials
SMALL GROUPS	NONFAT DRY MILK SMOOTH PEANUT BUTTER WAXED PAPER

Directions Children can work in small groups to make edible peanut butter "clay" by mixing together equal parts of nonfat dry milk and smooth peanut butter and kneading the clay on waxed paper until it has a doughlike consistency. Children can form clay letters to write their Spelling Words. Once a word has been checked as correct, they can "internalize" it as a tasty snack! Leftover dough can be refrigerated in a covered container and stored for several days.

WORD FAMILY HOUSE

Players
WHOLE CLASS
SMALL GROUPS
PAIRS

Materials
OAKTAG HOUSE WITH
   MANSARD ROOF AND
   SHUTTERED WINDOWS
CHART PAPER
MARKERS OR CRAYONS

Directions Draw a large house with a mansard roof and shuttered windows on oaktag. Cut along the shutters so they will open. Paste a large sheet of chart paper behind the house. On the roof, write a phonogram, such as -an. Invite children to open the shutters and write words that end with the phonogram— for example: *pan, can, man, ran, van, fan, plan, tan.*

Working in pairs, children can take turns opening a shutter, reading the concealed word, and asking the partner to spell it.

CLIMB THE LADDER

Players
WHOLE CLASS
SMALL GROUP

Materials
OAKTAG LADDERS

Directions Provide children with ladder cutouts. The rungs should be large enough to accommodate written words. To reinforce words in a phonogram family, have children write rhyming words on the rungs.

Turn this activity into a game by dividing a group into two teams and giving each a ladder. Have children race to see which team can "climb" a ladder first by filling the rungs with rhyming words.

SEE AND SPELL

Players
WHOLE CLASS
SMALL GROUPS

Materials
CHALKBOARD AND CHALK
PAPER AND PENCILS
OBJECTS ON A TRAY

Directions To play "See and Spell," place five or six objects whose names are Spelling Words on a tray. Have the child who is "It" mentally select one of these objects. He or she writes the name of the object on a slip of paper and gives it to you or another child. The remaining children have to guess the name by spelling it within a given number of turns. Children start by guessing the first letter, then the second, then the third, and so on. The child who is "It" writes the correct letters on the chalkboard as they are guessed. The child who completes the word becomes "It."

If a child feels able to identify the object after the first few letters have been guessed, he or she may challenge "It" and complete the spelling of the word. If the challenger is incorrect or misspells the word, other children continue guessing the letters. If the challenger is correct, he or she becomes "It."

LADY BUG

Players	Materials
WHOLE CLASS (TWO TEAMS)	CHALKBOARD AND CHALK
	PAPER AND PENCILS
SMALL GROUPS	PICTURE OF LADY BUG
PAIRS	PAPER BAG OR SMALL BOX

Directions To play "Lady Bug," divide the class into two teams. The object of the game is to be the first team to draw a complete lady bug. (Note: You may modify the game by changing the animal that children draw to reflect a story character or a class pet.) Give the first player of one team a Spelling Word. If the player spells it correctly, he or she draws one part of the lady bug's body on the chalkboard. If the word is misspelled, another team member can provide the correct spelling, but the team does not draw the bug's body. Continue playing by alternating between the two teams until one team has completed a lady bug. A completed figure might look like this:

This game may also be played by pairs of children. Have the Spelling Words written on folded pieces of paper and placed in a paper bag or small box. One player selects a piece of paper and reads the word. The other player spells the word. The first player to create a complete bug wins.

SPELLING BASEBALL

Players	Materials
WHOLE CLASS (TWO TEAMS)	4 CHAIRS WITH SIGNS IDENTIFYING HOME PLATE AND EACH OF THE BASES (OR 4 OAKTAG BASEBALL PLAYERS THAT CAN BE ATTACHED TO CHALKBOARD WITH ROLLED MASKING TAPE)
	CHALKBOARD AND CHALK

Directions To play "Spelling Baseball," arrange four chairs in a diamond shape in an open area of your classroom. Children can help you create signs for the chairs to identify home plate and each of the bases. Divide the class into two teams, and invite them to select team names. Assign each team member a number to indicate the "batting order." Explain that you will be "pitching" words to the batters on a team. When you "pitch" a word, the batter is to spell the word.

Begin the game by "pitching" a word to the first batter on Team A, who is seated on "home plate." If the player spells the word correctly, he or she moves to the "first base" chair. Then say a second word. If the second batter spells the next word correctly, he or she moves to first base and the first runner advances to second base. If a batter misspells a word, that player makes an "out." As play continues, keep track of the runs scored and the number of outs for each inning. After three outs, the side is "retired" and the other team comes to bat.

(Note: Depending on classroom space, you may prefer to draw a diamond on the chalkboard. In this case, players can draw and cut out "runners" and attach masking tape to the back of the figures so they can move them around the diagram.)

SPEEDY SPELLER

Players
WHOLE CLASS

Materials
CHALKBOARD AND CHALK
THREE-MINUTE TIMER

Directions Tell the children that you are going to write a common spelling for /ā/ on the board. At the count of three, they are to write as many words as they can that contain that spelling. Write *a-consonant-e* or *ay* on the board, and count to three. After three minutes, say "Stop." Have the children count the number of words they wrote. Make a master list of all the words on the board and have the children check their spellings. You can use the same activity for the spellings of other vowel or consonant sounds.

BUILD A WORD

Players
WHOLE CLASS

Materials
CHALKBOARD AND CHALK
CLEAN HALF-PINT MILK
  CARTONS
WOODEN OR CARDBOARD
  LETTER BLOCKS
CONSTRUCTION PAPER
MARKERS

Directions Write three columns of letters on the board. In the first column, write beginning letters; in the second column, write middle letters; and in the third column, write ending letters. For example:

f	a	p
w	e	n
l	i	t
h	u	d

Have children see how many words they can spell by combining the letters. When they are finished, make a master list of words on the board to see how many words were formed. Possibilities include *fan, fat, fad, fed, fin, fit, fun, wad, wet, wed, win, wit, lap, lad, let, led, lip, lit, lid, hat, had, hen, hip, hit, hid,* and *hut.*

Other beginning, middle, and ending letters may be used to play the game. You may also wish to provide wooden or cardboard letter blocks for children to manipulate as they build their words. Children can make their own sets of blocks by covering clean half-pint milk cartons with construction paper and using markers to write a letter on each side.

RHYMING WORD CONCENTRATION

Players
SMALL GROUPS
(PAIRS)

Materials
20 INDEX CARDS

Directions Have pairs of children write a list of ten pairs of different rhyming words. Then have them write each word on an index card.

To play "Rhyming Word Concentration," children should mix up the cards, divide them into two decks, and then place them face down. Children alternate turning up two cards at a time, one from each deck. If the words on the two cards rhyme, the child reads the words, keeps the pair, and continues. The other player may challenge if he or she thinks the words do not rhyme. If the two words do not rhyme, the cards are turned face down and put back in the deck. The player with the most cards wins the game.

Instead of keeping the cards in two decks, children can also randomly arrange all the cards face down on a desktop. Then, have children take turns turning up two cards at a time and attempting to match pairs of rhyming words. If the words rhyme, the child reads the words, keeps the pair, and continues until all cards are collected. This version of the game helps sharpen visual memory skills as children try to recall the positions of cards previously displayed.

WORD WHEELS

Players
WHOLE CLASS
SMALL GROUPS
(PAIRS)

Materials
2 OAKTAG CIRCLES (3" AND 6") PER STUDENT
FASTENERS
MARKERS, CRAYONS, OR PENCILS

Directions Have children construct "Word Wheels" to reinforce a specific phonogram. To begin, children can write on a sheet of paper words that contain a target phonogram. The words should be checked for correct spelling. Next, each child can make a word wheel by measuring and cutting out two circles, one approximately 6 inches in diameter and the other about 3 inches in diameter. Have children place the smaller circle on top of the larger one and fasten them together at their centers. Help children divide their larger circles into four, six, or eight equal parts, depending upon the number of words in the phonogram family. Have children write a different initial consonant in each section of the small circle and the phonogram on the large circle.

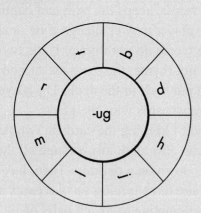

Have each child work with a partner and exchange completed word wheels. As a child turns the wheel, he or she writes the words that are formed. When all possible words have been made, the partner checks the list.

SPIN–A–VOWEL

Players
WHOLE CLASS
SMALL GROUPS

Materials
OAKTAG CIRCLE
PLASTIC LITER SODA BOTTLE WEIGHTED WITH SAND

Directions Draw a large circle on a piece of oaktag, and divide it into five equal sections. Have children write a vowel in each section of the circle. Place a one-liter plastic soda bottle weighted with sand in the middle of the circle, and have children take turns spinning it. When the bottle stops spinning, the player must identify the letter the bottle points to and then spell a word containing that vowel.

Other consonants or phonograms may also be used to construct this game.

HINK PINK RIDDLES

Players
SMALL GROUPS
(PAIRS)

Materials
PAPER AND PENCILS

Directions Have children make up "Hink Pink" riddles, using rhyming word pairs. For example, to reinforce the phonogram -*ig*, a child could think of the rhyming phrase *big pig* and write it on a piece of paper. He or she could ask a partner or small group to guess the "hink pink" by giving a clue, such as "My 'hink pink' tells about a large hog." The child who correctly guesses the "hink pink" can present the next riddle.

WORD LADDERS

Players	Materials
WHOLE CLASS	CHALKBOARD AND CHALK
SMALL GROUPS	(FOR EXAMPLES)
PAIRS	PAPER AND PENCILS

Directions Have children create "Word Ladders." In this activity, the children must change one letter in a word to create a different word; then, by changing a letter in the new word, they create a third word; and so on. Some "Word Ladders" can have many "rungs." For example:

not
pot
pat
pad
had
hat
cat
cab
tab
tub
rub
rib

After children write some "Word Ladders," have them find the solutions to the following puzzles:

Change *cat* to *dog* in three steps.

(**cat** *cot—dot—dog*)

Change *bat* to *pup* in three steps.

(**bat** *but—put—pup*)

There can be more than one solution to a "Word Ladder" puzzle. Accept any answers that change just one letter at a time and make an acceptable word for each step of the ladder.

Have children prepare "Word Ladder" puzzles for others to solve by using this format: Change *(word)* to *(word)* in *(number)* steps.

WORD CHAINS

Players	Materials
WHOLE CLASS	CHALKBOARD AND CHALK
SMALL GROUPS	(FOR EXAMPLES)
(PAIRS)	PAPER AND PENCILS

Directions This activity is similar to writing words as they appear in a crossword puzzle. Children make "Word Chains" by writing one word and then adding a second word perpendicular to the first that shares a letter in common with the first word, and so on.

c	a	t
		e
h	e	n
o		
m		
e		

Some children may be able to turn their "Word Chains" into actual crossword puzzles. Have them draw the outline of their "Word Chains" on graph paper. Show them how to add numbers and write clues for their puzzles. When they have finished, they can exchange puzzles with classmates and solve each other's puzzles.

For a simpler version of this game, have children write the letters of a word on narrow construction paper strips. Then have them give the letter strips to a partner and challenge him or her to use the strips to spell the word. Once the strips are in the correct order, have the partner staple the strips together to form links in a chain that spell the word.

INTEGRATING
Spelling and Literature

EACH SPELLING LESSON in *Integrated Spelling* corresponds to an anthology selection or trade book in *Signatures*. Every spelling lesson in Lessons 19–36 features a list of Spelling Words. The Spelling Words include words taken from the corresponding anthology selection. Each list of vocabulary WordShop Words features a different concept for children to explore.

Lessons 27 and 36 in *Integrated Spelling* are review lessons with activities that reflect the writing forms and language skills featured in the corresponding *Signatures* selections.

Lesson	Spelling Generalization	Corresponding Literature
1	Initial Consonants	"What I See"
2	Words with -ap	"Down on the Farm"
3	Words with -ot	"Sometimes"
4	Words with -an	"Five Little Rabbits"
5	Words with -at	"I Went Walking"
6	Words with -op	"Popcorn"
7	Words with -et	"Big Brown Bear"
8	Words with -ell	"The Chick and the Duckling"
9	Words with -en	"Cloudy Day, Sunny Day"
10	Words with -ick	"Moving Day"
11	Words with -ip	"Catch Me If You Can!"
12	Words with -ad	"Later, Rover"
13	Words with -in	"Hattie and the Fox"
14	Words with -ill	"And I Mean It, Stanley"
15	Words with -ug	"Best of Friends"
16	Words with -ig	"The Shoe Town"
17	Words with -un	"Making Friends, Keeping Friends"
18	Words with -ack	"Rex and Lily Playtime 'Let's Dance'"

Lesson	Spelling Generalization	Corresponding Literature
19	Words with Short e	"The Little Red Hen"
20	Words with Short u	"Henny Penny"
21	Words with Short i	"Little Lumpty"
22	Words with wh	"The Wild Woods"
23	Words with Short a	"Wonderful Worms"
24	Words with Short o	"Frog and Toad Together"
25	Words to Remember	"Lionel in the Winter"
26	Words to Remember with o	"Jenny's Journey"
27	REVIEW	
28	Words with Long a	"Dreams"
29	Words with th	"Henry and Mudge in the Green Time"
30	More Words to Remember	"Pets"
31	Words with Long e	"The Adventures of Snail at School"
32	Words with Long i	"Planets"
33	More Words to Remember	"Geraldine's Baby Brother"
34	More Words to Remember with o	"Julius"
35	Words with Long o	"New Shoes for Silvia"
36	REVIEW	

Spelling Word List Development

In a spelling program, the quality of the word lists on which instruction centers is a significant factor in making instruction match developmental levels. At every level, children should concentrate on learning to spell words they encounter most often in their reading and use most frequently in their writing.

Researchers have identified the words that children at different grade levels are most likely to encounter when reading and the words they use most often when writing. These words, along with selected words children encounter in *Signatures* anthology selections, form the basis of the Spelling Word lists in *Integrated Spelling.*

The lists of words to be taught in *Integrated Spelling* were compiled from no fewer than nine research-generated word lists. Three of these research-based lists rank words by frequency of occurrence in reading. Four others rank words by frequency of occurrence in children's writing. The others rank words according to how often they are misspelled.

Integrated Spelling is a complete developmental spelling program that integrates with *Signatures.* Words are grouped in accordance with the natural developmental flow of written language acquisition, and lists reflect common and consistent spelling patterns based on sound-letter relationships (phonology), word structures (affixes, inflections, syllable patterns, common roots, compound words), and word meaning.

Based on the sources that follow, and words selected from *Signatures,* the word-list selection used in developing the database for *Integrated Spelling* is one of the most systematic and comprehensive ever developed.

WRITING	Rinsland List (1945, Grades 1–8) 25,632 words
	Hillerich List (1966, Grades 2–6) 10,446 words
	Smith & Ingersoll (1984, Grades 1–8) 500,000 words from 4,000 compositions
	Farr List (1990, Grades 2–8) 3,080,831 running words from 21,697 essays
READING	Morris List (1987–88, 1993, Grades 2–adult) 10.2 million words from 1,500 publications
	Dolch List (1939, Grades 1–3) 220 words
	Kucera and Francis (1964, adult) 50,406 words from 500 samples
SUCCESS RATE	New Iowa Spelling Scale 5,507 words
	Farr Survey 3,080,831 running words

Cumulative Word List

This alphabetical list of 2,164 words includes all the Spelling Words that appear in Grades 1–6 of *Integrated Spelling*. Each word in the list is followed by two numbers. The first number indicates the grade in which the word appears. The second number indicates the lesson.

	Word	Grade	Lesson
Example:	able	3	33

Word	Grade	Lesson		Word	Grade	Lesson		Word	Grade	Lesson		Word	Grade	Lesson
ability	6	21		agree	3	35		another	6	10		at	2	3
able	3	33		agreement	4	30		answer	5	33		ate	3	16
about	4	13		ahead	3	21		answered	6	14		athlete	5	32
above	3	21		air	3	14		any	3	28		athletic	5	32
absent	6	32		airplane	3	29		anyway	5	16		attention	5	19
accept	6	13		aisle	5	33		any way	5	16		attractive	6	33
accident	6	26		alarm	4	35		apart	3	35		audience	6	20
accounts	6	26		alike	3	35		apartment	6	21		August	4	22
accurate	6	26		alive	3	35		apparent	6	26		author	3	32
accused	6	26		all	2	16		appear	5	25		authority	6	21
accustomed	6	26		allow	4	13		appearance	6	20		automobile	6	29
achieve	6	8		allowance	6	20		applause	6	26		autumn	4	22
acrobat	5	35		allowed	6	11		apple	3	33		available	5	18
act	3	1		all ready	5	16		application	5	32		Ave.	2	35
action	5	19		all right	5	16		applies	6	7		avoid	4	13
active	6	33		all together	5	16		apply	5	32		awake	3	35
activities	6	7		almost	3	10		appointed	6	26		aware	3	14
activity	6	21		alone	3	21		appreciate	6	26		away	2	8
adapt	6	13		along	3	21		approach	6	26		awful	4	30
add	2	16		a lot	5	16		April	3	17		babies'	3	23
addition	5	19		aloud	6	11		are	2	25		baby's	3	23
admire	6	15		already	5	16		area	4	9		back	2	20
admission	5	19		also	3	10		aren't	4	4		background	5	31
admit	6	1		although	5	26		argued	6	3		backward	6	19
admitted	6	14		altogether	5	16		argument	6	21		backyard	5	31
adopt	6	13		always	3	10		arm	2	25		bacon	4	34
adore	4	9		am	1	23		around	4	13		bad	2	3
advance	6	1		amazing	5	12		artist	6	25		bait	6	2
adventure	5	10		ambulance	6	20		artistic	6	25		baked	2	33
advise	6	28		America	5	34		as	2	3		balance	5	27
affair	6	26		American	5	34		ashes	2	23		ball	2	16
affect	6	13		among	6	4		Asia	5	34		ballet	6	5
affection	6	26		amount	3	35		Asian	5	34		balloon	4	8
afford	5	25		an	2	3		ask	5	1		bang	2	5
Africa	5	34		ancient	5	9		asleep	3	21		bank	4	35
African	5	34		and	1	23		assembly	6	26		barbecue	5	4
afternoon	4	18		angel	6	13		assign	6	28		barefoot	6	9
again	3	21		anger	6	10		assigned	6	26		baseball	2	34
age	4	7		angle	6	13		assignment	6	28		basic	4	34
agent	6	16		animal	5	15		assistant	6	26		basin	5	27
ago	3	21		annoyed	4	13		association	6	26		basis	6	16

Word			Word			Word			Word		
basket	4	31	boom	2	5	called	2	27	chicken	2	17
bat	2	3	boot	4	10	calves	4	26	chief	4	15
bath	2	19	born	2	28	came	1	28	child	3	8
batter	4	31	boss	4	35	can	1	23	children	4	26
battle	5	15	both	2	11	cannon	4	32	chili	5	4
beach	4	2	bottle	4	25	cannot	3	29	chimney	4	19
beans	2	17	bottom	3	26	canoe	5	4	chin	3	8
bear	3	14	bought	5	7	can't	2	22	chip	4	10
beauty	4	33	box	2	1	canyon	5	14	chocolate	5	4
beaver	4	34	boxes	2	23	capable	5	18	choice	4	13
because	5	9	boyfriend	6	8	capital	6	11	choose	3	8
become	3	21	boy's	3	22	Capitol	6	11	chop	4	3
becoming	5	12	boys	2	23	captain	3	34	chosen	5	27
bedroom	3	29	boys'	3	23	capture	5	10	church	3	19
bedtime	2	34	braille	6	17	car	2	20	circle	5	8
beef	4	35	brain	5	2	caravan	6	29	circus	5	25
beep	2	5	brake	4	27	card	4	9	cities	6	7
before	3	15	brand-new	5	31	care	2	20	city	4	7
beggar	5	29	bread	3	1	careful	3	27	civil	5	15
begin	3	21	break	4	27	careless	4	30	clapped	2	32
beginning	4	14	breathe	6	2	cargo	5	4	classroom	3	29
behave	3	35	breeze	5	4	carried	3	25	class's	3	23
behind	3	21	bridge	4	7	cartoon	4	35	clean	3	4
being	2	27	brief	5	2	castle	3	33	click	2	5
belief	6	8	bright	2	26	catch	6	1	client	6	19
believe	4	15	bring	2	19	catcher	5	29	climate	6	16
belong	3	35	broken	3	34	cattle	5	15	climbed	4	28
below	3	21	brook	5	7	caught	5	7	clock	3	2
beneath	3	35	broom	4	8	cause	3	10	close	3	3
berries	4	21	brother	2	11	cedar	4	33	closer	3	11
berth	6	11	brother's	3	23	ceiling	6	8	cloth	5	7
beside	3	35	brought	5	7	celebration	5	19	clothes	5	9
besides	3	21	brown	3	13	cellar	4	24	clouds	5	6
best	3	1	brush	2	31	Celsius	6	17	clown	4	13
better	3	26	bubble	3	33	cent	4	27	clue	5	3
between	3	35	buffalo	6	35	center	4	7	coach	4	3
beyond	3	35	build	5	1	central	4	25	coarse	6	11
bicycle	6	29	building	6	4	centuries	6	7	coast	2	10
big	1	21	bully	4	8	century	5	35	coat	2	10
bigger	3	11	bun	2	7	certain	3	34	coin	4	13
biggest	3	11	burglar	5	29	chain	5	2	college	4	7
bird	3	19	buried	3	25	chair	2	31	colonel	6	11
birth	6	11	burn	4	12	champion	6	29	colonies	6	7
birthday	3	29	burst	3	5	championship	6	21	color	3	32
biscuit	6	4	bus	2	7	chance	3	8	colored	4	14
black	2	20	bush	5	7	change	2	31	colorful	4	30
blanket	4	32	business	6	4	changed	5	12	column	5	33
blew	3	16	busy	5	1	chaos	6	19	comb	5	3
blow	2	14	but	1	20	chapter	5	14	come	1	26
blue	3	16	butter	4	24	charge	6	3	comfort	6	22
boat	2	10	button	5	14	chase	4	35	comfortable	5	18
bodies	6	7	buzz	2	5	chattering	5	23	coming	3	20
body	4	19	cabin	6	16	check	4	2	command	4	10
boil	5	6	cage	4	7	cheeks	5	2	commander	6	22
bold	5	3	cake	2	17	cheerful	4	30	comment	6	22
bomb	4	28	calendar	4	24	cheese	5	2	commercial	6	22
bone	2	15	California	4	16	cherries	3	25	committed	6	14
book	2	20	call	2	16	chewing	4	14	committee	6	22

Word			Word			Word			Word		
common	5	25	cried	5	12	devise	6	13	drip	2	5
communicate	6	22	cries	3	25	didn't	2	22	drive-in	4	18
community	6	21	cross	5	7	diesel	6	17	driven	6	10
companion	6	25	crowd	4	13	diet	5	28	driver	5	29
company	6	25	cruel	5	28	difference	6	20	driving	4	14
compare	6	25	crumbs	4	28	different	6	32	drop	3	2
comparison	6	25	cry	2	26	difficult	5	35	drown	5	6
compete	5	32	crystal	6	19	digging	4	14	dry	2	14
competitive	5	32	culture	5	10	dinner	3	26	duck	2	7
complete	6	22	curb	6	3	dinosaur	5	35	due	6	4
complex	5	26	cure	4	12	direction	5	19	dumb	4	28
conclusion	6	22	curious	6	33	director	5	29	duties	4	34
conference	6	20	curl	4	12	dirt	5	8	duty	4	8
confusion	5	19	current	6	32	disability	5	22	each	2	9
Congress	5	26	cursor	4	10	disadvantage	5	22	eager	4	34
connected	6	22	curve	4	12	disappear	4	20	earlier	4	21
consider	6	22	cut	2	7	disappointed	5	22	earn	4	12
considerable	5	18	cute	2	15	discomfort	4	20	earnings	5	8
constant	6	32	dad	2	3	discount	5	22	earth	4	12
constantly	6	22	dance	5	1	discovery	4	20	earthquake	5	31
constitution	6	22	danger	6	10	dishes	4	6	easiest	4	21
construction	6	22	dare	4	9	disk	4	10	easy	4	34
contact	6	22	dark	2	25	dislike	4	20	eat	2	9
contain	6	22	data	4	10	display	5	26	eaten	4	25
contest	4	32	date	3	17	dissatisfied	5	22	edge	4	7
continued	6	22	daughter	5	14	distance	6	20	education	5	19
contract	6	1	day	2	8	distant	6	15	effect	6	13
controlled	5	13	days	2	23	disturbed	5	22	effective	6	33
cook	3	9	debug	4	10	divide	5	32	effort	5	25
cookie	3	28	December	4	22	division	5	32	egg	2	2
cool	3	9	decent	6	13	do	1	30	eight	3	16
cooling	6	14	decided	5	22	dock	4	35	eighteen	4	15
copies	4	21	declare	5	8	doctor	4	24	eighth	6	4
copper	4	31	deduct	5	22	does	5	1	eighty	4	15
corn	2	28	deep	3	4	doesn't	4	4	either	4	15
corner	4	24	deer	4	26	dog's	3	23	electricity	6	21
cotton	3	26	defense	5	22	doing	2	27	element	6	32
couldn't	4	4	degree	5	22	doll	2	1	elephant	6	32
council	5	15	Delaware	4	16	dollar	3	32	eleven	4	25
count	6	5	delicious	6	33	done	2	11	else	4	2
countries	6	7	delight	5	22	don't	2	22	embarrassed	6	35
country	4	19	demand	5	22	door	2	28	employee	5	6
couple	5	15	denied	6	7	doorbell	2	34	employer	5	6
course	6	11	denim	6	17	doorway	5	31	empty	6	19
court	4	9	dentist	5	29	double	5	15	end	3	1
cousin	6	5	deny	4	19	doubt	4	28	endless	4	30
cover	4	24	depth	6	1	down	3	13	enemies	6	7
covered	5	13	descent	6	13	dozen	5	14	enemy	6	5
cowboy	4	18	describe	5	22	Dr.	2	35	energy	5	35
coyote	5	4	desert	5	27	dragon	5	14	engine	6	15
crackling	5	23	design	5	22	draperies	6	29	engineer	5	29
crash	2	5	designated	6	28	draw	3	10	England	5	34
creaking	5	23	designed	6	28	dream	5	2	English	5	34
create	5	28	destroy	4	13	dress	2	16	enjoy	3	13
creative	6	33	details	5	22	dresses	2	23	enormous	6	33
creature	5	10	develop	5	22	drew	2	21	enough	6	4
credit	6	16	development	6	21	dried	3	25	entered	5	13
crew	4	3	device	6	13	drink	3	2	entrance	6	20

word			word			word			word		
equal	6	25	favor	3	32	forth	3	15	girl's	3	22
equality	6	25	favorable	5	18	forty	5	8	give	1	33
equipped	6	14	favorite	5	35	forward	5	25	given	3	34
escape	6	19	feast	6	5	foul	6	11	giving	2	33
ethnic	6	1	feature	5	10	found	3	13	glad	4	1
even	5	27	February	4	22	four	2	29	glance	6	1
ever	3	32	feed	4	2	fowl	6	11	glass	2	16
every	3	28	feel	2	9	fox	2	1	glasses	2	23
everybody	5	31	fellow	5	25	foxes	2	23	gnaw	5	33
everyday	5	16	female	4	33	frankfurter	6	17	gnome	5	33
every day	5	16	fence	4	2	free	4	2	go	1	35
everyone	5	16	fever	4	33	Friday	3	17	goal	3	3
every one	5	16	field	4	15	fried	3	25	goalie	5	29
everything	3	29	fierce	6	8	friend	4	15	going	2	27
evil	5	15	fifteen	6	15	friendship	6	21	gold	4	3
examination	6	29	fifth	4	6	frightened	6	14	golden	4	25
example	5	35	fight	2	26	from	2	14	gone	5	1
excellent	6	32	figure	6	19	front	5	1	good	3	9
except	6	13	final	3	33	frown	5	6	good-bye	4	18
exchange	6	31	finally	6	35	frozen	5	14	goods	4	8
excited	5	9	fine	2	13	fruit	5	3	gorilla	6	35
excitement	6	31	finest	3	11	ft.	2	35	got	1	24
exhausted	6	31	finger	4	24	fuel	5	28	gotten	6	15
expand	6	31	finish	5	27	full	5	7	government	6	21
expected	6	31	fireplace	5	31	fun	2	7	grabbed	2	32
experience	6	20	fireworks	6	9	fun-loving	6	9	grade	4	1
experts	6	31	first	3	19	funniest	4	21	graffiti	6	35
explain	6	31	fish	2	31	funny	3	26	grammar	4	32
explode	5	26	five	2	13	fur	3	19	grandma	2	34
explore	6	31	fix	2	4	furious	6	33	grapes	2	17
express	6	31	flag	2	14	furniture	5	10	grass	2	14
extra	5	26	flash	2	31	furry	3	30	grasshoppers	6	9
eyes	4	6	flashlight	5	31	further	6	19	grateful	4	30
face	3	4	flavor	5	14	fury	4	12	gray	3	4
fact	5	1	flew	2	21	future	4	33	great	4	1
factor	5	14	flies	3	25	game	2	13	Greece	5	34
fair	4	9	float	4	3	garbage	4	32	Greek	5	34
fairy tales	6	9	floor	2	28	garden	4	9	green	3	4
fall	2	16	flow	4	3	gasoline	6	29	greenhouse	6	9
fallen	4	25	flower	3	13	gate	4	1	grew	2	21
false	5	7	flustered	5	13	gather	4	24	grief	6	8
familiar	6	25	flute	5	3	gathering	5	13	grind	5	23
family	6	25	fly	2	14	gave	2	13	gross	6	2
famous	6	16	focus	4	33	geese	4	26	ground	4	13
fanatic	6	29	foggy	3	30	general	6	10	group	2	21
fantastic	6	25	folks	5	3	gentle	4	7	grow	3	3
fantasy	6	25	follow	3	26	Georgia	4	16	grown	6	2
far	2	25	food	2	21	German	6	10	guess	4	2
farewell	6	9	fool	4	8	gesture	5	10	gum	2	7
farm	2	25	foot	3	9	get	2	2	gurgle	5	23
farmer	3	27	football	3	29	getting	2	32	gymnasium	6	29
farmland	5	31	for	2	29	ghost	4	28	habit	6	16
farther	5	26	force	3	15	giant	5	28	had	1	23
fast	2	14	foreign	6	8	giant's	3	22	hair	3	14
fat	3	1	forgetting	5	13	gift	4	6	half	5	33
father	4	24	form	3	15	giraffe	6	35	hamburger	6	29
father's	3	23	formal	5	15	girl	3	19	hammer	6	15
fault	6	5	fort	3	15	girlfriend	6	8	hand	3	1

Word			Word			Word			Word		
handle	3	33	hopeless	4	30	industries	6	7	Kentucky	4	16
happen	3	34	hopped	3	20	inexpensive	6	27	kernel	6	11
happened	5	13	horrible	5	18	influenza	6	29	keyboard	4	10
happiest	3	11	horse	2	28	informal	6	27	kids'	3	23
happiness	4	30	hospital	5	35	information	5	19	kind	2	20
happy	3	28	hot	2	1	inhale	6	23	king	2	19
hard	2	25	hotel	6	19	inject	6	23	kisses	2	23
hardware	4	10	hour	3	16	injustice	6	27	kitchen	3	34
harvest	4	32	house	3	13	innocent	6	32	kitten	3	34
hat	2	3	however	5	35	insist	6	15	kneel	4	28
hated	4	14	how's	4	4	instance	6	20	knees	3	7
have	1	30	huge	4	7	instant	6	32	knew	3	7
haven't	4	4	hugged	6	14	instead	5	26	knife	3	7
having	3	20	human	5	14	instinct	6	15	knight	5	2
hay	4	1	humor	4	34	instructions	5	19	knives	4	26
he	1	31	hunger	6	10	insurance	6	20	knob	4	28
head	3	1	hunt	3	2	intelligence	6	20	knock	3	7
health	5	1	hurried	4	21	intend	6	1	know	3	3
hear	3	16	hurry	4	19	intense	6	15	knowing	4	28
heard	4	27	hurt	3	19	intermediate	5	21	known	3	7
heart	2	25	husband	6	19	interrupt	5	21	label	4	34
heaven	4	25	hymn	5	33	interview	5	21	labor	4	24
heavier	4	21	ice	1	32	into	4	8	ladder	4	31
heaviest	4	21	ice cream	4	18	invasion	6	23	ladies	3	25
heavy	3	28	icy	3	30	invented	5	21	lamb	4	28
he'd	3	22	I'd	3	22	invisible	6	27	large	3	14
height	4	15	Idaho	4	16	invited	5	21	lasso	5	4
hello	3	26	identified	6	7	Iowa	4	16	last	2	14
help	1	19	if	2	4	irregular	6	27	late	2	13
hen	1	19	I'll	4	4	is	2	4	later	6	13
her	3	19	illegal	6	27	island	5	33	latter	6	13
herd	4	27	illness	4	30	it	1	21	laugh	3	7
here	3	16	I'm	2	22	item	5	27	laughed	5	1
here's	4	4	impatient	6	27	its	2	29	lay	2	8
hero	6	19	impolite	6	27	its	3	22	leader	3	27
herself	2	34	importance	6	20	it's	2	29	leadership	6	21
he's	4	4	important	6	32	it's	3	22	learn	4	12
hidden	4	31	impossible	6	27	I've	2	22	least	4	2
hiding	4	14	improve	5	26	jam	2	17	leave	5	2
high	2	26	impulse	6	1	January	4	22	leaves	4	26
hill	2	4	in	1	21	Japan	5	34	leaving	4	14
him	1	21	in.	2	35	Japanese	5	34	lecture	5	10
his	1	33	inability	6	27	job	3	2	left	3	1
hiss	2	5	incident	6	32	jog	2	1	leg	2	2
historic	6	25	incision	6	23	join	4	13	legal	4	33
history	6	25	include	5	21	journey	4	19	legislative	6	33
hockey	4	19	incomplete	6	27	joy	3	13	leisure	6	8
hole	2	15	incorrect	6	27	joystick	4	10	lemon	4	25
holiday	4	22	increase	5	26	judge	4	7	leotard	6	17
home	1	35	incredible	6	27	juice	5	3	less	2	16
home run	4	18	indeed	6	15	July	3	17	lesson	4	32
homesickness	6	9	indefinite	6	27	jump	4	3	let's	2	22
homework	3	29	independence	6	20	June	3	17	letter	4	24
honest	4	28	independent	6	27	jungle	4	35	letting	3	20
honked	5	23	index	6	15	just	1	20	level	5	15
honor	6	19	Indian	6	10	kangaroo	4	35	liar	5	28
hood	5	7	Indiana	4	16	Kansas	4	16	librarian	5	29
hop	2	1	indigestion	6	27	keep	2	9	library	5	35

lick	4	6	mayor	5	29	most	4	3	no	1	34
lie	3	3	me	1	31	mother's	3	23	nobody	4	18
life	2	13	mean	4	2	motive	6	16	nodded	6	14
lifeguard	5	31	measure	5	10	motor	4	24	noise	5	6
life jacket	4	18	meat	2	17	mouse	4	10	none	6	4
lifted	6	14	meet	3	4	mouth	5	6	nonsense	6	1
light	2	26	members	5	25	moved	3	20	noon	3	9
like	1	32	memories	4	21	movement	4	30	normal	3	33
liked	2	33	men	2	2	movie	3	28	nose	2	15
lion	5	28	men's	3	23	moving	2	33	nosy	3	30
liquid	6	1	menu	4	10	Mr.	2	35	not	1	24
listen	4	28	merchant	5	26	Mrs.	2	35	note	2	15
little	3	33	mercury	6	17	much	3	8	nothing	4	18
live	1	30	merry	4	19	muddy	3	30	noticed	4	14
lived	5	12	mess	2	2	mule	2	15	noun	5	6
living	2	33	met	2	2	multiplied	4	21	novel	6	16
load	2	10	metal	5	15	multiply	4	19	November	4	22
local	6	10	meters	4	33	mummies	6	7	now	1	26
lonely	3	27	Mexican	5	34	murmur	5	23	number	3	32
long	3	10	Mexico	5	34	music	4	34	numerous	6	33
longer	3	11	mice	4	26	musical	6	10	nut	2	7
look	1	25	middle	3	33	musician	5	29	oak	5	3
looked	2	27	middle-aged	6	9	must	1	20	obey	6	4
looking	2	27	middle school	4	18	my	2	26	object	5	25
loose	3	9	midnight	6	23	myself	2	34	occupied	6	7
lose	5	3	midway	6	23	mysterious	6	33	occurred	6	35
lost	3	10	might	2	26	named	5	12	ocean	5	9
lot	2	1	milk	2	17	nap	3	1	October	4	22
loud	3	13	mind	4	6	narrow	5	25	odor	5	14
love	1	34	mine	4	6	nation	5	19	odyssey	6	17
love	2	11	minutes	5	27	native	4	34	of	1	26
loved	5	1	mirror	3	32	natural	4	25	offer	5	7
low	2	10	misbehave	4	20	nature	4	34	office	5	25
loyal	4	25	mischief	6	8	necessary	6	35	officer	6	5
luck	4	3	miserable	5	18	nectar	4	24	often	4	28
luncheon	6	29	miss	2	16	need	2	9	Ohio	4	16
machine	5	9	Mississippi	4	16	needle	5	15	oil	3	13
made	1	28	misspelled	4	20	negative	6	33	old	1	35
magazine	5	35	mistake	4	20	neighbors	4	15	on	1	24
maiden	6	19	mixture	5	10	neither	4	15	once	4	7
mail	2	8	model	5	15	nerve	6	3	one	1	26
Maine	4	16	modem	4	10	nervous	6	33	one	3	16
major	4	34	moist	5	6	nest	4	2	only	2	11
majority	6	21	moisture	5	10	never	3	32	opening	5	13
make	2	13	mom	2	1	nevertheless	6	9	opponent	6	32
make-believe	5	31	moment	5	27	new	2	21	or	1	34
making	2	33	Monday	3	17	New Jersey	4	16	orange	4	7
March	3	17	money	3	28	newspaper	4	18	orchard	5	26
marched	5	8	monitor	4	10	New Year	6	9	order	5	8
mark	3	14	monkey	4	19	New York	4	16	ordered	5	13
married	3	25	monster	6	15	next	3	1	Oregon	4	16
Mars	6	17	month	4	22	nice	2	13	original	6	10
master	4	31	moo	2	5	nicer	3	11	orphan	6	15
match	4	1	mood	4	8	nicest	3	11	ostrich	5	26
math	2	19	moon	3	9	night	2	26	other	2	11
mathematics	6	29	moose	4	26	nightmare	6	3	our	3	16
May	3	17	more	2	28	nine	1	32	out	3	13
may	2	8	morning	4	9	nine	5	2	outdoors	5	31

Word			Word			Word			Word		
outside	3	29	pick	2	20	precision	6	25	put	1	25
oven	5	14	picked	3	20	predict	5	20	putting	2	32
over	2	11	picnic	4	31	prefer	5	20	qualified	6	7
owe	5	3	pie	4	6	preferred	6	34	qualify	4	19
own	2	10	piece	4	27	prehistoric	4	20	quarter	5	8
owner	3	27	pier	6	8	prepaid	4	20	question	5	19
oxen	4	26	pierce	4	15	prepare	5	20	quickly	3	27
page	6	2	pillow	6	15	prepared	6	34	quiet	5	28
pail	4	1	pilot	4	33	presence	6	20	quit	5	1
paint	3	4	pin	2	4	present	5	9	quite	4	6
pair	4	27	pioneer	5	29	president	6	32	rabbit	4	31
pajamas	4	35	pirate	4	33	pressure	5	9	raccoon	6	35
palm	5	33	pizza	2	17	pretend	5	20	race	4	1
pantaloons	6	29	place	4	1	prettier	4	21	rain	2	8
panther	5	26	placed	2	33	pretty	3	28	rainy	3	30
paper	4	24	plain	4	27	prevent	5	20	raise	3	4
parade	6	5	plan	4	1	preview	5	20	ranch	4	35
pare	4	27	plane	4	27	previous	5	20	rang	2	19
parents	4	9	planet	6	16	priceless	4	30	rapid	6	1
park	2	25	plant	4	1	pride	6	2	rarely	4	9
parka	4	35	plastic	4	32	princess	6	5	rather	5	14
parrot	4	32	plate	5	2	principal	6	11	rattle	5	23
part	2	25	play	1	28	principle	6	11	rattlesnake	5	31
parties	4	21	played	5	12	printed	4	14	ray	5	2
partnership	6	21	player	3	27	printer	4	10	Rd.	2	35
party	3	28	playful	3	27	prior	5	28	reach	2	31
pass	2	16	playground	3	29	private	5	27	react	5	28
pasture	5	10	please	5	9	probable	5	18	read	2	9
path	4	1	pleased	5	12	probably	5	35	reader	6	10
patient	4	34	pleasure	5	10	problem	4	31	real	3	4
patio	5	4	plenty	4	19	process	5	20	really	3	27
pattern	4	32	plop	2	5	produce	5	20	reason	3	34
paws	3	10	poem	5	28	product	5	20	reasonable	5	18
pay	2	8	poet	5	28	production	6	34	receive	5	32
payment	4	30	point	3	13	professional	6	34	reception	5	32
peace	4	27	pointing	6	14	professor	6	34	recital	5	21
peach	3	8	poison	4	13	program	5	20	recommend	6	35
peanut	5	27	polar	4	33	progress	6	34	recycle	5	35
pear	4	27	police	4	7	project	5	20	red	1	19
pearl	5	8	political	6	10	promised	5	20	reduced	6	31
pencil	4	7	pond	2	1	propeller	6	34	referred	5	13
pennies	4	21	pony	4	19	protect	5	20	refrigerator	6	29
people	4	25	popping	2	32	protection	6	34	refuse	5	9
perceived	6	34	popular	5	32	protest	6	34	refused	6	31
percent	5	9	population	5	32	proud	5	6	regain	6	31
perfect	4	32	porch	5	8	prove	5	3	regretted	5	13
perfectly	6	34	portrait	5	26	provide	5	20	rehearse	5	21
perform	4	9	positive	6	33	provided	6	34	reign	5	33
performance	6	20	possible	4	25	public	4	31	reins	6	8
perfume	6	34	potato	5	4	pulled	3	20	relationship	6	31
perhaps	6	34	power	4	24	pupil	4	33	relax	5	21
permanent	6	32	practice	5	9	puppet	4	31	remain	6	31
permission	5	19	practicing	5	12	puppies	3	25	remarkable	5	18
permitted	5	13	prairie	6	8	purchase	5	26	remember	4	24
person	3	19	praise	6	2	pure	4	12	remembered	5	13
persuade	6	34	precaution	5	20	purple	3	33	remind	5	21
phone	3	7	precise	6	25	purse	6	3	repair	5	8
pianist	5	29	precisely	6	34	push	3	8	replied	4	21

Word			Word			Word			Word		
report	4	9	saxophone	6	17	shoe	3	9	so	2	11
represent	6	31	say	2	8	shone	4	3	soap	3	3
rescue	6	4	says	5	1	shook	3	8	soda	4	33
resolve	6	31	scar	6	3	shop	2	31	sofa	6	16
responsible	5	18	scarce	6	3	shopped	3	20	soft	3	10
return	5	21	scared	4	14	shore	2	28	soften	4	28
returned	6	14	scatter	3	26	short	2	28	software	4	10
review	5	21	scene	3	16	shot	5	1	soil	3	13
revised	6	28	scent	4	27	should	5	7	solar	4	33
reward	6	3	school	2	21	shout	4	13	soldier	6	10
rhyme	4	28	science	5	28	show	2	10	solemn	6	16
ribbon	4	25	scientist	5	29	shower	5	6	solid	5	27
rich	2	31	scoop	3	9	shut	3	2	some	1	30
richer	3	11	score	6	3	side	4	6	some	2	11
richest	3	11	scratch	3	5	sidewalk	3	29	somehow	4	18
ride	1	32	scream	3	5	sigh	6	2	someone	3	29
riding	2	33	screams	6	2	sight	3	3	something	2	34
right	2	26	screen	3	5	sign	6	28	sometimes	2	34
ring	3	2	sculpture	5	10	signal	6	28	song	2	19
riot	5	28	search	4	12	signature	6	28	soon	2	21
rise	3	3	seashore	6	9	significant	6	32	sorry	3	28
river	3	32	season	3	34	signing	6	28	sort	2	28
road	2	10	seat	2	9	silence	4	33	soul	5	3
roadside	6	9	second	6	16	silver	4	31	sound	5	6
roar	6	3	section	5	19	simple	5	15	soup	3	9
roaring	5	23	secure	4	12	since	4	7	source	6	3
roast	6	2	security	6	21	sing	2	19	south	4	13
robin	5	27	seen	3	16	single	5	15	space	5	2
rodeo	5	4	seized	6	8	sipped	2	32	spacecraft	4	26
Roman	6	10	sensible	5	18	sisters'	3	23	spare	5	8
rookie	5	29	sensitive	6	33	sit	2	4	speak	4	2
room	2	21	sent	4	27	sitting	2	32	speaking	6	14
rose	1	35	sentence	5	9	six	2	4	special	4	25
rough	3	7	September	4	22	sixth	4	6	spelling	6	14
round	5	6	servant	6	32	sizzle	5	23	spider	6	16
row	2	10	serve	6	5	skating	4	14	spied	4	21
royal	4	13	service	6	3	sketch	6	1	spike	6	2
rubbed	2	32	set	2	2	skin	4	6	spirit	6	19
ruin	5	28	seven	3	34	sky	2	26	splash	5	23
rule	5	3	seventy-five	5	31	sleep	2	9	splendid	6	1
ruler	4	34	several	4	25	sleeping bag	4	18	spoil	5	6
run	1	20	shape	2	31	sleepy	3	30	sport	3	15
running	3	20	share	3	14	sleigh	6	4	spot	3	2
rustling	5	23	shark	5	8	slept	4	2	spotted	4	14
sack	6	1	sharp	3	8	slice	6	2	spray	3	5
sad	2	3	she	1	31	slight	5	2	spread	3	5
sadness	4	30	she'd	3	22	slope	6	2	spring	4	22
said	1	25	sheep	4	26	slow	2	10	sprout	3	5
salad	2	17	sheet	4	2	slowly	3	27	square	3	14
salty	3	30	shelves	4	26	slurp	5	23	squawked	5	23
same	3	4	shepherd	4	28	small	3	10	squeak	5	23
sandwich	6	17	sheriff	6	35	smaller	3	11	squeeze	6	2
sandy	3	30	she's	4	4	smart	5	8	squirrel	4	32
sat	2	3	shiny	3	30	smell	4	2	St.	2	35
satellite	6	35	ship	2	31	smiled	2	33	stained	6	14
Saturday	4	22	shirt	6	3	smooth	4	8	stairs	4	9
saved	3	20	shiver	6	16	snack	2	17	stampede	5	4
saw	1	33	shock	4	3	snowstorm	4	18	stand	4	1

Word			Word			Word			Word		
star	4	9	supper	3	26	themselves	4	18	train	2	8
stare	3	14	supplied	6	7	then	1	29	transfer	6	23
start	2	25	supply	4	19	then	6	13	transport	6	23
started	2	27	support	5	25	there	2	29	travel	5	27
state	6	5	supposed	5	12	there	3	14	treasure	5	10
statement	6	21	sure	5	9	therefore	4	9	tree	2	14
station	5	9	surface	4	32	there's	5	16	trial	5	15
stay	4	1	surprise	6	5	these	3	4	trickled	5	23
steak	6	4	surprised	5	12	they	1	29	tries	3	25
step	4	2	survive	5	25	they're	2	22	trip	4	6
stepped	4	14	swam	4	1	they're	2	29	triumph	5	28
stew	4	3	swimming	4	14	they've	3	22	trouble	4	25
stick	2	20	switch	5	1	thief	4	15	truck	3	2
sticky	3	30	sword	5	33	thieves	6	8	true	5	3
still	3	2	system	6	4	thing	4	6	truth	4	8
stolen	5	27	table	3	33	think	3	2	try	2	14
stomach	6	5	tail	2	8	thinner	3	11	trying	2	27
stone	3	3	take	2	13	third	3	19	Tuesday	4	22
stop	1	24	taken	3	34	this	2	4	tuna	5	4
stopped	2	32	taking	3	20	those	2	15	tune	2	15
store	3	15	talk	3	10	though	6	2	tunnel	4	32
stories	6	7	tall	5	7	thought	5	7	turkey	3	28
storm	2	28	tangerine	6	17	threatening	6	14	turn	3	19
story	3	15	tap	2	3	three	2	9	turned	5	12
stove	4	3	taste	6	5	threw	4	3	tuxedo	6	17
straight	5	2	taught	5	7	throat	5	3	twirl	5	8
strange	3	5	tea	4	35	throne	6	11	two	2	29
stranger	6	19	teacher's	3	22	through	4	8	type	4	6
street	3	5	teachers'	3	23	thrown	6	11	ugly	4	31
strike	3	5	teaching	5	12	thumb	6	1	umbrella	4	35
string	3	5	team	2	9	thunder	4	32	unable	4	20
strong	3	5	tearing	6	3	thunderstorm	6	9	uncover	5	21
structure	5	10	tease	5	2	Thursday	4	22	underground	6	23
student	4	34	teenager	6	9	tie	3	3	underhand	6	23
studied	3	25	teeth	4	26	tiger	4	33	underline	6	23
study	6	5	telephone	3	7	tight	3	3	underneath	6	23
stuff	4	3	televised	6	28	time	2	13	uneasy	5	21
stupid	4	8	television	5	19	tiny	4	19	unexpected	4	20
style	5	2	tell	3	1	tired	4	14	unfair	4	20
subdued	6	23	temper	4	31	to	2	29	unfolds	4	20
submarine	6	23	ten	2	2	tobacco	6	35	unhappy	4	20
submerge	6	23	tennis	5	25	toes	4	3	united	5	32
substitute	5	35	terrible	5	18	together	3	32	unity	5	32
subway	6	23	terrific	6	35	told	2	11	unknown	5	21
success	6	35	terrified	4	21	tomato	5	4	unpleasant	5	21
such	3	2	terror	5	14	tomorrow	6	35	untie	4	20
sudden	4	31	Texas	4	16	too	2	29	unusual	4	20
suddenly	5	35	than	6	13	took	2	20	up	2	7
suffered	5	13	thankful	3	27	tooth	4	8	upon	2	34
sugar	3	32	thanks	4	1	top	2	1	upstairs	5	31
suit	5	3	Thanksgiving	5	31	tornado	5	4	us	2	7
suitable	5	18	that	1	29	total	3	33	U.S.A.	2	35
summer	3	17	that's	4	4	tourist	5	29	use	2	15
sun	2	7	the	1	29	towel	4	35	used	2	33
Sunday	3	17	their	2	29	tower	5	14	useful	3	27
sunrise	2	34	their	4	15	town	5	6	useless	4	30
super	4	34	theirs	5	16	toys	2	23	vacant	5	27
supervise	6	28	them	2	19	traffic	4	32	vacation	5	19

valentine	6	17	went	1	19	would	5	33
valley	4	19	went	3	1	wounded	6	4
valuable	5	18	we're	2	22	wrap	5	33
vanilla	5	4	weren't	4	4	wreck	5	33
various	6	33	we've	3	22	wrinkled	5	33
velvet	6	15	what	1	22	write	3	7
very	3	28	what's	3	22	writing	5	12
veterinarian	6	29	wheat	3	8	written	3	26
vice-president	4	18	wheel	4	2	wrong	3	7
victor	6	19	when	1	22	wrote	3	7
Vietnam	5	34	where	1	22	yard	3	14
Vietnamese	5	34	where	3	8	yd.	2	35
village	3	26	which	2	19	year	3	17
visible	5	18	while	2	19	years	5	9
vision	6	28	whispered	6	14	yellow	3	26
visit	6	28	white	3	3	yes	2	2
visiting	5	13	who	1	34	yet	2	2
visitors	6	28	whole	6	2	yield	6	8
visual	6	28	whom	4	8	yolk	5	33
vital	6	16	who's	5	16	you	2	21
voice	4	7	whose	5	16	you'll	4	4
volcano	5	35	why	1	22	young	6	4
voyage	6	5	wiener	6	17	your	3	15
wagging	3	20	wild	4	6	you're	2	22
wagon	3	34	will	2	4	yours	4	9
waist	4	27	win	2	4	you've	4	4
wait	1	28	window	5	25	zero	4	35
waited	2	27	windy	3	30	zoo	3	9
walk	3	10	winning	2	32			
walking	5	12	winter	3	17			
wallet	4	31	wisdom	5	32			
wanted	2	27	wise	5	32			
war	3	15	wishes	2	23			
warlike	6	9	with	1	25			
warm	3	15	witness	6	15			
warn	5	8	wives	4	26			
was	1	33	woke	2	15			
wash	3	8	wolf	5	7			
Washington	4	16	wolves	4	26			
wasn't	2	22	woman	5	14			
waste	4	27	women	4	26			
watch	5	1	won	3	16			
watched	5	12	wonder	6	4			
water	3	32	wonderful	4	30			
watt	6	17	wondering	5	13			
way	3	4	won't	4	4			
we	1	31	wood	3	9			
weapon	6	10	wooden	4	8			
wear	3	14	wool	4	8			
we'd	4	4	word	3	19			
Wednesday	4	22	wore	3	15			
week	2	20	work	3	19			
weekend	4	22	worker	4	12			
weigh	4	15	world	4	12			
weight	4	15	worm	4	12			
weird	4	15	worse	4	12			
welcome	5	25	worst	6	3			
we'll	4	4	worth	4	12			

Bibliography

PROFESSIONAL LIST FOR TEACHERS

Allred, Ruel A. "Integrating Proven Spelling Content and Methods with Emerging Literacy Programs." *Reading Psychology: An International Quarterly* v14 (1993): 15–31.

Bear, Donald R. "'Learning to Fasten the Seat of My Union Suit Without Looking Around': The Synchrony of Literacy Development." *Theory Into Practice* v30 n3 (Summer 1991): 149–157.

Bear, Donald R., and Diane Barone. "Using Children's Spellings to Group for Word Study and Directed Reading in the Primary Classroom." *Reading Psychology: An International Quarterly* v10 (1989): 275–292.

Bolton, Faye, and Diane Snowball. *Teaching Spelling: A Practical Resource.* Portsmouth, NH: Heinemann, 1993.

Cunningham, Patricia M. *Phonics They Use: Words for Reading and Writing.* HarperCollins, 1995.

Cunningham, Patricia M., and James W. Cunningham. "Making Words: Enhancing the Invented Spelling-Decoding Connection." *The Reading Teacher* v46 n2 (October 1992): 106–115.

Farr, Roger, Cheryl Kelleher, Katherine Lee, and Caroline Beverstock. "An Analysis of the Spelling Patterns of Children in Grades Two Through Eight: A Study of a National Sample of Children's Writing." Center for Reading and Language Studies, Indiana University, 1989.

Fry, Edward, Ph.D. *Spelling Book: Words Most Needed, Plus Phonics, for Grades 1–6.* Laguna Beach, CA: Laguna Beach Educational Books, 1993.

Gentry, J. Richard. *SPEL . . . Is a Four-Letter Word.* Portsmouth, NH: Heinemann, 1989.

Gentry, J. Richard, and Jean W. Gillet. *Teaching Kids to Spell.* Portsmouth, NH: Heinemann, 1992.

Gill, J. Thomas, Jr. "Development of Word Knowledge As It Relates to Reading, Spelling, and Instruction." *Language Arts* v69 n6 (October 1992): 444–453.

Hillerich, Robert L. *Teaching Children to Write, K–8: A Complete Guide to Developing Writing Skills.* New York: Prentice Hall, 1985. (excerpts)

Hodges, Richard E. "The Conventions of Writing" in *Handbook of Research on Teaching the English Language Arts,* 775–786. Macmillan, 1991.

Holdaway, Don. "Shared Book Experience: Teaching Reading Using Favorite Books." *Theory Into Practice* v21 n4 (Fall 1982): 293–300.

Jongsma, Kathleen Stumpf. "Reading-Spelling Links: Questions & Answers." *The Reading Teacher* v43 n8 (April 1990): 608–610.

McAlexander, Patricia J., Ann B. Dobie, and Noel Gregg. *Beyond the "SP" Label: Improving the Spelling of Learning Disabled and Basic Writers.* National Council of Teachers of English, 1992.

Morris, Darrell. "Editorial Comment: Developmental Spelling Theory Revisited." *Reading Psychology: An International Quarterly* v10 n2 (1989): iii–x.

___. "Meeting the Needs of Poor Spellers in the Elementary School: A Developmental Perspective." *National College of Education Occasional Paper No. 14* (November 1986): 3–30.

___. "The Relationship Between Children's Concept of Word in Text and Phoneme Awareness in Learning to Read: A Longitudinal Study." *Research in the Teaching of English* v27 n2 (May 1993): 132–154.

___. " 'Word Sort': A Categorization Strategy for Improving Word Recognition Ability." *Reading Psychology: An International Quarterly* v3 n3 (July-September 1982): 247–259.

Routman, Regie. *Invitations: Changing as Teachers & Learners K–12.* Portsmouth, NH: Heinemann, 1994. (excerpts)

___. "The Uses and Abuses of Invented Spelling." *Instructor* v102 (May/June 1993): 36–39.

Schlagal, Robert C., and Joy Harris Schlagal. "The Integral Character of Spelling." *Language Arts* v69 n6 (October 1992): 418–424.

Strickland, Dorothy S. "Emergent Literacy: How Young Children Learn to Read and Write." *Educational Leadership* v47 (March 1990): 18–23.

Swisher, Karen. "An Action Model for Research in the Classroom: Developmental Spelling K–2." Paper presented at the annual meeting of the College Reading Association, Crystal City, VA, October 31, 1991, to November 3, 1991.

Templeton, Shane. "New Trends in an Historical Perspective: Old Story, New Resolution—Sound and Meaning in Spelling." *Language Arts* v69 n6 (October 1992): 454–463.

___. "Teaching and Learning the English Spelling System: Reconceptualizing Method and Purpose." *The Elementary School Journal* v92 n2 (November 1991): 185–201.

Weaver, Constance. "On the Teaching of Spelling." *Michigan Literacy Consortium Journal* (Spring 1995): 24–25.

Wilde, Sandra. "A Proposal for a New Spelling Curriculum." *The Elementary School Journal* v90 n3 (January 1990): 275–289.

___. *You Kan Red This! Spelling and Punctuation for Whole Language.* Portsmouth, NH: Heinemann, 1991.

Yopp, H.K. "Developing phonemic awareness in young children." *The Reading Teacher* v45 (1992): 696–703.

___. "A longitudinal study of the relationships between phonemic awareness and reading and spelling achievement." Paper presented at the annual meeting of the American Educational Research Association, San Francisco, CA (1992).

___. "Read-aloud books for developing phonemic awareness: An annotated bibliography." *The Reading Teacher* v48 (1995): 538–542.

___. "The validity and reliability of phonemic awareness tests." *Reading Research Quarterly* v23 (1988): 159–177.

Zutell, Jerry, and Timothy Rasinski. "Children's Spelling Strategies and Their Cognitive Development." In *Developmental and Cognitive Aspects of Learning to Spell: A Reflection of Word Knowledge.* Edited by Edmund H. Henderson and James W. Beers, 52–73. Newark, Delaware: International Reading Association, 1980.

___. "Reading and Spelling Connections in Third and Fifth Grade Students." *Reading Psychology: An International Quarterly* v10 n2 (1989): 137–155.

▶ WORD PLAY AND LANGUAGE-RELATED READING LIST FOR STUDENTS

Albert, Burton. *Code Busters!* Niles, IL: Albert Whitman & Company, 1985. WORD GAMES

Bayer, Jane. *A My Name Is Alice.* New York: Dial Books for Young Readers, 1984. ALLITERATION

Cameron, P. *"I can't," said the ant.* New York: Coward-McCann, 1961. ALLITERATION

Ciardi, John. *The Hopeful Trout & Other Limericks.* Boston: Houghton Mifflin & Company, 1992. LIMERICKS

Cole, William E. *Poem Stew.* New York: HarperCollins Children's Books, 1981. SPELLING-RELATED BOOKS

Durant, Alan. *Mouse Party.* Cambridge, Massachusetts: Candlewick Press, 1995. STORIES IN RHYME

Ehlert, Lois. *Feathers for Lunch.* San Diego: Harcourt Brace & Company, 1990. STORIES IN RHYME

Hepworth, Cathi. *Antics! An Alphabetical Anthology.* New York: Putnam Publishing Group, 1992. ALPHABETICAL LINEUP OF WORDS CONTAINING *ANT*

Keller, Charles. *Tongue Twisters.* New York: Simon & Schuster's Children's Books, 1989. TONGUE TWISTERS

Kellogg, Steven. *Aster Aardvark's Alphabet Adventures.* New York: Morrow Junior Books, 1987. ALPHABET BOOK

Martin, Jerome. *Carrot-Parrot.* New York: Simon & Schuster's Children's Books, 1991. RHYMES

Parish, Peggy. *Good Work, Amelia Bedelia.* New York: Avon, 1980. SPELLING

Rosen, Michael. *Walking the Bridge of Your Nose.* New York: Kingfisher, 1995. WORDPLAY; POEMS; RHYMES

Schwartz, Alvin. *Flapdoodle: Pure Nonsense from American Folklore.* New York: HarperCollins Children's Books, 1980. JUMP-ROPE RHYMES; AUTOGRAPH VERSE

Seuss, Dr. *Dr. Seuss's ABC.* New York: Random House, 1963. ALLITERATION

Seuss, Dr. *There's a wocket in my pocket.* New York: Random House, 1963. ALLITERATION

Terban, Marvin. *The Dove Dove: Funny Homograph Riddles.* New York: Clarion, 1988. SPELLING

INTEGRATED SPELLING:
Scope and Sequence

Grade	1	2	3	4	5	6
SPELLING GENERALIZATIONS						
Sound-Letter Relationships						
Consonants	X	X	X	X	X	X
Consonant Digraphs	X	X	X	X	X	X
Consonant Clusters		X	X	X	X	X
Short Vowels	X	X	X	X	X	X
Long Vowels	X	X	X	X	X	X
Vowel Diphthongs/Vowel Digraphs/Variant Vowels		X	X	X	X	X
R-Controlled Vowels		X	X	X	X	X
"Silent" Letters	X	X	X	X	X	X
Schwa			X	X	X	X
Double Letters		X	X	X	X	X
Spelling Patterns	X	X	X	X	X	X
Word Structure						
Contractions	X	X	X	X	X	X
Plurals/Possessives		X	X	X	X	X
Inflected Forms/Comparatives/Superlatives		X	X	X	X	X
Prefixes			X	X	X	X
Suffixes			X	X	X	X
Greek and Latin Word Parts					X	X
Word Analysis						
Invented Spelling	X	X				
Phonograms	X	X	X	X	X	X
Compound Words		X	X	X	X	X
Syllable Patterns				X	X	X
Letter Patterns				X	X	X
Pronunciation				X	X	X

Grade	1	2	3	4	5	6
SPELLING GENERALIZATIONS						
Spelling Strategies						
Rhyming Words	x	x	x	x	x	x
Word Shapes	x	x	x	x	x	x
Word Families	x	x	x	x	x	x
Study Steps to Learn a Word	x	x	x	x	x	x
Picture/Sound Out a Word		x	x	x	x	x
Related Words		x	x	x	x	x
Mnemonic Devices			x	x	x	x
Spell/Proofread with a Partner		x	x	x	x	x
Try Different Spellings/Best Guess		x	x	x	x	x
Dictionary/Definitions		x	x	x	x	x
Proofread Twice		x	x	x	x	x
Apply Spelling Rules		x	x	x	x	x
Vocabulary Development						
Classify/Categorize Words	x	x	x	x	x	x
Antonyms	x	x	x	x	x	x
Content-Area Words	x	x	x	x	x	x
Synonyms		x	x	x	x	x
Homophones		x	x	x	x	x
Multiple Meanings/Homographs		x	x	x	x	x
Dictionary (for meaning)		x	x	x	x	x
Word Origins		x	x	x	x	x
Analogies			x	x	x	x
Idioms			x	x	x	x
Denotation/Connotation					x	x
Parts of Speech					x	x
Root Words					x	x
Writing						
The Writing Process	x	x	x	x	x	x
Proofreading	x	x	x	x	x	x
Frequently Misspelled Words	x	x	x	x	x	x

Grade 1 Index

a, **long,** T183–T188

a, **short,** T153–T158

Accessing prior knowledge, T130, T136, T142, T148, T154, T160, T166, T172, T184, T190, T196, T202, T208, T214, T220, T226

-ack, T123–T128

Activities and games, T316–T321
See also Integrated curriculum activities.

Activities with WordShop Words, T24, T30, T36, T42, T48, T54, T60, T66, T72, T78, T84, T90, T96, T102, T108, T114, T120, T126, T132, T138, T144, T150, T156, T162, T168, T174, T186, T192, T198, T204, T210, T216, T222, T228
See also Vocabulary adventures.

-ad, T87–T92

Add Your Own Word
developing spelling lists, T166, T196, T214
recognizing patterns, T130, T136, T142, T148, T154, T160, T172, T184, T190, T202, T208, T220, T226

-an, T39–T44

Answer key
for Home activities master, T304
for lessons, T255–T260

-ap, T27–T32

Applying spelling strategies, T23, T29, T35, T41, T47, T53, T59, T65, T71, T77, T83, T89, T95, T101, T107, T113, T119, T125, T131, T137, T143, T149, T155, T161, T167, T173, T185, T191, T197, T203, T209, T215, T221, T227

Art
See Integrated curriculum activities.

Assessment
assessment options, T308–T309
informal, T21, T27, T33, T39, T45, T51, T57, T63, T69, T75, T81, T87, T93, T99, T105, T111, T117, T123, T129, T135, T141, T147, T153, T159, T165, T171, T183, T189, T195, T201, T207, T213, T219, T225
placement inventory, T14–T17
portfolio conferences, T311–T313
posttests, T133, T139, T145, T151, T157, T163, T169, T175, T187, T193, T199, T205, T211, T217, T223, T229
practice tests, T178, T232
pretests, T130, T136, T142, T148, T154, T160, T166, T172, T184, T190, T196, T202, T208, T214, T220, T226
self-assessment, T130, T136, T142, T148, T154, T160, T166, T172, T178, T184, T190, T196, T202, T208, T214, T220, T226, T232

Assignment guide, T11, T21, T27, T33, T39, T45, T51, T57, T63, T69, T75, T81, T87, T93, T99, T105, T111, T117, T123, T129, T135, T141, T147, T153, T159, T165, T171, T183, T189, T195, T201, T207, T213, T219, T225

-at, T45–T50

Auditory modality
See Learning differences.

Bibliography, T335–T337

C

Children acquiring English

building vocabulary, T24, T30, T36, T48, T54, T66, T84, T96, T137, T147, T155, T189, T210, T215, T219

comparing and contrasting, T21, T27, T33, T39, T45, T51, T57, T63, T69, T75, T81, T87, T93, T99, T105, T111, T117, T123, T129, T135, T141, T153, T159, T171, T183, T207, T213

practicing pronunciation, T72, T102, T108, T120, T126, T191

reinforcing self-esteem, T60, T204, T228

understanding idioms, T143, T167

understanding word meaning, T78, T90, T114, T131, T149, T173, T185, T201, T222, T225

See also Meeting individual needs.

Classifying

See Sorting.

Concept of word, T23, T29, T35, T41, T47, T53, T59, T65, T71, T77, T83, T89, T95, T101, T107, T113, T119, T125

Consonants, digraphs

th, T189–T194

wh, T147–T152

Cooperative learning

See Working together.

Copying masters, T263–T304

answer key for, T304

class record-keeping chart, T267

home activities masters, T268–T303

percent conversion chart, T265

spelling progress record, T266

using, T264

Cumulative word list, T325–T334

D

Descriptive words

See Vocabulary WordShop Words.

Developing individual spelling lists, T166, T196, T214

Developmental levels, T8–T10

challenge, T31, T91, T131, T143, T161, T163, T191, T197, T203, T209, T221, T227

children acquiring English, T21, T24, T27, T30, T33, T36, T39, T45, T48, T51, T57, T60, T63, T66, T69, T72, T75, T78, T81, T84, T87, T90, T93, T96, T99, T102, T105, T108, T111, T114, T117, T119, T123, T125, T129, T131, T135, T137, T141, T143, T147, T149, T153, T155, T159, T165, T167, T171, T173, T183, T185, T189, T191, T195, T201, T204, T207, T210, T213, T215, T219, T222, T225, T228

emergent spellers, T8, T10, T11

extra support/children acquiring English, T23, T29, T35, T41, T47, T53, T59, T65, T71, T77, T83, T89, T95, T101, T107, T113, T125

phonetic spellers, T8, T10, T11, T132, T138, T144, T150, T156, T162, T169, T185, T191, T192, T197, T203, T209, T216, T223, T227

semi-phonetic spellers, T8, T10, T11, T131, T137, T143, T149, T155, T167, T186, T191, T197, T203, T215, T221

strategic spellers, T9

syntactic-semantic spellers, T9

transitional spellers, T9, T10, T11, T132, T138, T144, T150, T156, T162, T168, T186, T192, T204, T210, T216, T222, T228

See also Learning differences; Meeting individual needs.

Dictionary, Spelling Picture

for spelling, T237–T244

Drafting

See Process writing steps.

e, **long,** T201–T206

e, **short,** T129–T134

-ell, T63–T68

-en, T69–T74

Error analysis chart, T310

-et, T57–T62

Extra help
See Meeting individual needs.

Fun with words, T131, T137, T143, T149,
T155, T161, T167, T173, T185, T191,
T197, T203, T209, T215, T221, T227

Graphic organizers
chart, T37, T61, T91, T103, T126, T127,
T134, T145, T175, T194, T205, T206,
T229
list, T121, T147, T188, T217
sentence frame, T25, T37, T55, T73, T85,
T127
web, T55, T151, T163, T169, T193

Home activities masters, T268–T304
answer key for, T304
See also Resources, home activities.

i, **long,** T207–T212

i, **short,** T141–T146

-ick, T75–T80

-ig, T111–T116

-ill, T99–T104

-in, T93–T98

-ip, T81–T86

Informal assessment
See Assessment.

Initial consonants, T21–T26

**Initial consonants, review of with phono-
grams,** T23, T29, T35, T41, T47, T53, T59,
T65, T71, T77, T83, T89, T95, T101, T107,
T113, T119, T125

Integrated curriculum activities
art, T32, T104, T116, T176, T230
language arts, T26, T32, T38, T44, T56,
T80, T92, T98, T104, T110, T128, T146,
T152, T170, T194, T218, T224
math, T86, T164, T194
music, T140, T200, T218
physical education, T122
science, T50, T68, T74, T158, T164, T188,
T212
social studies, T62, T80, T134, T176, T206,
T230

Integrated spelling and literature,
T322–T323

Introduction
introducing the lesson, T130, T136, T142,
T148, T154, T160, T166, T172, T184,
T190, T196, T202, T208, T214, T220,
T226
introducing the page, T22, T28, T34, T40,
T46, T52, T58, T64, T70, T76, T82, T88,
T94, T100, T106, T112, T118, T124
warm-up, T22, T28, T34, T40, T46, T52,
T58, T64, T70, T76, T82, T88, T94, T100,
T106, T112, T118, T124

Kinesthetic modality
See Learning differences.

Language arts
See Integrated curriculum activities.

Language Handbook, T180, T234

Learning differences
auditory modality, T26, T32, T38, T44, T50, T56, T62, T80, T86, T92, T98, T110, T116, T122, T128, T134, T140, T158, T164, T170, T176, T188, T200, T206, T212, T224, T230

kinesthetic modality, T26, T32, T38, T44, T50, T56, T62, T68, T74, T86, T92, T110, T116, T128, T134, T140, T164, T176, T188, T194, T200, T212, T230

visual modality, T68, T74, T80, T104, T140, T146, T152, T158, T164, T188, T194, T218, T230

Lesson planner
See Assignment guide.

Lesson wrap-up, T26, T32, T38, T44, T50, T56, T62, T68, T74, T80, T86, T92, T98, T104, T110, T116, T122, T128, T134, T140, T146, T152, T158, T164, T170, T176, T188, T194, T200, T206, T212, T218, T224, T230

Limited-English-proficient students
See Children acquiring English; Meeting individual needs.

Math
See Integrated curriculum activities.

Meeting individual needs
challenge, T31, T91, T131, T143, T161, T163, T191, T197, T203, T209, T221, T227

children acquiring English, T21, T24, T27, T30, T33, T36, T39, T45, T48, T51, T57, T60, T63, T66, T69, T72, T75, T78, T81, T84, T87, T90, T93, T96, T99, T102, T105, T108, T111, T114, T117, T119, T123, T125, T129, T131, T135, T137, T141, T143, T147, T149, T153, T155, T159, T165, T167, T171, T173, T183, T185, T189, T191, T195, T201, T204, T207, T210, T213, T215, T219, T222, T225, T228

extra support/children acquiring English, T23, T29, T35, T41, T47, T53, T59, T65, T71, T77, T83, T89, T95, T101, T107, T113, T125

phonetic spellers, T8, T10, T11, T132, T138, T144, T150, T156, T162, T169, T185, T191, T192, T197, T203, T209, T216, T223, T227

semi-phonetic spellers, T8, T10, T11, T131, T137, T143, T149, T155, T167, T186, T191, T197, T203, T215, T221

transitional spellers, T9, T10, T11, T132, T138, T144, T150, T156, T162, T168, T186, T192, T204, T210, T216, T222, T228

Modalities
See Learning differences.

Music
See Integrated curriculum activities.

o, **long,** T225–T230

o, **short,** T159–T164

o, **words to remember,** T171–T176

-op, T51–T56

-ot, T33–T38

Optional writing ideas
See Writing.

Pacing
See Assignment guide.

Philosophy of *Integrated Spelling*, T7

Physical education
See Integrated curriculum activities.

Picture Dictionary, T237–T244

Placement inventory, T14–T17

Planning instruction, T12–T13

Portfolio conferences
See Assessment.

Posttests
See Assessment.

Practice activities
See Copying masters; Resources.

Practice tests, T178, T232

Pretest/posttest context sentences, T129, T135, T141, T147, T153, T159, T165, T171, T183, T189, T195, T201, T207, T213, T219, T225

Pretests
See Assessment.

Prewriting
See Process writing steps.

Process writing steps
drafting, T245–T248
prewriting, T245–T248
proofreading, T180, T234, T245–T248
publishing, T245–T248
revising, T245–T248

Proofreading, T180, T234
See also Process writing steps.

Publishing
See Process writing steps.

Recognizing patterns, T130, T136, T142, T148, T154, T160, T172, T184, T190, T202, T208, T220, T226

Recognizing phonic elements, T130, T136, T142, T154, T160, T172, T184, T202, T208, T220, T226

Resources
activities and games, T316–T321
bibliography, T335–T337
cumulative word list for grades 1–6, T325–T334
home activities, T22, T28, T34, T40, T46, T52, T58, T64, T70, T76, T82, T88, T94, T100, T106, T112, T118, T124, T130, T136, T142, T148, T154, T160, T166, T172, T179, T184, T190, T196, T202, T208, T214, T220, T226, T233
integrating spelling and literature, T322–T323
scope and sequence, T338–T339
spelling word list development, T324

Reteach
learning differences, T26, T32, T38, T44, T50, T56, T62, T68, T74, T80, T86, T92, T98, T104, T110, T116, T122, T128, T134, T140, T146, T152, T158, T164, T170, T176, T188, T194, T200, T206, T212, T218, T224, T230

Review words, T177, T231

Revising
See Process writing steps.

Rhyming words, T177, T231
See also Strategy Workshop, rhyming words.

Science
See Integrated curriculum activities.